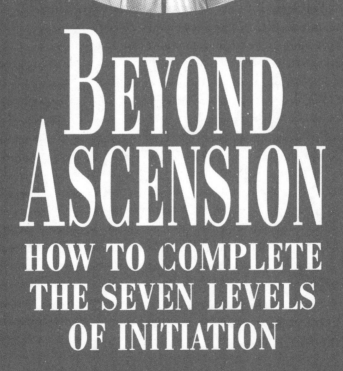

BEYOND ASCENSION

HOW TO COMPLETE THE SEVEN LEVELS OF INITIATION

JOSHUA DAVID STONE, Ph.D.

Also by Joshua David Stone, Ph.D.

The Easy-to-Read Encyclopedia of the Spiritual Path

BEYOND ASCENSION

How to Complete the Seven Levels of Initiation

Joshua David Stone, Ph.D.

THE EASY-TO-READ ENCYCLOPEDIA of the SPIRITUAL PATH
✦ Volume III ✦

Published by
Light Technology Publishing

Cover design by
Fay Richards

ISBN 0-929385-73-X

Published by
Light Technology Publishing
P.O. Box 1526 • Sedona, AZ 86339

Printed by

**MISSION
POSSIBLE**
Commercial
Printing

P.O. Box 1495 • Sedona, AZ 86339

Dedication

I would like to dedicate this book to my ascension buddies, Caryn Ogroskin and Marcia Dale Lopez. These two wonderful beings are not only my best friends but are also wonderful Lightworkers and spiritual sisters on the path. It is through my work with Caryn and Marcia that I have truly learned and experienced what group consciousness is at the level of the ascended master. What a delight it has been to work together in service to God and humanity as one unit with no ego, selfishness, or competition. We have worked together almost as one being. It was no accident that we all ascended in the same moment.

I thank you, my treasured friends, and look forward to our continued service together, not only during the rest of this incarnation but also in our future cosmic evolution.

Namasté.

Contents

Introduction

This book has had an interesting birthing process. After taking my ascension and the beginning of my sixth initiation, I decided that it was time to write my spiritual autobiography. Within six months' time the autobiography was so packed with information it was clear that it could no longer be just one book. As I was going for my morning "ascension walk," channeling the energies of Melchizedek, a spiritual birth took place and this book was born.

I had, just ten days previously, taken my seventh initiation and could not have conceived of writing a book by this title unless I had achieved that about which I was writing. Actually taking my seventh and final initiation had a profound effect on me, an effect even more powerful than my actual ascension had had. I recognize now that it was because the ascension, the sixth initiation, is really just the beginning of the ascension process. The seventh initiation is the completion of ascension and the true graduation as you move through the seventh and final seal.

Since my ascension there has been an incredible downpouring of spiritual information. This book contains the essence of that material, along with a dash of autobiographical flavor. It is unusual in that it is written from the perspective of one who has completed the full seven levels of initiation. As a person on Planet Earth, if you are attempting to achieve liberation, salvation, self-realization, and ascension, you must move through these seven levels of initiation, regardless of what religion, spiritual path, spiritual teacher, or mystery school you are involved with. Some of you may choose to leave Earth after your ascension, or sixth initiation; however, the initiation process will continue on the spiritual planes. There are three hundred fifty-two initiations that must eventually be moved through to return back to the Godhead at the highest cosmic level. For now, it is more than enough to deal with the seven initiations required to graduate from this school called Earth!

This book teaches you how to complete all seven levels of initiation in the most expedient and effective way possible so you may be of greater service to all sentient beings.

I have seriously debated whether I should share some of the things included in this book because they are so advanced. I have made the choice, however, to share all and trust the divinity within each of you, my readers. I do not mean to create fear in any way, shape, or form. What I am trying to say is that what you are receiving is not a toy. Once energies such as these have been invoked you can pass the point of no return. Lack of responsibility, self-discipline, and mastery and giving in to your lower self and negative ego will have much more serious consequences as you move up the pyramid. The higher up you are, the narrower it becomes. That is why the spiritual path has often been referred to as the short and narrow path to God. Faster is not better. Being in the Tao is the best. Consult your intuition as to the divine timing; ask when you will be ready to use each of these advanced ascension tools. If you are ready, then so be it. Make your invocation and take up the rod of power. Move forward with confidence and grace. If your inner guidance tells you to work on another aspect of self first, to prepare yourself for higher levels of understanding, then trust that guidance.

This book contains much divine food. It is essential to use your divine intelligence and intuition and some kind of systematic, methodical approach in applying all this material so you do not make yourself sick from overeating. I suggest that you begin applying a certain sequence of material each week. Over a period of nine months (for inner birth) to two years, all can be absorbed.

Many of the tools I have presented in this book are actually like spiritual surgery and are much more profound than you yet realize. So move forward with joy, confidence, centeredness, and divine intelligence, listening to your intuition and inner guidance at all times. God within you will answer all your questions. All you have to do is listen.

Now, let us begin.

1

The Seven Levels of Initiation

*It is potentially possible for a person to
move from the third to the sixth initiation
in only six years.*

Djwhal Khul

In this chapter I have included a brief synopsis of the seven levels of initiation. For a more detailed account, see my first book, *The Complete Ascension Manual: How to Achieve Ascension in This Lifetime.*

The spiritual path really begins prior to the seven levels of initiation. This period has been esoterically called the Path of Probation. It could be likened to the nine months of gestation in the womb prior to birth, but it refers to spiritual gestation, of course. The spiritual birth is the taking of the first initiation.

The first initiation deals with developing mastery over the densest body, or vehicle, which is the physical body. To pass this initiation you are required to develop a beginning level of mastery over the body and its appetites, requirements, sexual urges, sleep habits, and so on, in service of the soul, or higher self, which at this point would hold the ideal of balance and moderation.

The second initiation is concerned with developing mastery over the second densest vehicle, which is the emotional, or astral, body. To pass this initiation you must develop mastery over your emotions and desires to a certain degree, in service of the soul. It is not so much perfection that is required but, rather, conscious intent and continual choice-making to move in this direction. Material desires are beginning to be transformed into the spiritual desire for liberation and God-realization. As a disciple, you are learning to avoid being a victim of your desires and emotions and instead be a master and cause. (See my book *Soul Psychology* for help in this area.) This is the level of initiation at which you are most likely to stay stuck the longest.

The third initiation is related to mastery of the next densest vehicle, which is the mental body. To pass this initiation you must develop some level of mastery over your mind and your thoughts. This is the first major initiation, for it leads you to achieve what is called soul merge, or soul infusion. Mastery of the physical body, astral body, and mental body allows you, the disciple and personality on Earth, to merge with your soul. You then desire to be loving, forgiving, and to be of service, as well as wanting to begin the process of liberation from the wheel of rebirth.

It must be understood here that initiation is a process. It doesn't happen all at once, although there is one moment when you receive the Rod of Initiation from the Lord Maitreya (the "president" of the Spiritual Hierarchy). There are seven sublevels within each of the seven major initiations. When you take any given initiation you become a kindergarten disciple at that level. You must then move through all seven sublevels to fully complete that initiation. I had taken my sixth initiation but hadn't fully completed it until I realized the seventh sublevel of the sixth initiation. Then I took my seventh initiation. It wasn't until then that I really felt as though I had graduated and fully mastered my ascension.

Once you merge with your soul at the third initiation, things begin to speed up very rapidly. The fourth initiation is a major marker point. It is at this initiation that the soul body, which is also esoterically referred to as the causal body, burns up, and the higher self, or soul, which has been your guide throughout all your incarnations, merges back into the monad, or spirit. (The monad has also been referred to by some schools as the Mighty I Am Presence. From that moment on, the monad is your guide and teacher rather than the soul, which had been serving as an intermediary teacher until that moment. The soul has served as the repository for all your good karma from all your past lives and your current life. This repository is burned up over a period of time as you move toward completion of this initiation.

The fourth initiation has also been esoterically referred to as the initiation of renunciation. This is so because prior to taking it you are required on some level to let go of all attachments to the material world, including fame, fortune, power, selfishness, people, family, and reputation. I often think of this as the "Job initiation" — everything is stripped away as a test to see if you remain righteous in the eyes of the Lord.

Even though previous teachings said that the fourth initiation meant complete liberation from the wheel of rebirth, it is now known that while this is an important step, initiates continue the reincarnation process in another body after this one or through the continuation of this life until full ascension is achieved. I, personally, did not feel fully freed from the wheel of rebirth until I had completed the seventh sublevel of the sixth initiation. It was during that initiation ceremony that I finally felt fully freed for eternity. The fourth initiation requires a 65% Light quotient in your four-body system.

The Fifth Initiation

The fifth initiation is, in a sense, similar to the third initiation: in the third you begin the soul merge; in the fifth you begin the monadic merge, which could also be called the merge with spirit or with the I Am Presence. So this initiation might be considered a very early glimpse of your actual ascension, which is the sixth initiation.

Ascension really means that the personality, the soul, and the monad all become one unified being on Earth. The fifth initiation merges the monad in consciousness, but not in full actuality. At the fifth initiation you have to have a 75% Light quotient in your field.

You might not understand that these initiations occur on the inner plane and are very subtle. I would say most people are not even consciously aware they have taken them. This is very often true even in the case of those people who are aware of the seven levels of initiation and are working on them consciously. It is even true of actual ascension. I must admit that the process of completing seven levels of initiation was very different from what I'd expected. I, personally, happened to be quite aware of my later initiations and they were all quite wonderful, but I am learning that is rare. I am acquainted with a great number of people now who are beginning to take these initiations and everyone agrees that the actual initiation experience is more subtle than they had expected it to be. This is not to say that the experiences are not profound. I was deeply impacted by my fifth, sixth, and seventh initiations, but not in the way that I expected to be, and I was most deeply affected by the seventh initiation in which I felt the largest and most extraordinary transformation took place.

The Sixth Initiation, Ascension

The taking of the sixth initiation is the actual ascension experience for which everyone is waiting and working. In the past, when people took their sixth initiations they usually left their bodies and passed on to the spiritual world. On rare occasions they were able to dematerialize their physical bodies and take them along; however, this was more the exception than the rule. The new goal of the Spiritual Hierarchy and Sanat Kumara is to have people ascend and continue serving on Earth to help bring in the New Age.

Ascension is full merger with the monad or I Am Presence or spirit while on Earth. There is a ceremony that takes place on the inner plane involving Sanat Kumara even though most people do not remember it. The actual experience is subtle, while the implications of taking this initiation are quite profound.

There are seven planes through which you must evolve. The seven planes are connected with the seven levels of initiation and are, according to Djwhal Khul in the Alice Bailey material, as follows:

Physical plane . . . . First initiation
Astral plane . . . . Second initiation
Mental plane . . . . Third initiation
Buddhic plane . . . . Fourth initiation
Atmic plane . . . . Fifth initiation
Monadic plane . . . . Sixth initiation
Logoic plane . . . . Seventh initiation

As you can see from this little diagram, ascension is movement toward the monadic and logoic planes. Each initiation you go through stabilizes you at the next higher plane. I am using the word "plane" here rather than "dimension" because there are seven planes and nine dimensions with which you deal here on Earth.

Ascension, the sixth initiation, is movement into the fifth dimension. The seventh initiation is movement into the sixth dimension. As you can see, the dimensions are different from the seven subplanes that make up the cosmic physical plane. There are also seven cosmic planes. (See *The Complete Ascension Manual: How to Achieve Ascension in This Lifetime.*) Even the seventh initiation is less than one inch up a ten-inch ruler in terms of how far you still have to go to fully realize God at the highest cosmic level. Evolving through these seven major initiations is a major step, however.

The first cosmic initiation, from the point of view of the higher university on Sirius, is the fifth initiation. The second cosmic initiation from that point of view is the sixth initiation, ascension. The third cosmic initiation is the seventh initiation. There are two more initiations that can be taken after leaving the Earth: the eighth and the ninth. The completion of the ninth is the doorway for leaving the cosmic physical universe altogether.

Getting back to the sixth initiation: when you take this initiation you are considered a kindergarten-level ascended master. You do have a choice as to whether you want to leave Earth or remain here and serve. At this time, most are choosing to stay. Just because you have ascended, it does not necessarily mean that you can walk on water, raise the dead, or turn water into wine. These are potential abilities that can be developed;

however, you probably won't develop them until some time after fully completing your seventh initiation.

You will be happy to know that you do not have to have perfect health in order to ascend; you can even have chronic health lessons. I know this for a fact because I did. You also do not have to be totally free of all negative emotions and/or totally free of the negative ego and lower self. This may surprise some of you; however, I also know this to be a fact.

I know people who have taken their ascension whom I would consider to be emotional victims, although they also happen to have been extremely gifted in other spiritual areas. Their victimization by their emotional bodies and desire did not prevent their ascension. You have to balance only 51% of your karma to ascend.

After you ascend you will feel like exactly the same person you were before you ascended, but you will be in a higher octave. You will be carrying more Light, and you will be more connected to spirit and to the ascended masters.

I had been under the assumption that freedom from the wheel of rebirth occurred at the beginning of the sixth initiation. If this were not the case, then why would people of past centuries have physically died when they took this initiation and ascension? When my wife, Terri Sue, was channeling Djwhal Khul just recently during one of our Wednesday night classes, he said that the discrepancy exists because freedom from the necessity of rebirth actually occurs at the completion of the sixth initiation. My own experience tells me that true graduation occurred at the completion of the sixth. What I do know is that liberation from the wheel of rebirth happens somewhere during the sixth initiation, either at the beginning or at the end. It is also somewhat individual, in that some even choose to return to resolve the small percentage of remaining karma or to strengthen some aspect of self while continuing to serve the Earth and humanity.

Djwhal Khul has suggested that if you happen to die physically just prior to taking the sixth initiation or during the middle of it, you should call to the ascended masters to help you to complete your initiation process. They can work with you on the inner plane to help you finish up. I should also emphasize here that you can physically die even though you are ascended.

Ascended masters are not invulnerable and, in truth, are far from perfect. There are many different kinds of ascended masters. Some ascended masters (you may officially call yourself one upon taking the sixth initiation) are emotional types, some mental types, some physical types. The same strengths and weaknesses you had in your four-body system before your ascension will be there after you ascend. You will, however, have greater Light, energy, and consciousness with which to heal yourself more quickly.

To ascend and take your sixth initiation you will need an 80% to 83% Light quotient in your four-body system. This issue of the Light quotient is extremely important and I have dedicated a chapter in this book to ways of building it. The ascension ceremony often occurs in a group situation, often at the Wesak Festival, which occurs at the full moon of Taurus in May.

A planetary window for mass ascension is occurring on this planet between 1995 and the year 2000. Ascensions will continue on a large scale after that, but that is the main window. In the past, it used to take whole lifetimes to take just one initiation. I know for an absolute fact that a person can move through whole levels of initiation in as short a time as five months because I did it. I am not saying everyone will evolve at that rate; it all depends upon your commitment and focus. If you are really committed and very focused, I would say intuitively that during this most extraordinary time, if you use all the techniques in this book and my other books, it is reasonable to expect that you could move through the initiations at the rate of anywhere from one to five years per initiation. I am putting myself out on a limb by saying this because people are so different, but if you use the tools and ideas given here, I think it is a reasonable prediction, especially given what is happening to the planet at this time.

The issue then is how to know your level of initiation. Your intuition can tell you. If you are proficient in the use of a pendulum, that can be a useful tool. Ask during your meditations. Ask for a dream to tell you. As a last resort, you can ask a qualified channel of the ascended masters. This is not my favorite method because it is always better to get it from within yourself; however, it can be useful at times.

I recommend that you be discerning about whom you talk with about this subject. There is a great tendency to compare and compete and that is not good. It is antithetical to the whole process. There is also a tendency to judge yourself and others. It is essential to understand that everyone is God, regardless of his or her level of unfoldment, and everyone should be treated as such. I am not saying that you can never talk about it, but be extremely discerning and examine your motives for doing so.

This is actually the first time I have openly discussed my own initiation process. I have not talked about it in our classes, workshops, or seminars at all. I have just kept it to myself and tried to be it instead of talking about it. My inner guidance, however, told me that for the purposes of this book and for the benefit that might come to you, the reader, from my personal experiences, it would be appropriate. The key question is always whether sharing the information is a service or is for the gratification of the ego. Is it serving spirit to share or serving the negative ego? If it is of service, do share. Just be discerning, for you do not want others to feel inferior. As the Bible says, "Pride goeth before a fall."

In the system of initiation delineated by Brian Grattan in *Mahatma I & II*, ascension is still the sixth and its completion is the ninth initiation. The seventh initiation in the Alice Bailey system is level nine and one-half of Brian Grattan's system. The completion of the seventh initiation is the same as saying that you have completed the seven sublevels of the seventh initiation. It is at this point (at the twelfth initiation in Grattan's system) that all initiations stop for the rest of the incarnation. Your total focus from that point forward is service and helping humanity and the lower kingdoms to share in the grace.

There is also a correlation between the initiations and the anchoring of the higher chakras. When you ascend, your sixteenth chakra has descended and is anchored in your crown. The sixteenth chakra is the beginning of the fifth-dimensional chakra grid, chakras sixteen through twenty-two. At the completion of the seventh initiation, the thirty-sixth chakra has descended and is fully anchored and actualized in the crown chakra. One of the most important ways of accelerating your spiritual progression is to call forth the anchoring of the fifth-, sixth-, and seventh-dimensional chakra grids during meditation (and before sleep every night).

At the time of writing this chapter I have installed all of my thirty-six chakras; however, I am currently actualizing up to the beginning of my thirty-fifth. The reason I bring this up is so I can share that the anchoring, activation, and actualization of the individual chakras and the entire chakra grid are scientifically connected to the initiation process. In other words, each chakra can be associated with one of the seven sublevels between each major initiation. As each individual chakra is anchored, activated, and then actualized, you move up to another sublevel.

Prior to your ascension, during every meditation, you should call forth the full anchoring, activation, and actualization of your twenty-two chakras and of your fourth- and fifth-dimensional chakra grids. The masters will do this for you upon your request and invitation. Though there may be one, I don't know of any technique other than building your Light quotient that will accelerate your evolution.

It is at the sixth initiation that you make the choice of which of the seven paths of higher evolution you will follow upon leaving this plane. These seven paths are:

> The Path of Earth Service
> The Path of Magnetic Work
> The Path of Training to become a Planetary Logos
> The Path to Sirius

The Ray Path
The Path on which the Logos is found
The Path of Absolute Sonship

There is very little information on this plane about these seven paths. Djwhal Khul, in the Alice Bailey books, is almost the only master to bring forth any information at all. One of the services I have tried to render in this book is to share with you my research, in easy-to-understand language, into these seven paths.

Ascension is basically merging with the Clear Light of God, much like what is recommended during the bardo, or after-death experience. The only difference is that ascension is merging with the Clear Light of God while still retaining a physical body. The monad, at the time of ascension, is able to fully anchor Light at the 80% to 83% level. As you complete your ascension the Light quotient is up to the 92% to 94% level. At the time of writing this book my Light quotient is at the 94% to 95% level. I have been guided that within three-and-a-half months' time, which falls on the 12:12 ceremony (December 12, 1994), my Light quotient will be at the 97% level and I will be at the beginning of the seventh sublevel of the seventh initiation (at the beginning of the twelfth initiation in Brian Grattan's system). I have also been told that by the Wesak Festival on May 14, 1995, my Light quotient will be fully stabilized at the 98% level and I will have completed the seventh initiation (Brian's twelfth initiation). I share this personal information with you to give you a sense of how the process works and a feel for the time frame of taking these initiations and building your Light quotient.

The Seventh Initiation

The seventh initiation has to do with the movement from the monadic plane of reality up to the logoic, or seventh plane of reality. Where the sixth initiation deals with merging with the monad, the seventh initiation concerns greater merger with Sanat Kumara and Shamballa. Djwhal Khul told me that the seventh-degree initiate is usually one who becomes a teacher on a global level in a very visible way.

Sixth-degree initiates and ascended masters often have this service path; however, that is not required. Djwhal Khul also told my friend Marcia, who heads Djwhal Khul's ashram on the East Coast, and me during one of our meditations since taking the seventh initiation, that much has been given and much is now expected. This was fine with us, for as *A Course in Miracles* says, "True pleasure is serving God."

After taking my sixth initiation I asked Vywamus how long it would take for me and the core ascension group with which I am working to achieve our seventh initiation. At that time he said from one to five years. He also said that the taking of our seventh initiation might be affected by planetary events. One element was the geographic location in which we live. (Terri Sue and I live in Los Angeles at the time of this writing — not the best place in the world to be, energetically!)

Vywamus also said that a second factor is the fact that an asteroid is heading toward this planet. It will not directly hit the planet but will pass very close by. The exact timing was not clear, but he said that September 1997 was what he was seeing at the time of the conversation, early in 1994. Vywamus said it would cause a spiritual quickening for the planet. He said that a good metaphor for understanding its effects would be to imagine being in a car parked on a freeway, when all of a sudden an eighteen-wheeled truck goes speeding by. I don't need to explain the effects. The asteroid will have similar effects on the Earth.

Vywamus said another planetary event that could have an effect on when we take our seventh initiation is the alien situation. He said that extraterrestrials will begin making much more overt contact with Planet Earth around September of 1995. Depending on how overt this contact is, it could send shock waves reverberating around the entire planet.

I share these personal conversations with you because they might also affect you, my reader. Until now, I had never considered that these planetary events might have any effect on my own initiation process. As it turned out, they did not. I took my ascension on March 23, 1994, and I took my seventh initiation on August 23, 1994.

The seventh initiation causes a complete implosion of energy in the heart chakra. It creates a whole new chakra system. All the chakras become one column of Light, connected with the antakarana and the ascension column. This new chakra system, metaphorically, is like the creation of a new star system. The ascension of the sixth initiation is centered in the throat chakra. The seventh initiation occurs in the heart chakra; it is a merger with the monad at approximately the 94% Light quotient level.

The seventh initiation is not truly complete until the Light quotient is stabilized at the 97% to 98% level. Djwhal Khul told us that the very beginning stages of the seventh initiation can occur when you reach the 89% to 91% Light quotient level. You aren't really into the seventh initiation until you reach the 94% Light quotient level. I, personally, took the seventh initiation when I was at the 94% Light quotient level. Djwhal said that some could take it when they are between the 92% and 94% levels.

The seventh initiation is the beginning of the transcendence of all physical laws. It is also a complete and total commitment to service and a relinquishment of all negative ego. Djwhal also told us that even though the monad is fully anchored into the four-body system after ascension, it would not be completely merged in its full totality until after taking the seventh initiation. The seventh initiation means merging with the sixth dimension of reality and with the seventh-dimensional chakra grid, or chakras thirty through thirty-six.

The seventh initiation is divorced from all considerations of form and the initiate becomes a concentrated point of living Light. The seventh initiation gives the initiate the right to come and go in the courts of Shamballa. It has been referred to, esoterically, as the initiation of resurrection. Lord Maitreya took his seventh initiation on the cross at the death of the master Jesus. Lord Maitreya, of course, shared Jesus' physical body during the last three years of his life. Jesus took his fourth initiation on the cross.

The seventh initiation is the one in which the child of God has found his way back to the Father and to his originating Source, or that state of existence known as Shamballa. The seventh initiation begins the full opening of involvement with the extraplanetary existence with which our Planetary Logos, the Lord of the World, is involved.

At this initiation Sanat Kumara is attended by two groups of beings. The first is called Knowers of the Purpose, Custodians of the Will. This is the smaller group. The second group is much larger and is called The Wise Ones and Attractive Energies of Shamballa. These beings operate on a high level of the cosmic plane, corresponding to the ajna center of humankind, and embody the Will to Good. More succinctly, they are the ajna, or third eye center, for Sanat Kumara, the Planetary Logos. In a larger context, Shamballa is the crown center; the Spiritual Hierarchy is the heart center, and humanity is the creative throat center. It is also to Shamballa that the seventh-degree initiate goes for periods of cyclic recharging.

At the seventh initiation, an even higher electrical force is transmitted to the master through Sanat Kumara's Rod of Initiation, which signifies full completion. The master has become a full-fledged seventh-degree Melchizedek (as the ancient Egyptian teachings described the process). This, again, is the highest initiation that can be taken on the Earthly plane.

After you take the seventh initiation, work still remains to be done in terms of fully realizing or completing this initiation. You have moved from being an advanced sixth-degree initiate to being a beginning seventh-degree initiate. It is most likely in the seventh initiation that the more advanced and transcendent ascension abilities will be developed — that is to say, those that defy physical laws. At the seventh initiation your Light quotient is high enough (minimally 94%) to master these abilities with ease.

The eighth initiation has been referred to as the Great Transition; it will be taken on the inner plane after leaving the material world. The ninth initiation has been esoterically called the Refusal; it indicates the master's last contact with what has been referred to as cosmic evil as it relates to this planet.

I took my seventh initiation sitting on top of a physical mountain with my wife, Terri Sue. Upon the completion of a brief ceremony, Djwhal Khul said, "Welcome to the eighth school." Each initiation you pass welcomes you to the school above. Melchizedek referred to this seventh initiation as going through the final seal, which reminds me of the seven seals of which Peter spoke in the Revelation.

There was a tremendous feeling of celebration and joy after this experience. It really felt like a marker point, like a complete graduation. Terri Sue had had a dream three days earlier regarding the completion of our ascension, or sixth initiation. In the dream we were meditating together under the full moon when all of a sudden a sniper shot Terri Sue in the heart and she died. I picked her up and took her to a more comfortable spot and then I was shot in the third eye. (Where we were shot is significant.) I died and we both ascended. The completion of the ascension and the taking of the seventh initiation are like a death. Physical existence is never again the same, for you have totally ascended and are now remaining in the physical vehicle as a bodhisattva for service purposes.

More Information on the Higher Initiations

My friend Marcia channeled some very interesting information on initiations three through seven.

Third initiation	=	Desire to know your true self
Fourth initiation	=	Desire for complete knowledge of self
Fifth initiation	=	Complete unification with peace and harmony
Sixth initiation	=	Service
Seventh initiation	=	Complete liberation from Earthbound functions; development of advanced and transcendent ascension abilities.

Planetary Initiations

Just as humanity goes through initiations, so do the Earth Mother and Sanat Kumara, who ensouls the Earth as the Planetary Logos. The Earth Mother, or the heavenly body known as Earth, has recently taken her third initiation, the soul merge initiation. This is why Earth has moved into what has been termed sacred status. It is a recent occurrence, for in Djwhal Khul's writings in the Alice Bailey material, it had not yet happened.

Vywamus gave me a fascinating piece of information about this process that I had never before realized. I asked Vywamus what happens when the Earth Mother completes her seventh initiation. He told me that the Earth Mother will experience a nova — in other words, will turn into Light. That is to say that the Earth Mother will ascend. The planetary body known as Earth will experience a type of ascension similar to that of humans upon completion of the seventh initiation.

I also asked Vywamus about Sanat Kumara's initiation process, for Sanat Kumara has recently taken another initiation. When Sanat Kumara takes an initiation as the Planetary Logos, all evolution on the planet — human, animal, plant, and mineral — moves up another octave with him.

I asked Vywamus to explain Sanat Kumara's initiations. He was not allowed to explain too much, but what he did say was that there were twelve further initiations on a more cosmic level which Sanat Kumara was in the process of working through. So there are the seven basic cosmic initiations and then the five higher cosmic initiations that correspond to the five higher rays. I asked if these initiations relate to what might be termed the first twenty-four initiations of the three hundred fifty-two levels that make up the Mahatma. Vywamus said that he was using a different system. It is interesting to me that the initiation process is still in effect at this cosmic level, at least for the training of a planetary logos.

Vywamus said that the Earth Mother was still relatively young, rather like a radiant adolescent, and the Earth being is a very sought-after planet for the incarnation process. He also said that the life forms on this planet would probably return to an etheric state before the actual nova, or ascension, effect. That is interesting, for it is also how life began on this planet in pre-Lemurian times. Life was not always physical in the way that we now understand it to be. Earth is a very tough school, Vywamus said. However, the potential for spiritual growth and evolvment is enormous and that is why incarnating here is so desirable.

2

How to Open, Anchor, and Activate
the Fifty Chakras

*At the completion of the seventh initiation
the thirty-sixth chakra will be anchored
in the crown chakra.*

Melchizedek

There exists a completely new understanding of the chakras that has never before been written about. Most spiritual schools teach that there are seven major chakras and many minor chakras. Some New Age mystery schools teach that there are twelve chakras. Well, I am here to tell you that, in truth, there are thirty-six major chakras that must be dealt with if you plan to complete the seven levels of initiation. There are also some beyond that.

The best way to understand the chakras is to see that they basically come in sets of seven, according to the dimensional grid with which they are associated:

Third-dimensional chakra grid	Chakras one through seven
Fourth-dimensional chakra grid . .	Chakras eight through fifteen
Fifth-dimensional chakra grid	Chakras sixteen through twenty-two
Sixth-dimensional chakra grid.	Chakras twenty-three through twenty-nine.
Seventh-dimensional chakra grid . .	Chakras thirty through thirty-six
Eighth-dimensional chakra grid . .	Chakras thirty-seven through forty-three
Ninth-dimensional chakra grid	Chakras forty-four through fifty

As you evolve spiritually, these chakras naturally descend, just as the soul and monad naturally descend in the process of initiation and ascension. The world has not known of these higher chakras because few humans have, until now, evolved beyond the third and fourth dimensions of reality. As Wesak of 1995 approaches with its first wave of mass ascension, the situation will change dramatically. That is why the new information about the chakras is coming forward now.

Vywamus, through Janet McClure, was the first to come out with some detailed information on the twenty-two chakras. Since I have written about the third-, fourth- and fifth-dimensional chakra grids in other books, I am not going to repeat myself here. What I do want to say is that when you ascend and take your sixth initiation, your sixteenth chakra becomes anchored in the crown. What ascension really is, from the frame of reference of the chakras, is the complete anchoring into the four-body system of the third and fourth chakra grids — that is, chakras one through fifteen. When the sixteenth chakra (the first chakra of the fifth-dimensional chakra grid) anchors, you have ascended and are in the first stage of the fifth dimension. To complete your ascension you must then anchor and actualize the entire fifth-dimensional and sixth-dimensional chakra grids.

Now, you would think that to take the seventh initiation all you would have to do would be to complete the fifth-dimensional chakra grid and anchor the first of the sixth-dimensional chakras. However, that was not my experience. When I took the seventh initiation, I had already installed and actualized the thirty-third chakra. The seventh initiation is the entrance into the sixth dimension; the thirty-third chakra is actually in the seventh-dimensional chakra grid. I don't know if I was a little precocious or if this is the level all must attain in order to take the seventh. I tend to think this is a standard level, just as a certain Light quotient needs to be achieved.

To complete the seventh initiation it is required that all initiates fully install, anchor, and actualize all thirty-six chakras. In other words, at the completion of your seventh initiation, your thirty-sixth chakra will be in your crown, and so on. Following is a list showing the chakras and their corresponding areas:

Chakra thirty-six . . . . . Crown
Chakra thirty-five . . . . Third eye
Chakra thirty-four . . . . Throat
Chakra thirty-three . . Heart

The chakras from the previous sixth-dimensional grid will move down through your thighs, knees, ankles, and feet and into the Earth.

The most important thing to understand here is that the process of anchoring your chakras can be speeded up. This is one of the main reasons I was able to move through the fifth, sixth, and seventh initiations so quickly. I began working with the ability to collapse time. Melchizedek recently told Marcia and me that the evolutionary process has never before moved so quickly in the history of this planet. In that sense we are prototypes and guinea pigs. The masters are watching this process of speeded-up evolution with great interest.

It is important to know that there are three levels of understanding in the process of anchoring the higher chakras: the first is installation; the second is actualization; the third is accessing the chakras' abilities, or utilization.

The first step in speeding up your evolutionary process is to request, in every meditation you do, the full anchoring and installation of your twenty-two chakras and your fourth- and fifth-dimensional chakra grids. Upon your invocation and request, these chakras will descend like bodies of Light. You can even channel the individual chakras and talk to them. Each has a consciousness. As they descend they will overlay the previous chakra grid.

I recommend that you request the anchoring and installation of the chakras through the completion of the fifth-dimensional chakra grid which is chakra twenty-two. You are allowed to work a little ahead of yourself. Always ask for this (and this is important) under the guidance and direction of your own Mighty I Am Presence and monad. These are, in truth, very powerful electrical energies and you don't want to "spontaneously combust" from too much spiritual current.

If you are just beginning your spiritual path, then begin anchoring chakras one through twelve. If you are more advanced, begin anchoring up to chakra fifteen. If you are very advanced and extremely devoted, then do all twenty-two chakras. No matter where you are, ask your Mighty I Am Presence to monitor and calibrate the whole process so you stay in the Tao.

Never forget that faster is not better; slower is not better. Staying in the Tao is the most efficient way to God-realization and, in truth, the *only* way to God-realization. People who have tried to force the evolution of their kundalini unwisely have sometimes set themselves back entire life-times becaues of the damage they have caused to their etheric bodies. I am not trying to scare you here, for this process is totally safe as long as you follow these instructions, but do not attempt, under any circumstances, to anchor chakras twenty-two through thirty-six until after you have taken your sixth initiation. You can always activate one grid above where you are, but no more than that.

I recommend asking the ascended masters, especially Djwhal Khul and the Arcturians, for help in this process, for the installation of the chakra grids is much like spiritual surgery. The masters will not install the entire chakra grid, or all seven chakras of that grid, all at once. They will usually do two chakras at a time. This is the reason for the second phase of this process, which is actualization. The chakras might be installed but that does not mean that you have actualized them in the slightest. For example, as I mentioned previously, I have had all thirty-six chakras installed, but I am actualizing, at the moment of writing this, only up to the very beginning of the thirty-fifth.

The key question here is, "How do you actualize the chakras that have been installed?" It is done by living a God-inspired lifestyle. Meditation, I would say, is the key. You can pray to the ascended masters and the Arcturians for help in actualizing your chakras as well as to have them installed.

The third step is being able to access the chakra's abilities. For example, I have now actualized almost all thirty-six chakras; however, I have not yet learned to utilize all of their abilities. Someone like Sai Baba is an example of one who has. His ability to materialize things, to be physically in two places at once, to teleport, and so on, are examples of utilization, the next step after installation and actualization.

You cannot go higher than the top of the sixth dimension while still retaining a physical vehicle. When you take the seventh initiation you are in the sixth dimension. The completion of the seventh initiation means you are accessing the top level of the sixth dimension without yet having switched over to the seventh dimension. You can, however, still access dimensions seven through nine in meditation and in the dream state. I am currently doing that. After the ninth dimension you are no longer dealing with physical existence. The most important point here is that you can continually ask in meditation for this anchoring to occur.

If you feel a need to know about the progress of the work, and if you can channel or if you have a friend who can channel, talk with the masters. If not, it does not matter. You are God, and if you ask for this it will be done.

There is so much that goes on in the spiritual world about which humans have not the slightest idea. A lot of what I am sharing with you here I ask you to take on faith, judging with your intuitive knowingness that what I am sharing with you is true and effective. To a third-dimensional scientist, this whole book might seem like hogwash; to a disciple and initiate, the information makes perfect sense and is as real as anything perceivable with the physical senses.

After taking your sixth initiation and ascension you can begin calling in the sixth-dimensional grid of chakras twenty-three through twenty-nine. The act of calling them in and anchoring them is no different from calling in one of the ascended masters. The process is not dangerous. Having them installed is the next step; again, I suggest you have Djwhal Khul, the Arcturians, or Vywamus help you. Your good lifestyle, meditations, and Light-quotient-building work will help you to actualize the installation.

It took me eight months to install and actualize chakras twenty-three through thirty-six — an unusually short time. The process has moved so quickly for me because of my extraordinary wife and friends. Our ascension buddy system has formed a kind of group mind that has accelerated the process.

I am also in the unique position of being in charge of Djwhal Khul's ashram on the West Coast, along with Terri Sue. I have hesitated to share my experiences here because I do not want to give you unrealistic expectations; I share with you what is potentially possible so that it can motivate you to discipline yourself and get down to business so you can achieve full God-realization and hence be of greater service to humanity, as well as sharing in the extraordinary joy of it all.

We have just recently been given permission to anchor all fifty chakras. The process begins with a request for installation. Then follows the slow anchoring and activation of the eighth- and ninth-dimensional chakra grids.

The Chakra Chambers and Facets

The next major understanding about the chakra system came as a result of an advanced ascension workshop which Terri Sue and I were hosting. During the workshop Djwhal Khul, for the first time, spoke of the seven chambers in each of the chakras, including the ascension chakra, that needed to be opened. The ascension chakra is a chakra located toward the back of the head where a ponytail might begin. It is the key chakra in the ascension process. As you know, each of the seven major chakras is connected to a gland: the crown to the pineal; the third eye to the pituitary; the throat to the thyroid, and so on down the line. The ascension chakra, Djwhal told us, is connected to the hypothalamus.

For full God-realization, each of the seven chambers in each chakra must be open and active. Djwhal told us that just completing the seven levels of initiation does not automatically ensure their opening and activation. The picture on the next page is based on a sketch Terri Sue drew showing an individual chakra and its seven chambers from two angles.

The cone shape is the whole chakra; as you move down the seven levels, the chambers are smaller and harder to open and activate. In the second drawing you are looking down at just one chamber of the seven in any given chakra. The chamber is like a pie that has been sliced for serving. Then each slice is cut horizontally into three pieces. The numbered pieces total forty-eight, the number that Melchizedek told Marcia and me was the best model with which to work.

I am calling each one of these forty-eight pieces a facet of the chamber.

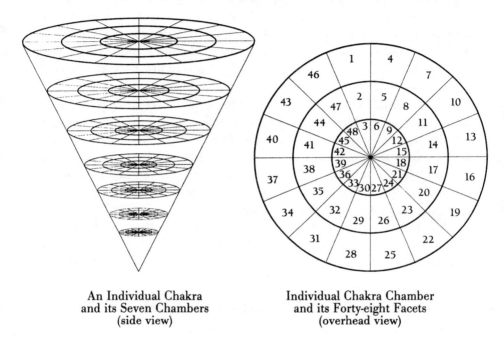

An Individual Chakra
and its Seven Chambers
(side view)

Individual Chakra Chamber
and its Forty-eight Facets
(overhead view)

When the chambers are opened by your spiritual work, your Mighty I Am Presence, or the ascended masters, they are not opened all at once. They are opened, in a sense, one facet at a time. The opening of one facet leads to the opening of another. The facets could be likened to the facets of a diamond or the triangles that make up a merkabah or geodesic dome. During the workshop Djwhal activated certain facets of these chambers. He also does so in individual sessions through Terri Sue. It is all done very mathematically and scientifically. For example, he might say something like, "Activate and open crown chakra, level one, facet thirty-five." This is not exactly the way he does it, but it does make the point. The whole process gets more complicated because although Melchizedek told us that a model of forty-eight facets was the best model to use, all the chakras do not necessarily have forty-eight facets. Nonetheless, it is enough to know that each chakra has seven chambers and they need to be opened for full God-realization.

Earlier I spoke of the stages of anchoring the thirty-six chakras — installation, actualization, and utilization of the abilities. The opening of the chambers is connected to the actualization and utilization of the abilities of the chakras. For example, teleporting will use certain chambers and facets that I have not as yet developed. This is the next step, and that is why the information is now being brought forward. The opening of all these chambers is the next step in my personal evolution. Now that I have installed and actualized nearly all thirty-six chakras (the fifth-, sixth- and seventh-dimensional chakra grids) it is time to move to the third stage of utilizing the abilities of all these chakras.

Marcia and I, in our meditations together, were quite fascinated with this whole process and we came up with some more information about it. First, when you complete your ascension and take your seventh initiation, the chakras become one column of Light rather than seven individual chakras. In addition, this chakra column combines with the antakarana, or rainbow bridge, when the kundalini rises within the ascension column.

Marcia realized that of the three facets in each pie piece, the smallest one closest to the center represents the future, the middle one, the present, and the one closest to the outside of the circle, the past. Ideally, all three are open, activated, and working together. What often happens, however, is that just the past is open; people then end up projecting their past misconceptions onto the present and future because the facets are not integrated properly. When all thirty-six chakras are anchored and all chambers and facets are open, twelve strands of DNA move from the etheric vehicle into the physical vehicle.

Now, some of the facets and chambers open automatically in the process of evolution on the spiritual path. Melchizedek told us that the invocation of all the fire letters, key codes, and sacred geometries (which you will find later in this book) aids in the opening of these facets and chambers. I believe that sitting in the ascension seats also helps in this regard, as do other forms of Light quotient building and meditation techniques.

In essence, all the varied spiritual practices, from journal writing to affirmations to prayer, have their effects on the chakra system. Melchizedek told us that basically all knowledge is stored somewhere within the chakra system. The meditation techniques I have included in this book will have a stunning effect on the activation and opening of these facets and chambers.

It is also possible to ask your own Mighty I Am Presence and the ascended masters to in a sense collapse time and accelerate the process by opening them for you. This cannot and will not be done all at once, for that would be too dangerous. Terri Sue, Marcia, Caryn, and I asked for it to be done effectively by using the Huna prayer method of which I am so fond. However, before sharing that with you there is one more piece of the chakra puzzle I must discuss.

Vywamus on the Chakra Chambers

As I continued to research this subject from as many points of view as possible, Vywamus had some interesting things to add. He said that the chakras are means of focusing Light; in other words, they are vibrational focusing tools. The totality of the chakras and their chambers helps to create a tonal quality and tonal frequency for each person. He said that the ultimate goal is indeed to open all the chambers and all the petals, or facets, including those of the minor chakras, to achieve your optimum octave and frequency. He said, however, that it was essential to under-stand, in the process of doing this, that there is a step-by-step process of chamber recalibration that must go on. If the chamber and petals are opened all at once the initiate would lose the physical vehicle. The recalibration process makes sure that a balance is kept among all energies to ensure the maintenance of a healthy and integrated Light frequency. The calibrating of Light should always be done in conjunction with your soul or monad. The relationship of the petals and chambers in the chakras is that a certain number of petals (for example one thousand in the crown chakra) are connected to certain chambers. The exact mathematics, he said, are too complicated to be more specific about.

At major initiations, recalibrations of Light frequency and chakra adjustment and opening take place. During minor initiations a similar process occurs but in a less intense manner. You can request a Light recalibration adjustment of the chambers and petals in the chakras to take you to the next step in your evolution. The Huna prayer at the end of this chapter offers just such a request.

The Chakras and the Petals

If you study Eastern spiritual literature and the Djwhal Khul/Alice Bailey books, you will find studies of the working of the chakra system. Among other things, Djwhal Khul says that each chakra has a specified number of individual petals which need to be opened.

Crown chakra . . . . one thousand petals
Third eye . . . . two petals
Throat chakra . . . . sixteen petals
Heart chakra . . . . twelve petals
Solar plexus chakra . . ten petals
Polarity chakra. . . . . . . six petals
Root chakra . . . . four petals

As you can see, there is a relationship here between the Eastern system of opening all the petals of each lotus, or chakra, and the opening of the chakra chambers. What the exact relationship is, I am not sure. The study of the chakra system is such a vast undertaking, I believe you could spend a liftime focusing on nothing else and you would just begin to scratch the surface. As Melchizedek said, "All knowledge is stored within the chakra system." In any case, I am choosing to use both systems in terms of the invocation and prayer work. I believe in covering all the bases.

One thing I do know is that the petals, chambers, and facets are connected to the etheric nervous system. They are also connected to the right and left hemispheres of the brain. The chakras themselves are connected to the glands which affect the organs and the functions of the entire physical body.

The astral, mental, and spiritual bodies also have their effects on the etheric nervous system, the nadis, or spiritual filaments that connect with the facets, or petals. As you can see, this is one very synergistic, holistic, integrated process. The key is to get the entire seven-body system, the thirty-six chakras, the personality, soul and monad, all chambers, facets, and petals, the ascension column, kundalini, antakarana, heart and cosmic heart, upper spiritual triad, and lower spiritual triad, all working in perfect unison, harmony, integration, and balance as one unified system with no separate parts.

The metaphysical science of breaking all that down into its component parts, showing cause-and-effect relationships, can be quite complex and even, in some cases, incomprehensible, given the complexity of all the different functions that are taking place simultaneously. For current purposes, the most important thing is to open the chambers, facets, petals, and chakras so you can more fully realize God and be of greater service. This is the bottom line.

Huna Prayer for Opening

The prayer below is the prayer I used with Terri Sue to open and activate the chambers and petals of my chakras. My recommendation is to ask to go to the ascension seat in Shamballa first. Then read the prayer three times out loud. If you do it with an ascension friend it is even more powerful, but that is not necessary. After repeating the prayer three times aloud, then say the second paragraph, which is addressed to the subconscious mind, one time. Wait thirty seconds to allow the subconscious mind to take the prayer where it needs to go. Then say the last paragraph and be silent for another thirty seconds to receive the initial blessing.

The exact wording of the prayer can be changed if you like. The timetable I used was what was right for me, given the coming of the 12:12 celebration and Wesak in May 1995; you must use your own intuition to determine what is right for you. What is nice about this prayer is that it applies not just to one meditation but invokes help on an ongoing, everyday basis for a substantial period of time.

The use of Huna prayers has been absolutely invaluable and is one of the main reasons Terri Sue, Marcia, Caryn, and I have moved forward so quickly. I write one for whatever dispensation we need or are looking for and we all say it. This action really locks the prayer in and makes it official. The prayers work every time.

Beloved Presence of God, Sanat Kumara, Vywamus, and Djwhal Khul: We hereby call forth a divine dispensation on our behalf. We call forth, over the next _____ months to _____ months, a full opening and activation of the seven levels of chambers in each of our chakras, including the ascension chakras. We ask that this work go on every night while we sleep and during our meditations and receptive periods during the day. We also ask that this work continue until fully completed [and, if possible, that it be completed some time between the 12:12 and Wesak of 1995].

We also ask at this time for a full opening and activation of all the individual petals that make up each of the individual chakras. [For example the one thousand petals in the crown, two in the third eye chakra, sixteen in the throat, twelve in the heart, and so on down the line.]

We thank you and accept this as done in the name of the fully realized Christ so we may be of greater service.

Amen.

(Repeat three times.)

Our beloved subconscious minds, we hereby ask and command that you take this thought form prayer, with all the mana and vital force that are needed and necessary to manifest and demonstrate this prayer, to the Source of our being.

Amen.

(Repeat only once. Then wait for twenty or thirty seconds while visualizing a fountain or some other suitable imagery shooting upward from within you and going straight to God, or Source.)

Sanat Kumara, Vywamus, and Djwhal Khul, let the Rain of Blessings fall!
Amen.
(Visualize the Rain of Blessings as it falls upon you.)

3

How to Build Your Light Quotient

I Am the Light of the World.
A Course in Miracles

One of the subjects I have been most interested in is the issue of how to build your Light quotient. I have questioned Djwhal Khul, Vywamus, and other ascended masters extensively on this point and I would like to share with you what we have come up with.

First of all, it is important to understand that at every moment of your day, you are either building or decreasing your Light quotient. Every thought you think, every word you speak, every action you take has its effect. The key, in my opinion, is to "keep your mind steady in the Light," as Djwhal Khul would say. If your mind is held steady in the Light at all times, then your emotional body will be held in the Light and your actions will be held in the Light, for it is your thoughts that create your reality.

The Light quotient is built in masculine and feminine ways. If you are on Earth, regardless of your level of initiation, you receive energy from Source or you would not be alive. This energy is received through the silver cord which is connected to Source through your monad, or I Am Presence. You receive this pure, unadulterated God energy; then, depending on the nature of your consciousness, you qualify it in either a positive or a negative manner, in terms of Light or darkness, in terms of serving your lower self and negative ego or your higher self, soul, and Christ consciousness. Does not the Bible say, "Let this mind be in you that was in Christ Jesus." It could also be called the Buddha mind or Krishna mind or spiritual mind.

Assertive Ways of Building Light

One of the keys to creating more Light in a masculine, or assertive, way is to constantly qualify all incoming energy to create only Light, love, joy, positivity, godliness, Christ consciousness, appropriate spiritual action, and so on. Unceasing spiritual practices such as meditating, praying, repeating positive affirmations and visualizations, reading spiritual material, chanting God's names, visualizing forms, listening to spiritual tapes, attending spiritual lectures, workshops, and seminars, doing spiritual journal writing, performing service work, and practicing the presence of God are ways of creating enormous amounts of Light quotient in your field.

Vywamus told me that one of the best ways to build your Light quotient is to clear the subconscious mind through etheric work, sound, and color. This can also be done through visualization or just self-inquiry on a thought level. Another method Vywamus shared with me for raising the Light quotient is to achieve a deeper view of self in meditation. When you are able to really look deeply into your essence in a clear manner, an enormous influx of Light is released into yourself from the very core of your being. I experience this strongly when I write in my journal, for example.

Building your Light quotient is extremely important for all seven levels of initiation. It is one of the requirements for passing each initiation. The third initiation requires 56%, the fourth initiation requires 63%, the fifth initiation requires 75% Light quotient. The sixth initiation, ascension, requires 80% to 83% Light quotient. The seventh initiation requires 94% Light quotient.

In every interaction you have with self, with other people, and with life in general, you should be asking yourself this question: "Am I creating Light or darkness in my consciousness in this moment? Am I serving God or my negative ego at this moment?" When you realize you are creating inappropriately, just forgive yourself and immediately change your thinking, feeling, and behavior. As Sai Baba says, "It is your mind that creates bondage and your mind that creates liberation."

When your mind or lower self starts putting you in bondage, immediately change your mind and put yourself in liberation. If you find yourself holding a grudge, immediately change your mind and forgive, hence creating more Light and love (which are the same). Your mental and visual functions can be greatly enhanced by using the breath. Enormous amounts of Light can be created by supporting your mental and spiritual work with proper breathing; Djwhal Khul says it is the foundation of all Light work.

Intention and desire to build your Light quotient will help to build more Light because they give you a goal and keep you focused on it. The ideal is to shine your Light all the time, regardless of other people's behavior and regardless of circumstances. It is important to realize that everyone, including the ascended masters, Sanat Kumara, Vywamus, and even Lenduce, still has a tiny bit of darkness, or lack of Light, within himself. The term "darkness" is another way of referring to the remnants of negative ego, separation, fear, selfishness, or material overidentification within. As you evolve through the seven levels of initiation and then up through the cosmic levels of initiation and evolution, you will move closer and closer to pure Light. The ideal is to eventually become pure Light, pure Love, pure Joy, pure God, which are all ways of saying the same thing.

It is also important to understand that your Light quotient fluctuates according to what is going on in your consciousness and in your life. You might move three points up and then drop three points during a crisis period. The key is to strive for even-mindedness and consistency in your efforts and emotional nature.

Receptive Ways of Building Light

The more receptive, or feminine, ways of building the Light quotient have to do with allowing the ascended masters and/or the positive extraterrestrial groups to help you. Vywamus speaks of "receiving a Light shower" from one or more of the ascended masters or angels. Metatron is an especially proficient archangel in this regard, for he is the creator of all outer Light in the universe, according to *The Keys of Enoch*. However, any of the masters can help.

The ascension seats of which I spoke in *The Complete Ascension Manual: How to Achieve Ascension in This Lifetime* are really Light-creating machines. They can be found on spacecraft in the Ashtar Command, in Telos (the underground city beneath Mt. Shasta), inside Mt. Shasta on the etheric level, and in Luxor, the ascension retreat of Serapis Bey. These ascension seats run Light through your four-body system; it feels like a tingling over the entire body. In the past, I have gone to these ascension seats in meditation. What I have been doing more recently is asking the Arcturians, throughout my day, even if I am watching television, sleeping, walking, or working, to run the higher Light quotients through my four-body system. At the time of writing this particular section I have been told that my Light quotient is somewhere around the 88% level. I have worked out a system with the Arcturians in which I just say, "Arcturians, 98% Light quotient, please." Son-of-a-gun, not more than two or three seconds later, I feel a tingling sensation begin to move throughout my body, and I feel the blood in my veins begin to pump faster. It has the added benefit of making me feel more awake and alert, which I really like. It is kind of like the feeling I have after exercising. Clairvoyantly, my hands look red in color because of the increased circulation. It feels like more energy is running through my etheric body and into all my cells and organs. It is a wonderful feeling!

The Arcturians have the most advanced technology in this galaxy. Djwhal Khul told me that even the Hierarchy uses some of their technology. Caryn and I spend a lot of time on the phone chatting, while absorbing this Light. We call it the spiritual jacuzzi, for that is literally what it feels like. I have been amazed at how substantial the feeling is.

I usually find that the flow of energy varies throughout the day. Sanat Kumara is overseeing this process for Caryn and me, which I also feel good about. I might ask for 98%, but they will send only that which my body can handle and absorb in a safe manner. Apparently there are teams of Arcturian temple workers on the ships and they take turns monitoring us. They have also graciously agreed to help me strengthen my digestive system on electrical and energetic levels, which I feel very excited about.

The Arcturians are wonderfully loving, service-oriented beings. Their entire civilization is at the level of an ascended master. They have physical bodies that are different from humans', but do not let that deter you from asking them for help. They are literally the Light of the galaxy. I am so amazed by their technology and the results I am getting that both Caryn and I are focusing on them most of the time for building our Light quotients. They have told us that they are happy to assist whoever asks for their help. However, they will never intervene without an invitation; they operate according to the Prime Directive, as publicized by *Star Trek*. They will send a level of Light that is appropriate for your path or level of evolution and will watch you closely on their computer screens.

Since they have begun to work with me in this manner I have felt a definite increase in my overall physical health. I am currently having them do some intensive healing work on my pancreas and liver functions. Both Caryn and I feel we have hit a spiritual gold mine in finding the Arcturians. They also told us that they can accommodate any number of people, however many might ask for their help. If they have to, they will send for more starships. I hope to keep them very busy, for I think they are "the best thing since apple pie."

I usually find that they will run the energies at the highest possible frequency appropriate for my level of evolution and then slow it down for a while to let me integrate that which I have received. The highest they have sent is 98% for not more than an hour or two. I usually find that it fluctuates between 90% and 98%. After working with them quite intensively for the past month, I feel I am able to handle a much higher Light quotient than I was previously handling, but this is just an intuitive feeling on my part.

I have requested that they send me energy all night while I am sleeping.

However, they said I was very busy on the inner plane at night and had a rather regimented schedule – which does not surprise me – so they are meeting my request as my schedule allows. I have given them a blanket invitation to work on me all through the day indefinitely, or at least until I take my seventh initiation. I am sure I will be taking advantage of their services after that too, but this is just my short-term goal and focus. They are having an enormously accelerating effect on my consciousness and whole being and I am eternally grateful for their selfless service.

I usually find, also, that they slow down the Light quotient building while I am eating and just afterwards to allow the food to be digested. I keep telling them to continue even then, but then I tend to be a little bit of a "Light hog." In truth, I totally trust the Arcturians and Sanat Kumara in this process. I do find that it will stop at times; then when I ask for it to return, it does. I am beginning to get an intuitive sense of what level they are running. If a person is at the 56% Light quotient level they would probably run 58% to 62% Light quotient and then see how the person is reacting to and integrating the energy. There is no rush! It just feels really good. Caryn and I often meditate together on the phone, marveling at the experience.

The Arcturians told me this morning that the energy is sent through their machines into the etheric body grid, which then transfers it to the physical level. They recommended requesting each night to travel to their Arcturian starship where they will work on you. This is what I do in terms of the strengthening of my digestive system and the building of my Light quotient. This procedure is a little different from what I mentioned before because this method has me leaving my physical body and going to their ship, whereas most of the time, my etheric body remains with my physical body while they are working on me.

If you have health problems, or emotional, mental or spiritual problems, call out to the Arcturians before retiring and ask them to work with you on their starship. They are lovingly allowed to do this if you consciously ask for it.

Altogether, the best way to increase your Light quotient is to go through your day alternating between using assertive and passive methods of increasing it. That way, every moment of your day will be devoted to raising your vibration!

Other Techniques for Building Your Light Quotient

Another very powerful technique for building your Light quotient is to ask the combined force of Metatron, the Mahatma, and Melchizedek, the Universal Logos, for help in building it. The combination of these cosmic beings seems to be ideal. The Huna prayers are an example of how to invoke such beings on an ongoing basis.

I also recommend calling on the Ashtar Command, asking Commander Ashtar and, in particular, Soltec, for help. The Ashtar Command ascension work seems to come in through the crown, whereas the Arcturians' Light quotient energy seems to come through the whole body simultaneously. Both of these groups will happily work with you for this noble purpose.

Another technique for Light quotient building is to use consistently the ascension meditation and treatment in the back of *The Complete Ascension Manual: How to Achieve Ascension in This Lifetime*. You might want to put that meditation on tape. The combination of the meditation and the other ascension techniques in the book will build your Light quotient like nothing else you will find on this planet.

Still another technique that is especially good for Light quotient building is calling for your personal merkabah during each meditation and having the masters and your own monad help to spin your merkabah like a top to raise your vibration and Light quotient to the ascended master state. Even if you cannot see it, you will feel like a slight tingling sensation over your entire body. In every meditation be sure to ask that your ascension chakra and all your brain centers be fully opened and illumined; this will allow you to receive more Light.

Every morning upon awakening, call to your soul or monad to fully anchor and merge with you, the personality on Earth. Ask your monad, or I Am Presence, to remain merged with you all day. Every morning also request the full anchoring of your soul, or monadic, Lightbody. Call in all your higher chakras to descend, anchor, and remain with you all day long.

Each morning, call in the Mahatma and all three hundred fifty-two levels of the Mahatma to merge and blend with your four-body system and to remain with you all day long. Also call forth your mayavarupa body, or monadic blueprint body, to fully anchor and blend. This will allow your physical and etheric vehicles to work from a more perfect blueprint for your overall health. To this end, I would add the calling forth of your golden solar angelic body and your solar body of Light which will also build your Light quotient. Then ask Metatron to anchor the Microtron, which will allow you to integrate all this Light more effectively. Lastly, I would call forth a tube of Light, a pillar of Light, an ascension column of Light to surround and protect you all day long.

The invocation of these energies to blend with your four-body system each morning as you start your day will increase your Light quotient and accelerate your ascension process like nothing else. The invocation of these energies just while you are reading this section, for example, would take only a minute or so. A few moments of spiritual practice will bring you enormous spiritual acceleration. You might even want to write the names of these energies on a card to keep in your wallet or purse until they become fully integrated into your consciousness so you can invoke them at lunch and in the evening.

The using of these simple techniques, which take almost no time at all, will build your Light quotient in a most accelerated manner. Since our ascension, the Light quotient of our core ascension group has gone up about five points in seven weeks, which is mindboggling. A lot of this had to do with Wesak and the astrological configuration from Sirius in April of 1994, which brings me to the next method.

This method of Light quotient building has to do with taking advantage of astrological configurations and the holy days of the Spiritual Hierarchy. I am speaking here of the extra incoming spiritual energies at full moons, new moons, and major astrological configurations. These include the Wesak Festival (the festival of the Buddha at the full moon in May, the Festival of the Christ which occurs at the previous full moon in April, and the Festival of Humanity, which is the full moon of June. You can also use the extra spiritual energy of eclipses, comets, and so on, as well as taking advantage of the great spiritual events such as the Harmonic Convergence, the 11:11, and the 12:12. Another special event is the World Peace Meditation each year on December 31 at noon Greenwich Mean Time. Organized by John Randolph Price, it is also referred to as "Project One, a vision of Global Peace and Planetary Brotherhood, an expression of Unity, a worldwide demonstration of Harmony, as millions around the globe are joined in a celebration of sound, Light and motion."

All of these events have great spiritual significance. Meditate at these times and ask to receive the spiritual benefits of the occurrences. It is even better if you can meditate with a group. Enormous energies flow in on days such as these. At the Wesak celebration in May of 1994, Lord Maitreya came to our group and planted a "Rod of Light" down through our crown chakras and into the whole chakra column. The Light was later to be absorbed into the entire four-body system. This was another great boon and blessing for our Light quotient building.

Yet another Light quotient building tool is to ask Djwhal Khul to officially enroll you in the Light quotient building program about which I will speak in more detail later. I have humorously called it the "intravenous Light quotient building program." They literally drip Light into you as an intravenous needle would drip medication. I think much of it occurs at night while you sleep.

An important understanding in regard to the Light quotient building is that the four bodies — physical, emotional, mental, and spiritual — will necessarily be at the same level of Light quotient at a given moment. If you are the emotional type you might have more Light quotient in that body and less in your mental body. If you are the mental type, it might be the opposite. The ideal is to try to integrate the four bodies on a daily basis in an even and balanced manner so as to keep them evolving at pretty much the same speed. Realistically, however, in most people there will be some differences. Your overall Light quotient is an averaging of all the bodies.

The best ways I have found for building the Light quotient are working in the Light Synthesis Chamber, working with Archangel Metatron, and visiting the ascension seats. I have referred previously to such ascension seats as those in Luxor and Telos and those aboard Ashtar's and the Arcturians' ships. Recently I have discovered three more ascension seats which I highly recommend experimenting with in your meditations. The first one is in Shamballa. It is a large cylinder that sits in a courtyard. Just ask to be taken there by your own I Am Presence or by one of the ascended masters. Step inside it and ask that it be activated for the completion of your ascension. Also ask that you retain in your conscious daily life the consciousness and activation you receive.

I learned about the second new ascension seat from Saint Germain. It is a Lemurian ascension seat which, believe it or not, is in a mountainous area of southern California. I plan to do much more meditating there. The last ascension seat is in Africa in an extraterrestrial spacecraft that is buried underground.

In an advanced ascension workshop that Terri Sue and I held in our home, Archangel Metatron spoke through Terri Sue and brought forth some incredible information on building the Light quotient which I would like to share with you. First of all, he said that the Light quotient was the single most important factor in terms of whether you are ready to take your next initiation. The first thing the masters look at when they examine your level of evolvement is how much Light you have in your field.

Archangel Metatron said that your Light quotient can be built regardless of whether you have physical health problems, emotional instability and emotional problems, or even mental problems. He recommended that you ask him at first for an increase of "12% Light quotient." Use these exact words.

The one thing you might notice, as I have in my experience, is that with Archangel Metatron the process of building the Light quotient will occur very slowly at first. When I asked for the same process from the Arcturians, the increase seemed to occur much more quickly and more powerfully. Maybe this is because the Arcturians are using technology of a kind that I find more easily discernible. One is not better than another. Metatron purposely builds up slowly so as to be safe and not burn out your body. It is like physical exercise. If you have ever been a jogger, you know that the first day you do not run twenty-six miles. You build up to it. This is what Metatron is doing with the Light quotient building process. So start by asking for a 12% increase. Then after a bit, ask for that to be doubled. Then ask for a 50% buildup; then you can even ask for a 100% Light quotient increase — with a qualification: "as long as it is safe for my four-body system." Metatron might progress slowly. However, within fifteen minutes of beginning your meditation, you will be amazed by how powerful and intense the energy flow is. Sometimes it feels electric. If it gets too intense, just ask Metatron to tone it down. This is also true of any of the ascension seats or other practices I have mentioned.

The other thing that Metatron did with us was to have us ask for the increase in specific bodies. For example, ask for the Light quotient to be increased in your emotional body. Ask for a 100% increase just on the emotional level and see how that feels. Then do it for the mental body, the physical body, and the spiritual body. Then, using a symbol of infinity,* blend the four bodies together so they function as your one body. This is the same as the seven major chakras blending together to form one unified chakra. Certain people will have more Light in one body than another. It is fun to experiment with this.

I can not emphasize strongly enough the importance of building the Light quotient. In my opinion, it should be one of the main focuses of every meditation. In using the Light quotient, you gain in loving kindness and service in the demonstration of God in your daily life. This Light can also be used in your individual and group meditations and for world service work such as healing Mother Earth, activating and energizing the planetary grids, and healing trouble spots on the planet. You will be amazed at how powerful these processes are.

One other interesting thing that Archangel Metatron suggested was to call in the angels who deal specifically with building the Light quotient. Ask these angels to blend with your body and help in this process while Archangel Metatron is working with you.

Djwhal Khul told us that Sai Baba is past the 99.99% Light quotient, as is the Lord Maitreya. Djwhal said no one is really at 100% because there is always a little margin for error.

---

* The infinity symbol is a figure eight turned sideways (∞) and there is a twist in the ribbon so that when tracing it with your finger, you touch every part of it.

The Ultimate Golden Key to Building Your Light Quotient

After you take your ascension you are ready to step up to a new level. You are ready to begin working more closely with Shamballa, the Galactic Core, and the Universal Core. It is for this reason I am recommending that if you have become a kindergarten ascended master, you spend most of your day in the ascension seats of Shamballa and Sanat Kumara or in Lenduce's ashram in his ascension seats, and then travel up another level to the Golden Chamber of Melchizedek and sit in his ascension seat at the Universal Core level. I am currently spending most of my time in these three seats and have been guided not to use the other ascension seats but to focus just on these, since I am about to complete my ascension.

Prior to ascension much work needs to be done in the ascension seat in Luxor with Serapis Bey, in the ascension seat on Ashtar's command ship, and in the ones in Telos beneath Mt. Shasta, in the King's Chamber in the Great Pyramid, and in the Arcturians' ships. I spent a full year working with my wife before completing the ascension. (In the past many have spent an entire lifetime doing this.) Then we were told we were ready to move to the next level.

Prior to ascension you can ask to experience the galactic and universal seats. However, I would recommend that your base of operations be the others mentioned above. You cannot build the second and third floors of a house until the first floor is properly established.

There might also be an ascension seat in the Solar Core in relationship to Helios. I have gotten some preliminary information, but I am still checking this one out.

What I have been doing is going to Luxor in my morning meditations. I then continue this meditation during my morning ascension walk, so I have a kind of walking meditation. In the late mornings and afternoons I usually focus on the ascension seat in Shamballa. However, when I go out to do errands I go to the Light Synthesis Chamber on the Arcturian ship and have a type of bilocation experience. Before bed I like to go to the Golden Chamber of Melchizedek. I try to be in the ascension seats as much as possible. I like being in the ascension seat in Shamballa or the Arcturian Light Synthesis Chamber while watching television before bed. Some of my best Light quotient building, in fact, has occurred while watching television. Many times, once you get into a schedule like this, the energies come on their own; then I don't consciously invoke any particular ascension seat.

Meditation for Building Your Light Quotient

The following meditation is specifically designed to build your Light quotient. It is the best and finest technique I have found for the most enjoyable and effective results. Use this meditation every day, or at least parts of it every day, and you will be guaranteed success in this endeavor.

It can be used in a group or the words can be adjusted so that it is appropriate for you to use when alone.

Beloved Presence of God, Sanat Kumara, Metatron, and Djwhal Khul,

We call forth the tube of Light, the ascension column of Light, and a pillar of Light to surround the group.

We call forth the golden-white ascension energies, that they might come down through our crown chakras.

We call forth the complete opening of our ascension chakras.

We call forth the complete opening and activation of all our brain centers.

We call forth the complete anchoring of the fourth-dimensional chakra grid and chakras eight through fifteen.

We call forth the fifth-dimensional chakra grid — chakras sixteen through twenty-two — to now anchor, under the guidance of the monad.

We call forth the full anchoring of the three hundred fifty-two levels of the Mahatma.

We call forth the full anchoring of our souls and monadic Light-bodies.

We call forth the full anchoring of our mayavarupa bodies.

We call forth the full anchoring of our solar bodies of Light.

We call forth our golden solar angelic bodies.

Let us also call forth the full anchoring of the Microtron by Metatron.

Let us call forth, inwardly, our personal merkabahs, under the guidance of Sanat Kumara or Djwhal Khul. We ask that they begin spinning to raise our vibrational frequencies to the full realization of the ascended master state of consciousness.

We now call forth the Greater Flame to descend and merge with the lesser flame.

We now call forth the Arcturian temple workers and the Arcturian starships under the guidance of Sanat Kumara to give us an energetic experience of their Light quotient building technology. We ask that they run the energies at the appropriate level for each person present.

We now call forth a group merkabah to travel to Commander Ashtar's ship under the guidance of Sanat Kumara and Djwhal Khul and to sit upon the ascension seats there.

As our last experience of building our Light quotient, we call forth Sanat Kumara, Vywamus, and Lenduce and ask that they give us an experience of the Light quotient, a Light shower.

Another Golden Key to Building Your Light Quotient

After working with this process for almost a full year in a very focused manner, I have come up with what I consider to be the golden key to building the Light quotient and accelerating spiritual growth. The golden key is this: throughout your day, switch back and forth between your normal activity and focusing on one or the other of these wonderful sources – the Arcturians, Archangel Metatron, the Mahatma, Melchizedek, or the ascension seats. I have learned this can be done in a bilocational manner so that you are doing two things at once – watching television, working, eating, sleeping, or socializing, as well as increasing your Light potential.

The one danger here is that it is possible to do too much and this is where the issue of staying in the Tao, or maintaining balance, is important. If you ever start overheating or running a fever where too much heat is coming out of your body, then take a vacation immediately. It is okay to want to accelerate your program, but only to a point. Ask that the whole process be monitored carefully by your monad.

Ascension Walks and the Environment

One of my favorite ways of building my Light quotient and running the ascension energies is to go for a walk. I begin the walk by calling forth one of the ascension seats or Metatron for a Light quotient increase. Sometimes I also call in Djwhal Khul to help run the energies.

Such a walk is very enjoyable and is one of my favorite daily activities. I did, however, learn a little lesson recently. In Los Angeles, where I live, as in most large cities, there is an enormous amount of environmental pollution. It is hard to escape, and there is much more of it around than can be perceived with the five senses. I had been taking my daily ascension walks for some time when Djwhal told me that my aura was filled with environmental pollutants. I had never before thought about it, but I would walk through the neighborhood in a receptive mode, channeling the Light. Unbeknownst to me, I was also channeling the environmental pollution into my aura.

Djwhal told me to drink more water and to use Hanna Kroeger's iron ring after each walk. This is a ring in which you stand for a couple of minutes while it pulls the environmental toxins out of your aura. You can read about it in her book. The only problem is that you will probably have to make it yourself, which is not really that difficult if you are handy.

I also use a specific homeopathic remedy called Enviroprotect, which is distributed by Futureplex and can be ordered from Capitol Drugs, a homeopathic pharmacy in Sherman Oaks, California, by calling (818) 905-8338. You can try to walk in natural areas and parks as much as possible, but even then, if you live in a city there is no avoiding the pollution. I still go for the same walk every day, but I do take these preventive measures now.

Another measure I take is to avoid coddling myself. This is a trap I see many Lightworkers fall into. They become so sensitive and fragile that they end up in a prison of their own creation. It is important to find the perfect balance between taking care of yourself and becoming ultrasensitive and a hypochondriac.

Every city has a certain energy pulse and auric field. It is a good idea, in terms of your future plans, to try to live in that geographic area which resonates best with your pulse. After scanning the United States, I found that Arizona is the area that resonates with and strengthens my personal aura the best. It is certainly preferable to live in a place that strengthens your personal energies rather than depleting them.

Vywamus has said that geography even has an effect on the initiation process. For example, think about the results of being in the energy of Mt. Shasta or Sedona, Arizona. Imagine the effect living there all the time would have on you. I am not saying living in these places would be right for everybody, but even to vacation in this kind of energy can have an uplifting effect. Certain areas are large vortexes of energy and have much clearer energy fields, so that you are naturally uplifted and the energy flows in much more easily. Lightworkers are needed in all areas, so wherever you are, make that place work for you. I have completed my ascension in Los Angeles and there have been many great benefits to being here; the pollution factor was not one of them!

4

New Ascension Techniques

*Spend as much time sitting in the ascension
seats on the inner plane as you
possibly can.*

Melchizedek

Since ascending, I have come across some new ascension techniques that I would recommend adding to your meditation program along with the forty-eight techniques listed in *The Complete Ascension Manual.*

New Ascension Technique Number One

Call forth in meditation the full anchoring and integration of the twenty-four dimensions of reality into your four-body system. Also request that any and all Lightpackets of information be anchored and disseminated into your computer banks.

New Ascension Technique Number Two

Call to the Arcturian temple workers, the Arcturian elders, and the Arcturian starships for help in running the higher Light frequencies through your four-body system and meridians. Ask for this at whatever Light quotient percentage you are currently working on. For example, I am currently focused on realizing the seventh initiation so I am requesting that they run the energies at the 94% Light quotient level. If you haven't ascended, then I would recommend that you ask them to help you run the energies at the 80% to 83% level to prepare you for ascension. At the end of your prayer request, ask them to run the energies at the highest possible Light quotient level that is safe and comfortable for your four-body system. It may take them a month or two, or perhaps even longer, to build up to the 94% level.

New Ascension Technique Number Three

Call forth the full anchoring of the Cosmic Heart into your four-body system.

New Ascension Technique Number Four

Call to the Lightbeings from the Great Central Sun to help you build your Light quotient.

New Ascension Technique Number Five

Call to Helios, the Solar Logos, to help you build your Light quotient.

New Ascension Technique Number Six

In every meditation ask Sanat Kumara, Vywamus, and Lenduce to oversee and facilitate your meditation. This trinity is like the personality, soul, and monad, but on a cosmic level. If you want to ascend, make yourself known to Sanat Kumara, for he is the god of this planet and the conductor of all initiations. This is a particularly valuable technique for accelerating your spiritual growth.

New Ascension Technique Number Seven

Call forth in meditation the planetary ascension ray group with which you are connected and ask that they all receive the benefits of your meditation. If you don't know what ray and inner plane ashram you are connected to, then just ask to be connected to the planetary ascension group of all the rays and ask that they receive the benefits of your meditation if they choose to.

New Ascension Technique Number Eight

This technique is one I have mentioned before, but it is so important that I am going to reiterate it. Regularly call on the Great White Brotherhood Medical Assistance Program (MAP) healing team consisting of your monad, Pan, the Overlighting Deva of Healing, and the Great White Brotherhood Medical Unit.

Whenever I have not felt well during my day, I have called on them for help. (I also call to Serapis Bey, Star Master — who will remove etheric mucus from your energy field using his etheric crystals — the Arcturian temple workers, and Metatron to help.) I cannot put into words the debt of gratitude I feel to these most wonderful beings. Given that, for me personally, the physical vehicle was the weakest of my four-body system, I cannot tell you how many times they helped me. There is nothing worse than having responsibilities to large groups of people and not feeling well. I would constantly — and I mean constantly — call on them for help. It was like having my own personal healing team with me at all times, and I am very happy to be able to acknowledge them in this book.

All you have to do is call on them and/or any other masters or angels you want help from and they will instantly respond. You must remember that they evolve by being of service. You must ask, however, for them to be allowed to help you. They will also help with emotional challenges you are having. They will help to balance your energy body which will serve to balance your emotional body on an energetic level. I cannot recommend strongly enough that you call on your own MAP healing team for help.

New Ascension Technique Number Nine

Call forth an ascended master healing platform every night before bed to work on any minor or major health lessons you might have. If you are perfectly healthy, you can ask them to heal your emotional, mental, or spiritual body. The invocation of the ascended master healing platform calls forth a large group of ascended masters who will hold a particular point of focus for a specific period of time. I recommend that you ask them to hold the point of focus all night long. I often call on them to hold a focus for the healing and strengthening of my digestive system. In conjunction with that, I also call for an axiatonal alignment and cosmic integration and alignment. I would also recommend that if you are having physical health lessons, every night before bed you call on the MAP healing team to assist, in addition to the healing platform.

New Ascension Technique Number Ten

Three times a day, call forth the numerical sequence nine-one-one, either out loud or in meditation. The stating of this number sequence balances and readjusts the space-to-motion ratio in the atomic structure of the body. It is no accident that 911 is the number used on Earth for emergencies. Whoever came up with that number, of all numbers, was clearly channeling. Any time you feel out of balance, just state these three numbers out loud and you will feel the balancing effects.

New Ascension Technique Number Eleven

Call forth Djwhal Khul in meditation or in a Huna prayer and ask to be placed in the Second Ray Light Quotient Building Program. Djwhal described it as being like an intravenous Light technology. The Light is dripped into your four-body system in the same way that a real IV would drip medication into your veins at a hospital. This is usually done while you sleep. You are closely monitored so you get exactly the right amount of Light. Describe this in your prayer and Djwhal Khul will sign you up on the inner plane. Request that it occur every night while you sleep.

New Ascension Technique Number Twelve

Prior to ascending I was focusing on bringing in the eleven other soul extensions of my soul group to participate in my meditations. Now that I have completed that phase, I am bringing in the one hundred forty-four soul extensions of my entire monadic group so they can participate in the meditation if they so choose. In other words, in the beginning I call in the one hundred forty-four fellow soul extensions of my monad to join my meditation and get the benefit of it. This uplifts my entire monad. Before ascension I would recommend including only your soul group of twelve, of which you are one. (For a detailed explanation of this, please see *The Complete Ascension Manual.*)

My Ascension Buddy System

One of the ideas I came up with was to set up a buddy system with my ascension friends. It included Terri Sue, Marcia, and Caryn. The idea was that every time I would meditate and do inner plane spiritual work I would call them in to be a part of it, and they would do the same for me. The four of us became a core ascension group. The benefits were unbelievable. Counting all four of us, we were probably meditating twenty-four hours a day. It was no accident that we all ascended in the same moment. This relates to what I was saying earlier about how an enormous amount of work takes place on the inner plane without your conscious awareness. Ascension is a group consciousness experience.

I can honestly say that there was no feeling of competition or comparison or anything like that. This was confirmed to me in a dream I had some days after the major earthquake in Los Angeles. In the dream I was on a path in the mountains with my core ascension group. It was very cold and I did not have a jacket so I told the group I was going to sprint ahead with my flashlight to keep warm. I did so and felt exhilarated to be making such progress on the path. The next thing I knew, I was pleasantly surprised to see the group with me. We were running together as a unit. If one person would fall, he or she would be picked up and swung forward to the head of the group – total cooperation, total team effort, total group consciousness.

I recommend forming groups so you can meditate and share information with friends. I am absolutely convinced it accelerated our ascension process manyfold. Another aspect of the group is the weekly meetings of our ashram. If there is any way you can find a spiritual community of people to work with, it would be of great benefit to all concerned. If not, then be strong and do it on your own. Another possibility is to place your name on the mailing list to receive tapes of our regular weekly meetings. This can be done by contacting Raney Alexandre, 900 S. Mansfield Ave., Los Angeles, CA 90036. Raney handles the taping and mailing on an ongoing basis and many find that it helps to keep them connected and moving forward spiritually together with us, even though they are in different parts of the country.

Another dream that demonstrated this unity and cooperation came one night when I dreamt that I was the head of the three musketeers and all the other musketeers. In the dream I was leading "cheers," saying something to the effect of, "Hail to the Musketeers, all for one and one for all." I was also saying "Hail to King Charles," although I haven't the faintest idea why I was saying that. I often do think consciously, in my waking state, of this idea of all for one and one for all, and I do seem to be the cheerleader type, both on this plane and on the inner plane – an impassioned motivator for God and the Spiritual Hierarchy.

Advanced Ascension Skills

In the advanced ascension workshop Terri Sue and I recently hosted, the masters Djwhal Khul, Kuthumi, Sanat Kumara, and Saint Germain gave us some basic information on beginning to practice some of the advanced ascension skills. We began with shapeshifting. The idea was to set the intent in your mind and visualize yourself changing into another form such as an animal, bird, or one of the masters. We each chose a figure. In the beginning stages our form changed more in the energy body than in the actual physical body; in later, more advanced stages, the physical body can change too, as has been demonstrated by Sai Baba on many occasions.

The second advanced ascension skill we practiced was transfiguration. Here the masters had us change our faces to make them look younger. Then they had us make them look like the faces of angels. We then began a process of "youthing" our entire bodies. We were told to see an image of ourselves when we were younger. We went through our organs, glands, and entire bodies, energetically, emotionally, mentally, and visually youthing them. Again, in the beginning stages this occurs more on the subtle body level. However, in more advanced stages there can be an immediate transformation of the physical vehicle as well. Even in this beginning stage, the physical vehicle will be affected.

We then practiced telepathy. We were guided to do this from the third eye rather than from the solar plexus. We were guided to choose someone and send a beam of pink-gold Light to that person. We were then asked to become receptive and receive the Light or message that was sent back. It could come as a thought, an image, Light, or just as a feeling. We were taught to be very relaxed during this process and to send from our hearts in conjunction with our minds.

We then practiced bilocation. Djwhal told us an interesting thing: the very beginning stage of the process is really astral projection. That level is eventually transcended and you then move to soul travel; soul travel practice then leads to the practice of bilocation. Bilocation means maintaining the consciousness of being in two places simultaneously. It is different from teleportation in that you are sending your etheric, or subtle, body rather than your physical body, as you would when teleporting. Bilocation is like being on a seesaw and being balanced right in the middle. The tendency is to go too far one way or the other. If you go too far into the consciousness of the etheric body you have projected, you are actually doing soul travel rather than bilocation. The idea is to bounce back and forth between the etheric and physical states of consciousness. For bilocation you can go to a place on the planet such as Egypt or to one of the ascension retreats or to Djwhal Khul's ashram. Most of you have been bilocating for a long time without realizing that is what you were doing.

I find this last advanced skill to be the most interesting of all: teleportation. Teleportation is the actual sending of your entire four-body system, including the physical, to another location on the planet. Teleportation, the masters said, is not a required ability every person must learn. Master Kuthumi said it was optional. Wouldn't it be nice, however, not to have to travel by plane, but to be somewhere instantly by using the power of your mind and spirit.

One of the keys to being able to teleport is to maintain a consistently high Light quotient in your four-body system. Teleportation is one of the most advanced of all the ascension skills. It is actually a process of dematerializing the physical vehicle, transferring it, and rematerializing it in another place. Kuthumi has said that there will be ascended masters who will be physically materializing on the planet in the not-too-distant future to train the advanced initiates and the kindergarten ascended masters how to do this.

My intuition is that you need at least 94% to 95% Light quotient to do this. Bilocation is an essential development before you can teleport. One of the dangers of teleportation is that it is possible to teleport into a solid object like a mountain or a piece of furniture. This sounds funny, but it can actually happen. In the Philadelphia Experiment, the U.S. government actually developed the technology to dematerialize a battleship. The only problem was that during the second experiment, when Navy personnel were aboard, when the ship came back after having dematerialized for four hours, many of the Navy personnel were rematerialized within the actual metal of the ship. The government was soon wise enough to stop this experiment, for they were dealing with a technology far more advanced than they were prepared to handle.

One of the ways to prevent such an occurrence is to first bilocate and soul travel to the place you want to teleport to in order to check things out. This is also why, in the beginning, an ascended master usually tutors you in the actual development of this ability to make sure you don't get off the track. It is usually better in the beginning to choose a distance only about ten or twenty feet away instead of trying to go around the globe the first time, although, in reality, there is no time or space, and going to Egypt is just as easy as going across the room! When you go to Egypt, the idea is to see it as being only ten feet away.

The actual method provided by Kuthumi was to take a picture of yourself in your mind's eye, like a snapshot, and then to project that picture to the actual place you want to teleport to. The idea is to hold that picture in perfect clarity and then to transfer your energy and material body to the picture. Kuthumi said it was actually like being beamed up in *Star Trek*. The idea is to see yourself dematerializing into shimmering Light and then rematerializing wherever you have sent the picture. Kuthumi said it usually takes at least twenty minutes to actually do this in the beginning, but once you develop the ability, it can be done in an instant.

A tool that Djwhal told me about that can be used in teleportation is the spinning of the merkabah to raise your vibration to the level needed to teleport. Another method is to see yourself at the foot of your bed while you are lying down; then see yourself moving back and forth between your physical body and your projected body at a supersonic speed. You can also ask the masters, Arcturians, ascension seats, and Ashtar Command to help raise your vibration. It is always a good idea to ask the masters for help when practicing teleportation, anyhow.

Djwhal Khul told me yesterday that a 97% to 98% Light quotient was needed to teleport, but since it is one of the advanced ascension skills, it is not required as part of the initiation process.

The Ascension Seats

On the inner plane there are a great many ascension seats that are available to you in meditation. As I said earlier, the purpose of these ascension seats is to accelerate spiritual evolution by helping to build the Light quotient. Using them will accelerate your progress like no other spiritual process. The following is a list of the ascension seats I have discovered so far:

1. The ascension seat on Commander Ashtar's spacecraft;
2. The ascension seat in Serapis Bey's retreat in Luxor;
3. The atomic accelerator ascension seat in Table Mountain, Wyoming;
4. The ascension seats in the Arcturian motherships called Light Synthesis Chambers;
5. The ascension seat in Telos, the underground city below Mt. Shasta;

6. The ascension seat in Mt. Shasta;
7. The ascension seat in Shamballa, home of Sanat Kumara;
8. The ascension seat in Lenduce's ashram on the galactic level;
9. The ascension seat in the Golden Chamber of Melchizedek on the universal level;
10. The ascension seat in the Golden Chamber of Helios in the Solar Core;
11. The ascension seat in the Galactic Core and Chamber of Melchior;
12. The ascension seat of Melchizedek in the center of the Earth.

In each meditation you do by yourself or with friends, ask to be taken to these ascension seats in your spiritual body or etheric body. You will immediately feel the subtle spiritual current running through your body. Once you get the feel of the process, you can begin bilocating. In other words, go to an ascension seat while watching television, going for a walk, or running errands. This will be a very efficient use of your time – you will be building your Light quotient and accelerating your ascension process – and your life will become a meditation. If you feel you are losing the connection, just reaffirm your presence in the particular ashram you have chosen and you will immediately feel the current running again.

A Monadic Sweep

An effective spiritual centering and clearing method is to call forth three times a day and in your meditations a monadic sweep in which the monad, also known as the Mighty I Am Presence, sweeps through your chakras and four-body system, clearing them of all psychic debris and giving them a quick balancing.

I also recommend, along with this, calling forth an axiatonal alignment and cosmic integration and alignment. The axiatonal alignment will align your meridians with the planetary, solar, and galactic sources and will align your evolution with the actual ascension of Earth on a planetary level. The invocation of cosmic integration and alignment will align you with the universal and cosmic levels of evolution. Whenever you feel out of sorts, I recommend invoking one or all of these powerful and effective means of alignment.

The Golden Chamber of Helios and His Ascension Seats

A wonderful ascension seat to which you may request to be taken on the inner plane is the Golden Chamber of Helios in the Solar Core. This ascension seat is actually in the center of the sun which is not too hot to visit, as you might think it would be. There is a great galactic city there.

For our purposes of ascension activation it is to Helios' Golden Chamber and to his ascension seat that you ask to travel.

Once there, I suggest you call forth your ascension healing module. This is a double (base to base) geodesic dome made up of nine triangles. There are fire letters and key codes that are associated with each of the triangles. The fire letters are in the five sacred languages: Tibetan, Hebrew, Sanskrit, Chinese, and Egyptian. When invoked, the fire letters and codes in this healing module will beam into your four-body system and activate the keys within your own body, although this is not something that will happen all at once, as there is the danger of overwhelming and burning out the four-body system if it is done too fast.

Invoking the full firing of all the fire letters and key codes in your healing module will bring forth into your being whole packets of information in the form of Light. I recommend that you request this be done for the twelve dimensions of reality; even though the completion of ascension includes only the six dimensions of reality, these fire letters and key codes can be ignited for the higher dimensions and can be preparation for the future work you will be doing. It can be likened to a foreign language tape played while you are sleeping – the information is programmed into your subconscious mind so that when it is time for you to learn it consciously, that language is much easier to absorb. Ask Helios to take charge of this process for you.

As you sit in the ascension seat you will be surrounded by your own personal Kabbalah and by the ascension healing module. You can also ask for the spinning of your merkabah for greater ascension activation. As the ascension seats in Helios' chamber are activated, an ascension column of Light will descend, like cascading liquid Light. This flowing Light could be likened to food; it is the food of the future. Caryn and I discovered this chamber in our meditations together and would like you to take advantage of this wonderful dispensation now being made available to humanity.

The Golden Chamber of Melchizedek

In one of my meditations with Marcia, we connected with the Universal Logos, Melchizedek, and were invited into his Golden Chamber. A couple of weeks before that we had been working intensively in Lenduce's ashram in the ascension seats that are at a Galactic Core level. The intensive work we had been doing had prepared us to sit in the ascension seats in Melchizedek's Golden Chamber at the Universal Core level. Before the entrance there was a stream in which we were to bathe, letting it further refine us so we could enter such a high level of evolutionary vibration. There we sat in the seats, and Melchizedek's most beautiful energies began to pour into us.

He told us he would help us to build our Light quotients and would work with us on an ongoing basis, pouring in as much Light as we could handle. He also placed a ring of fire around our heads and a golden dome on the tops of our heads. The dome he had on his head was much larger; ours were only two or three inches wide. This seemed to allow us to be connected to the Universal Core level and his Golden Chamber and to receive his energies and Light quotient building process more easily.

He suggested that we visualize his energies as a golden-orange ball coming into us and said that we could also send this ball of Light through our third eyes into a glass of water. I asked Melchizedek if we could occupy this ascension seat while walking and he said it would be best to do it just in meditation until after September, which was then about two months away, when we seemed to be on schedule to complete our ascension.

He spoke of our connection to him in the past and of the future work we would be doing with him. We were invited to come back every day. He suggested that we spend part of each day in his ascension chamber, in Lenduce's ascension chamber, and in the ascension chamber in Shamballa. Marcia and I set up a schedule that would allow us to do this together three times a day, even though we live on opposite coasts of the United States.

Melchizedek appeared to have a long beard, and enormous Light was radiating from his third eye. He seemed like a wonderful wizard wearing white, flowing robes. He reminded me of Gandalf in the Tolkien trilogy. Later in the day I visited Melchizedek again with Caryn. He gave us his blessing and, after some heartfelt prayers, gave the four of us — Marcia, Caryn, Terri Sue, and myself — an envelope stamped by Sanat Kumara, Melchior, and himself that was apparently directly from the Great Central Sun and that granted us all the dispensations we had requested. I highly recommend visiting Melchizedek in his Golden Chamber.

The Atomic Accelerator

If you have read *The "I Am" Discourses* by Godfre Ray King, you will remember a reference to the atomic accelerator. The atomic accelerator is an ascension seat. What is unique about this ascension seat is that it has been brought down to third-dimensional reality; the other ascension seats of which I have spoken are etheric in nature. It is possible to physically experience this atomic accelerator, but you must have completed your ascension and be approaching your seventh initiation. You must get specific permission from Saint Germain, the Karmic Board, Sanat Kumara, and, of course the specific master who governs the ashram with which you work. Then you have to be inwardly guided to find it, for it cannot be found by searching for it.

Sitting in this machine integrates the ascension energies in a physicalized way that goes beyond what the other ascension seats can do. (The ascension seats in Telos are actually physical also.) You do not need to go to the atomic accelerator to complete your ascension — you can just as easily complete the whole process without it — but experiencing the atomic accelerator in the physical might accelerate the process a little bit. Great benefit can be received by traveling to Table Mountain, Wyoming, in your etheric body, too.

In my meditations with Caryn we began visiting the atomic accelerator in Table Mountain, Wyoming. We went etherically and the effect was much like the other ascension seats we had visited. I suggest that you include visiting the atomic accelerator in your daily meditation practice. Request Saint Germain to be your guide in this work.

I also recommend reading the first two books in Saint Germain's series of books, The "I Am" Discourses. The first book is called Unveiled Mysteries and book two is The Magic Presence. They are very much worth reading, for they tell the story of Godfre Ray King's ascension and the use of this amazing ascension machine.

Cosmic Fire Cleansing

Another ascension meditation that is quite useful is the invocation of the Cosmic Fire. This energy must be used with extreme caution. Djwhal Khul has recommended calling forth only a matchstick's worth. I suggest invoking this energy only under the guidance of your monad, Sanat Kumara, and/or one of the ascended masters so they can monitor the flow. I use this energy for cleansing myself when I feel a lot of psychic or spiritual debris or cloudiness in my aura. The Cosmic Fire burns it all up.

Building the Antakarana and Widening the Central Canal

One of the most important meditations with which to work has to do with building your antakarana to your soul and monad. This is the line of Light filament energy you build among the three spheres of consciousness — personality, soul, and monad. Before the three can become totally unified, which is ascension, the antakarana that connects them must be built. Work for a minimum of three weeks to three months to build this bridge of Light, following the material in the chapter on the subject in The Complete Ascension Manual. Then do the meditations in the same chapter that focus on widening the central canal, and call forth the spiritual vortex to cleanse your field. I recommend doing this exercise daily.

Connecting the Antakarana with the Ascension Column

Djwhal Khul shared with Marcia and me a wonderful spiritual invocation and meditation technique. The specific ascension technique has to do with invoking the seven ray masters, specifically El Morya, Kuthumi, Serapis Bey, Paul the Venetian, Hilarion, Jesus, and Saint Germain. The idea is to invoke their help in connecting your third eye with the rainbow bridge, or antakarana. This is the thread of Light the initiate has created from the personality back through the soul to the monad which then connects into and merges with the ascension column. So the antakarana is merged with the ascension column through all the chakras, one through twenty-two or one through thirty-six, and then continues to the monad. I have added to this invocation that the seven ray masters then perfectly open and balance all the chakras. The following is an invocation you can use to invoke this process:

> I call forth the radiance of all seven rays and the combined full power of the seven ray masters to shine through my third eye center and connect the force of the rainbow bridge into the Light of the ascension column, through all chakras and to the monad. I also ask for a perfect opening and balancing of all my chakras, now!

Widening Your Cosmic Antakarana

Call to the Cosmic Consultant, the Mahatma, Melchizedek, Lenduce, and Vywamus for help in building your antakarana all the way back to the Godhead. Normally, you might think of building the antakarana only to the soul and monad; it is time to enlarge that concept and build it all the way to Source Itself. After that is completed, ask that your cosmic and monadic antakarana be widened and enlarged to allow more God-current. Do this every day and, over time, that is exactly what will take place. It must be done slowly to make sure that your circuits don't get burned out from too much God-current.

Merging with the Nine Dimensions of Reality

Nine basic dimensions of reality are involved with physical existence. The specific ascension technique I am recommending here involves a full merger with these nine dimensions in meditation and a request that those aspects of self that are already realized on those levels be blended, integrated, and merged within you. The following is an invocation that can be used:

> I call forth the full merger with the nine dimensions of reality and with those aspects of self that are already realized at those levels!

Brain Illumination

One of the most important aspects of achieving ascension is the anchoring of brain illumination. The process of ascension really begins in the brain centers and then spreads throughout the four-body system. The following is an ascension technique and invocation that can be used to help accelerate this brain illumination:

> I call forth a full and permanent opening of our ascension chakras, and a full opening and activation of all our brain centers, leading to full brain illumination at the completed ascended master level of consciousness.

Spiritual Acupuncture

Call to Lord Maitreya and the Medical Assistance Program healing team and ask them to contact the specialized, inner plane acupuncture team. Share with them your particular health concern, and they will give you an acupuncture treatment with etheric needles instead of with physical needles. It saves money and works just as well.

Further Programming of Your Ascension Healing Module

A fantastic programming technique for your ascension healing module is to request that Helios and your own Mighty I Am Presence arrange for your module to automatically send you the color frequencies that your four-body system requires. In other words, instead of constantly needing to invoke the color frequencies you need, the ascension healing module will automatically do it for you.

Metatron and the Spinning Mini-Merkabahs

Another ascension technique is to call to Metatron to spin the mini-merkabahs throughout your entire chakra column to completely cleanse, open, and balance all your chakras. This can be seen clairvoyantly as miniature merkabahs which look like two very, very small pyramids placed together base to base. These mini-merkabahs spin through the chakras, getting rid of all the psychic debris and spinning them open.

Removing Etheric Mucus from the Etheric Body

In the process of living on Earth and learning lessons, it often happens that you accumulate etheric mucus, or dark clouds in your etheric body. There are several ways it can be removed. One very quick way is to ask that Vywamus, Lenduce, and/or Archangel Michael just suck it out magnetically with their golden hands. A most wonderful being by the name of Star Master is also willing to come in and remove it with his etheric crystals. The MAP healing team can also be helpful in this regard; all you have to do is make the specific request. The galactic and universal masters are able to clean it up quickly and efficiently.

Removing Alien Implants and Negative Elementals

The best way to get rid of alien implants and negative elementals is to have someone who is skilled in the process to remove them for you. Terri Sue and Marcia can help you with this. It is possible, however, to remove some of them on your own. I would recommend that on a regular basis in your meditations, you call to ascended masters Djwhal Khul and Vywamus to help you. Ask that Vywamus sweep through your four-body system with his golden hands (like a net) to remove as many as he is able to remove. Afterwards, call forth from him a golden dome of protection.

Anchoring the Twelve Strands of DNA

The first step in anchoring the DNA is to make an invocation and prayer request for the creation of the twelve strands of DNA in your etheric body. Contrary to what most people believe, it is only in the etheric body that these are created, and it is only after taking the seventh initiation that they can be fully anchored into the actual physical vehicle. Once you have created the twelve strands of DNA in the etheric vehicle, then the process of invoking their transfer into the physical vehicle can occur.

Cutting the Cords of Negativity

Another useful clearing technique is to call forth Archangel Michael and request that he cut all cords of negativity that are binding you to other people or to situations that are not of your soul and spirit's true desire. Ask that all these cords be cut, forgive any and all concerned, and call forth the Violet Flame of Saint Germain to transmute all negativity.

The Mini-Tornadoes

An effective ascension technique to utilize after you have invoked all the major energies you want to anchor is to then call forth mini-tornadoes. These mini-tornadoes are what they sound like – miniature swirls of energy that blend the higher bodies that have been invoked into the four-body system on Earth. It is almost as though the mini-tornadoes sew the higher bodies into the four-body system in some mystical fashion.

When I refer to the higher bodies, I am speaking of the Lightbody, the mayavarupa body, the Golden Buddha body, the Seamless Robe of the Christ, the higher chakra bodies, the Solar Body of Light, the Golden Angelic body, and all other higher energies that have been anchored, such as the three hundred fifty-two levels of the Mahatma. Once all these energies have been anchored, the mini-tornadoes weave the bodies and energies into your lower bodies to create less separation and more integration.

You can also call forth mini-tornadoes with the twelve strands of DNA inside them. They will help in the transference of the DNA from the etheric to the physical.

The Appropriate Spinning of the Electrons

Djwhal Khul has spoken of the appropriate spinning of the electrons in the four-body system. When you fully complete your ascension process the electrons will begin to spin in a perfect orbit. The absence of full God-realization could be seen in the way the electrons are spinning if we could look at them through a microscope. Their spin can be rectified to a great extent by invoking from spirit their proper orbit. I recommend using the following invocation:

> I call forth the perfect spinning of all my electrons in their perfect ascended-master-level orbits and according to the perfect monadic blueprint.

Ascension Blessing from Lord Sai Baba

Sai Baba in India, the Cosmic Christ, along with Lord Maitreya in London and another master on the East Coast of the United States who has not yet been named are the three most highly evolved beings on Planet Earth at this time. You can invoke an ascension blessing from one of the masters, either the ones mentioned here or, in truth, any master on the inner plane. A very special being to invoke for this type of blessing is Sanat Kumara, the Planetary Logos. The following example of this ascension technique illustrates such an invocation:

> I call forth a special ascension blessing from His Holiness, the Lord Sai Baba, to help me complete my ascension so I may be of greater service to all sentient beings.

You can use this technique with any of the masters to whom you feel drawn on the inner or outer planes. They will be happy to give you their blessings and help in any way they can.

Anchoring Your Higher Chakras

Prior to ascension, I recommend that in every meditation you request that your fifteen chakras be anchored into your crown chakra. You may also request that chakras sixteen through twenty-two be called in; even though they will not remain permanently anchored, it is a good idea to call them in. By doing this you are blending your energies with the masters' energies. The more you call in the energy, the more it becomes integrated into your four-body system.

After your actual ascension, you can begin calling in the sixth- and seventh-dimensional chakra grids which are chakras twenty-two through thirty-six. It is only after ascension that you are realistically ready to integrate these energies. When this process is complete, your thirty-sixth chakra will replace your seventh chakra. Your third eye will become your thirty-fifth chakra. Your present throat chakra will be the thirty-fourth chakra. This is the process with which I am currently working.

In a recent Wednesday night class, Djwhal Khul gave us permission to call in all fifty chakras in our meditations. Once you come close to completing your ascension, I suggest calling in all fifty chakras even though the fiftieth cannot be completely anchored while in the physical body. I believe this is a new dispensation because of the incredible spiritual acceleration occurring on Earth at this time.

The Unified Chakras

In your meditations, call for the unification of your chakras into one single column of Light. After you ascend, instead of there being seven separate chakras, they blend into one chakra column, just as the personality, soul, and monad blend into one being.

I hereby call forth my unified chakras and the complete unification of my four-body system so that my entire being may work in total unison and oneness, in perfect integration.

Preparing the Nervous System for Ascension

One of the most important preparations you must make to achieve complete ascension is to prepare your nervous system to receive the higher voltages of energy necessary to take the higher initiations. I recommend that you call forth Vywamus, the higher aspect of Sanat Kumara, in your daily meditations to prepare your nervous system for ascension. He will run a current of energy through your etheric body and etheric nerves on a daily basis to facilitate this work.

The Lightbeings from the Great Central Sun

Another very effective ascension tool for building your Light quotient is to invoke the Lightbeings from the Great Central Sun. They will come in as sparks of Light and enter your four-body system. Ask them for whatever help you need and they will be happy to serve.

Invocation of the Greater Flame

I recommend that in every meditation, you make the invocation that the Greater Flame merge with the lesser flame on Earth. The Greater Flame is the monad, the spirit, the Mighty I Am Presence. The process of ascension is, in essence, this merger. This constant invocation will, over time, lessen the separation bit by bit until final ascension occurs. I have continued to use this invocation even after taking my ascension, for the monad does not become fully anchored until after you complete your ascension. I will probably continue to use this invocation until the monad is anchored at the 98% Light quotient level which is the highest Light level it is possible to hold on this plane and still remain in a physical vehicle.

Grounding Spiritual Energy

For the grounding of spiritual energies during your meditations, I recommend calling for Archangels Sandalphon and Khamael. They are lesser-known archangels who are most helpful for grounding. It is of the greatest importance that Lightworkers bring Heaven to Earth and not remain out of their bodies, floating around. If this is one of your lessons, invoke these archangels for help.

The Anchoring of the Microtron by Metatron

I consider this particular invocation to be one of the most important invocations of all. The anchoring of the Microtron allows the entry of the highest level of ascension energy available to humankind on Earth. I will speak more about this later on, but for now, just use the following invocation in your meditation:

> I hereby call for Metatron to fully anchor the Microtron into my four-body system now.

Calling Forth Your Soul Extensions

In every meditation, I recommend calling forth the eleven other soul extensions that make up your soul group. Do not order them to come, for that would infringe upon their free will. Rather, invite them to join you in your efforts, according to their highest will. They are beings exactly as you are, who are currently either incarnated on this or some other planet or are on the inner plane. Your higher self evolves through the twelve of you, not just through one of you, as you might have imagined.

The purpose for calling these other soul extensions into your meditation is to allow them to take advantage of the energies you are invoking. By doing this, your meditation becomes twelve times more powerful. Your soul extensions will join you on the inner plane, and benefit is received by all.

After you ascend, you might want to call forth the other one hundred forty-three monadic extensions from your monadic group to join you in every meditation. That way, you are meditating for your entire monadic consciousness and not just for yourself.

You may also invite other groups of people or beings to join every meditation. There is a limitless amount of energy. It is just as easy to meditate for a billion people or for whatever group is appropriate for each meditation as it is to meditate for just yourself.

Aligning with the Planetary Kundalini

Call to the Earth Mother for help in aligning your personal kundalini with the planetary kundalini. This will facilitate the flowing in of the God-current from the Earth Mother, as well as from the Godhead.

The Light of a Thousand Suns

Another very effective ascension technique is to call forth the Light of a Thousand Suns to flow through your crown chakra into your four-body system. This will immediately expand your aura and Light quotient.

Calling Forth the Ascension Energies

Djwhal Khul has guided us that the ascension energies come down initially as a golden-white Light. I would recommend beginning every meditation by calling forth this particular frequency of energy. Let it flow through your crown chakra, through your entire four-body system, into your legs and feet, and into the Earth. Allow yourself to be a channel and column of pure ascension Light.

How to Get Spiritually Recentered

Any time you find yourself getting spiritually off center, I recommend calling for an axiatonal alignment. This will immediately invoke a pouring of energies through your meridians to align you directly with the soul and monadic aspects of self. I would also add to this the calling forth of cosmic integration and cosmic alignment. These two simple invocations will align your personal energies with the entire cosmos. It is like a superfast spiritual and cosmic chiropractic treatment from the great chiropractor in the sky!

The Elohim Computers

Call forth in your meditation the seven mighty elohim and the Earth Mother for an alignment and integration with the elohim computers that are now in the process of being activated in the Earth. With this invocation, your personal energies will be intensified as these elohim computers are ignited over the five years leading up to the end of the century. The ones already ignited will be immediately integrated.

The Monadic Mantra

Begin all meditation and spiritual work with the following mantra, which was created or brought forth by Djwhal Khul. In my opinion there is no more powerful mantra on the planet.

> I am the monad,
> I am the Light Divine,
> I am Love,
> I am Will,
> I am Fixed Design.

This simple mantra will activate you for spiritual work like no other. It is also a fabulous centering mantra whenever you feel out of sorts. It will immediately bring you back to your center. This and the axiatonal alignment, cosmic integration, and cosmic alignment are the simplest but most powerful tools imaginable.

Balancing the Threefold Flame

Call forth to your Mighty I Am Presence to balance the threefold flame in your heart. The threefold flame is the perfect integration of love, wisdom, and power. Also ask for the perfect balancing, energetically, of your male and female polarities within your four-body system.

Baptism by the Holy Spirit

Another ascension technique is to call forth in meditation a baptism by the Holy Spirit. It may be visualized or seen in many different ways and for that reason I will leave it to your own direct experience.

The Amrita and the Sacred Geometries

Call forth in your meditation the amrita (divine nectar) and the sacred geometries to pour into your field as God would have it be. Call to Sai Baba and he will sprinkle the sacred virbutti ash over you as he does in real life in his ashram.

The Raincloud of Knowable Things

Call forth in your meditations the raincloud of knowable things. I believe this term was coined by the great Eastern master, Patanjali, who is considered by some to be the initiator of the Aryan Age teachings through his famous sutras. The calling of the raincloud of knowable things, in truth, is the anchoring of your soul and monadic Lightbodies.

The Monadic Blueprint Body

Call forth in meditation the full anchoring of your monadic blueprint body and ask that it replace the tainted physical blueprint that you have been using for many of your past lives. Many people do not heal from chronic illnesses because their etheric bodies have been damaged or because the blueprint off which they have been working has been tainted by all their incarnations on the Earth plane. This can be easily remedied by calling to Djwhal Khul and Vywamus to help you bring in your monadic blueprint body on a permanent basis. Ask that all healing from this moment forward be based on this blueprint and none other, as God would have it be.

The Egyptian Dispensation

Call forth a full anchoring of the pyramid energies on the planet with the help of Thoth, Serapis Bey, Isis, Osiris, Horus, Amenhotep, and Akhenaton. Request to be taken to the King's Chamber in the Great Pyramid of Giza to be placed in the ascension seat there. Also call forth the Ark of the Covenant to be used on your behalf for the ascension acceleration of all those you are meditating with and praying for. Call forth an anchoring of the ascension temple energies from Luxor to add to this energy, under the guidance of Serapis Bey.

Ascension Meditations

Use the ascension meditations in this book, as well as those in *The Complete Ascension Manual*. These techniques are useless if you don't use them and practice them. The most important spiritual practice for achieving your ascension is meditation. Meditation can be tremendously fun and enjoyable. You might see things, you might hear things, you might just experience profound energies. Take advantage of this divine dispensation of information you are receiving. This is the incarnation to complete your ascension, achieve liberation, and be of the greatest possible service to humankind.

Permanent Monadic Anchoring

In meditation, call forth a full and permanent anchoring of your soul and monad into your physical vehicle. Make a special request of Sanat Kumara and Ascended Master Djwhal Khul in this regard. This can be done before you take your ascension.

The Alpha and Omega Chakras

Call for the activation and full opening of your alpha and omega chakras. These are specialized chakras that can be opened and activated through your conscious invocation.

The Planetary Grids

There are three main grids that overlie the planetary body. They might simply be called the A grid, the B grid, and the C grid. In your prayers and meditations ask to be merged and integrated with the A grid. Through continual prayer, invocation, and working with this material, the merging will take place.

The Etheric Healing Team

Over a period of a couple of months, call daily to the etheric healing team, which is different from the Medical Assistance Program healing team, to completely repair your etheric vehicle from any past damage that it has incurred in this life and in all your past lives. Contrary to many people's understanding, the etheric body can be damaged. It is a good idea also to call forth the MAP healing team in conjunction with the etheric healing team to clear your genetic line of any energies that are not in line with the monadic blueprint.

Request a repairing of your astral, mental, and soul bodies to reflect the perfect monadic blueprint. While you are at it, also request a complete clearing and healing of your atomic body. Call forth Archangel Michael to cut all cords of negativity that improperly connect you to family members or others. Ask that all people who are psychically and spiritually connected to you in an improper way be removed from your field.

Your Ascended Master Team

In another meditation, create a special ceremony on the inner plane and make a special prayer request to the ascended masters whom you wish to help you in your ascension. For example, the masters I specifically asked for help in this regard were Djwhal Khul, Sai Baba, Vywamus, and Sanat Kumara. They most graciously agreed to help. I recommend that you get in touch with the two or three with whom you are most aligned and do the same.

Keeping Spiritual Logs

One of the most effective ascension acceleration tools I have found is the keeping of spiritual logs. By this I mean keeping a dream log, a log of your spiritual successes, spiritual insights, spiritual experiences, meditation experiences, channeling experiences, and the channeled and meditation experiences of others that hold significance for you. You can then review this material whenever you so desire. Doing this gives me a sense of my progress and victories and helps me to remember all that I am learning. It is also helpful if you ever decide to write a book or teach. I review this material when I am in a slump, unmotivated, or feeling a bit beaten down by the lessons of life. Every day I add to it so that there is a sense of continuity and growth. This process of building is the process of moving through the initiations.

The Use of Burning Pots

A burning pot is for the purpose of clearing the negative energy and dark clouds that sometimes gather in the home or workplace. You can do this in each room of your home as often as once a week.

The burning pot is just a small cooking pot or any container that can hold fire and which you will use only for this purpose. (Do not use a large pot, as the energy of the fire is quite strong!) Into the small pot sprinkle just enough Epsom salts to cover the bottom. Just a few tablespoonfuls are sufficient. Over that, pour enough rubbing alcohol to just cover the Epsom salts. This is the inexpensive rubbing alcohol that may be purchased at a regular grocery or drug store. Set the pot on a trivet or some kind of insulating material to protect the surface it is sitting on, as the pot gets very hot. Then light a match and drop it into the pot. The flames will burn up about a foot high and are very beautiful. You might also envision it drawing any negativity from you as well as from the room and surroundings.

No other method I know of will cleanse the negativity from your home as effectively as this, not even sage or incense. Burning sage and incense certainly has its effects, but they are different from the effects of the burning pot. Having a clear energy space is essential for advanced and accelerated ascension work.

Meditation

I recommend meditating twice a day. Whenever you can meditate with a group you will find it even more powerful and beneficial. I used to be terrible at meditating, and I resisted it like the plague. Now it is my favorite thing in life. Working with the meditation tools suggested herein can make it much more fun and interesting. Meditation is the key to ascension. You want to energetically experience and merge with these energies, not just think about them!

Once you start experiencing the anchoring of the higher energies, it is almost like a drug. The drug is God-intoxication. Once you experience these higher energies running through your four-body system and anchoring within your being, you will eagerly anticipate your next meditation. If you skip one, you will miss the energies and realize that you want to experience them again and again! It is the process, done over and over again, that eventually merges you with the energies and higher aspects of self on a permanent basis. Once you experience God, all over-identification with worldly pursuits will become absolutely meaningless.

Audio Tape

You might want to make an audio tape of certain of the ascension meditations or techniques. Especially in the beginning, a tape often makes it easier to sit quietly and flow with the meditation. A tape will make it easier to integrate the material and make it your own.* Eventually, it is important that you set aside all tapes and everything else and simply *be* with the meditation energies.

If you do not want to make a tape, making out a list just to remind yourself of some particular process that appealed to you can also be very helpful. You can then go into your meditation and when you feel ready or feel the need, open one eye and peek at your list to see what else you wanted to include. Sometimes a chart or list in front of you is enough and it becomes unnecessary even to look at it.

Ascension Column

I recommend requesting of the masters that a specific ascension column be built in your home. Terri Sue's and my ascension column is in the living room where we hold all of our classes and workshops. The masters have told us that the living room is theirs and the rest of the house is ours, which is fine with us. This ascension column keeps being toned up and heightened in vibration as time goes on and we evolve. If you hold group gatherings in your house, then place the column in your meeting room; if not, then build your ascension column — or I should say, have the masters build it — in the place where you meditate and do most of your spiritual work.

Expanding Your Body

Begin to see your body as the whole Earth and see everyone and everything living inside of that one Earth Being. Do this for longer and longer periods of time. It will automatically increase your unconditional love, compassion, and understanding of karma and the law of oneness. This is the process of functioning as a planetary being and not just as an individual. It is also the understanding of group consciousness.

Attending Events in Your Spiritual Body

You might not fully realize how much of what you do spiritually is done on the inner plane. There are incredible spiritual events going on all

---

* I have made a tape called "Ascension Activation Meditation" which is available from Raney Alexandre, 900 S. Mansfield Ave., Los Angeles, CA 90036.

over the planet at this time in history. It is impossible to attend very many of them physically because of cost, time, distance, and various other obstacles. What I suggest is that you call to your Mighty I Am Presence to send your spiritual Lightbody to the workshop or gathering, be it in Hawaii or Egypt. You can absorb a lot of the energies and information on the inner plane.

You are a multidimensional being and are not limited to being where your physical body is located at any given time. You would be amazed to know how many spiritual beings attend these different events without their physical bodies! I recommend doing this, even though you might not be consciously aware of what is transpiring.

Practicing Channeling

One of the spiritual activities that will most effectively accelerate your ascension is channeling. Practice voice channeling with a friend or by yourself with a tape recorder anywhere from one to three times a week. This can be done in person or over the phone. Call in the specific ascended master with whom you wish to work. Bring that being down the tube of Light that connects you with the spiritual plane.

If you are practicing with an ascension buddy you might take turns channeling and asking questions. Look at it as role-playing in the beginning and go beyond resistance and fear. Having someone ask questions helps the process tremendously.

Service Work

Service can be summed up in Sai Baba's famous quote: "Hands that help are holier than lips that pray." Being of service is what the whole program is all about. The purpose of evolving and ascending is to be of greater service. Being of service to your fellow beings is the single greatest accelerator of the ascension process. It does not matter how you serve, just dedicate the appropriate portion of your life to doing so.

Traveling to the Govinda Galaxy

Another ascension acceleration tool is to request to be taken to the Govinda Galaxy in your personal merkabah under the guidance of one of the ascended masters. This is something I did in the dream state. It places into your aura a certain vibration of energy for the integrating of unconditional love. You possibly will not remember much about this experience when you wake up, but I recommend doing it anyhow, and do it on two consecutive nights.

The Spinning of the Cosmic Heart

This ascension tool deals specifically with prosperity and the laws of manifestation. What I recommend is imagining a cosmic heart in front of you which can be any size you want it to be. Place inside this heart your prayers for the material manifestations you are hoping to create. Then ask that the cosmic heart begin spinning. Place it on top of your home and enlarge it. The spinning of the heart will increase its vibration just as the spinning of your own personal merkabah increases your vibration.

Teleportation Classes on the Inner Plane

Request before bed to be enrolled in teleportation classes on the inner plane. You may also request to be enrolled in classes in the higher university on Sirius every night while you sleep. Leave the nature of the classes in which you are to be enrolled to the guidance of your monad and Mighty I Am Presence.

Merger with the Galactic Core

In meditation and before bed you can request a merger with the Galactic Core and the galactic level of consciousness. This can be invoked on an ongoing basis. It can also be done in relationship to Melchior, the Galactic Logos. Some of this work can also be done by visiting Lenduce's ashram and sitting in one of the ascension seats there. Some of it can be accomplished by traveling to Sirius and attending the higher university there.

The galactic level is actually about working with dimensions and initiations nine through twelve. This level has been newly anchored on Earth and I highly recommend working with it and calling it forth in meditation.

Light Information Packets from Sirius

Call forth in meditation the full anchoring of the Light information packets from Sirius. Also request the full anchoring of the Light information packets from the three hundred fifty-two levels of the Mahatma and from the twenty-four dimensions of reality, as well as the Light packets of information anchored from *The Book of Knowledge: The Keys of Enoch*.

These Light packets of information are exactly what the words say they are – they are advanced information in the form of Light that can be programmed into your computer banks and four-body system for future use. It is possible to receive Light packets way beyond the level of your evolution. The anchoring of the packets helps to build your Light quotient. It will also help you to evolve faster in the future when those higher initiations and levels are reached because you will have already integrated that information.

For this work I recommend that you call forth Mahatma, Lenduce, Vywamus, Sanat Kumara, Metatron, Enoch, and/or Djwhal Khul for help, along with your own Mighty I Am Presence. To fully integrate all the information will take many months. Also request that the material from *The Keys of Enoch* be anchored with the help of Helios in all five sacred languages.

Going before the Throne of Grace

This is perhaps the most profound meditation of all. Caryn and I asked to be taken in our merkabahs before the Throne of Grace. By this I mean not just Sanat Kumara (which is another great meditation), but before the Godhead Itself, the Cocreator Council of Twelve, and the twenty-four elders who surround the Throne of Grace. We went before them and then proceeded to pray aloud as we had never prayed before.

There was something really nice about doing this with a good friend, although it doesn't have to be done that way. We prayed for help in achieving our ascension, for healing, and to be of greater service. Instead of worrying and holding on to our burdens, we prayed to God and asked Him to lift them from us. When we had finished, we received God's blessing and the Council's blessing and then we traveled back to our physical bodies on Earth.

Whether it occurred in our imaginations or we were actually there does not matter. I know God heard our prayers, and we received a great blessing and divine dispensation to accelerate our ascension. God and the great masters that govern the omniverse, the universe, the galaxy, the solar system, and this planet are capable of giving dispensations to you. One of the keys is that you must pray and ask for them. Sometimes there is a discussion among the powers that be, such as Sanat Kumara and the Lords of Karma, the seven ray masters, and God, Himself; however, if the prayer is of pure intent and not selfishly motivated, it is often granted.

I also recommend that you do a similar type of meditation before Sanat Kumara, the Planetary Logos and personal god for this planet. Ask to be taken to Shamballa to stand before Sanat Kumara and the masters of Shamballa. Pray to Sanat Kumara as you have prayed to God. This has been my favorite place to go, among all the infinite places to travel in the universe on the inner and outer planes. Spend time in his ascension seat when you have finished praying and speaking to him.

Melchizedek's Golden Flame

Go to the Golden Chamber of Melchizedek and call forth Melchizedek's Golden Flame of Purification. There is nothing like it in the universe. It completely purifies everything it touches.

Metatron and His Rod of Initiation

Call forth Archangel Metatron and his Rod of Initiation and ask him to use his rod for Light quotient building and ascension activation.

The Spinning of the Double Merkabah

Call forth to your Mighty I Am Presence for your double merkabah. Spin the inner merkabah in a clockwise manner from left to right. Spin the outer merkabah in a counterclockwise direction from right to left. The spinning of the merkabahs in opposite directions is actually a teleportation technique as well as a technique to build your Light quotient and raise your overall frequency and vibration. It also serves to clear any unwanted debris from the chakra column. It can be helpful to ask Archangel Metatron and the Lord Maitreya to help with this particular ascension technique.

The Mahatma Coding Invocation

The Mahatma contains the blueprint, or coding, of all three hundred fifty-two levels of initiation leading back to the Godhead. I recommend calling forth this blueprint and coding from the Mahatma to be programmed into your computer banks and four-body system. The anchoring of this coding will make it easier to move through the cosmic initiations in the future.

The Eye of Horus

Ask to be taken to the Golden Chamber of Melchizedek, and ask Melchizedek to anchor the planetary, solar, and galactic Eye of Horus into your third eye. The Eye of Horus is a six-pointed star that is ideally anchored into the four-body system which deals with the union and integration of the upper and lower spiritual triad. The lower spiritual triad is the threefold personality of the physical, emotional, and mental bodies. The upper spiritual triad has been referred to by Djwhal Khul as intuition, spiritual will, and higher mind.

When these two spiritual triads are brought together in the ascended state and the Eye of Horus is anchored and activated, there is an opening in the very center of the star and in the third eye. This opening is the omnipresent Light which can be seen and demonstrated. It is the Great Central Sun that shines through this opening.

It must be understood that there are multiple levels of the Great Central Sun and, hence, multiple levels at which the Eye of Horus can be activated. It can be activated at the planetary, solar, galactic, universal, and cosmic levels. On Earth, the highest potential would be the galactic level Eye of Horus. The galactic level includes initiations seven through twelve. You are always allowed to reach ahead of where you are, to a certain degree. Melchizedek will gladly anchor the Eye of Horus for you upon your request.

The Atomic Doorway

Last night in class, Djwhal Khul spoke of something he had never spoken of before. He referred to a point above the third eye, at the very top of the third eye close to the hairline, which he called the Atomic Doorway. This particular ascension technique involves invoking from your own Mighty I Am Presence and from Vywamus and Djwhal Khul the full opening and activation of the Atomic Doorway. This particular point is very connected to the opening of the doorway for mass planetary ascension of the Earth!

The Physical Matrix for Ascension Anchoring

Another fascinating ascension technique deals with a new metaphysical matrix that was recently created on the inner plane and that has been anchored into a small number of Lightworkers. It is now available for the asking to all Lightworkers on the planet. It is a specific matrix that deals with the physical body. The calling forth of this matrix in meditation, with the help of Djwhal Khul, is the new blueprint for the fully ascended physical vehicle. This particular anchoring needs to be called in only once. Request, in meditation, that it be fully anchored into your whole body — that is, every cell, molecule, and atom in your physical body.

The Raising of the Kundalini

Request in meditation a very gentle — and I mean gentle — raising of your kundalini by your own Mighty I Am Presence. Do not, under any circumstances, do any breathing practices or any other types of practices to try to raise it. Let it just naturally rise on its own with this gentle prayer request to your monad. Other than this prayer, your kundalini is something that you want to allow to unfold naturally!

Meditation and Treatment for the Completion of the Sixth and Seventh Degrees

The following is a meditation and treatment I recommend doing twice a day. It is a powerful meditation and treatment for spiritual growth, and you are sure to feel the effects. Marcia and I adopted the practice of doing it twice a day and then would do it together on the phone, taking turns saying the sentences, which makes it even more powerful.

Some of the numbers have to do with the Light quotient level and will need to be amended to suit your specific level of work and focus. Usually about once a month the numbers should be changed to signify growth made in this regard. If your intention is to really accelerate and super-charge your path of ascension, then work consistently with this meditation treatment. When you have finished this invocation, sit quietly and experience the effects.

I, _____, and I, _____, humbly request to be taken to Lenduce's ashram and placed in the ascension seats.

We call forth this day, during this meditation, the combined help of Lenduce, Vywamus, Sanat Kumara, Djwhal Khul, Kuthumi, Lord Maitreya, Sai Baba, Metatron, Melchizedek, the Mahatma, the Cosmic Consultant, Babaji, Archangel Michael, the Arcturians, Christ, Buddha, and the Divine Mother energies of God.

We call forth the full anchoring of all three hundred fifty-two levels of the Mahatma into our four-body systems.

We call forth the full anchoring of and merger with the Cosmic Consultant.

We call forth the full anchoring and blending with Sanat Kumara and the logoic plane of consciousness.

We call forth the full merger with the nine dimensions of reality and those aspects of self that are already realized at those levels.

We call forth the full and permanent anchoring of the Cosmic Heart and the connection to Shamballa.

We call forth an axiatonal alignment.

We call forth cosmic integration and cosmic alignment at the highest possible source level.

We call forth a full and permanent opening of our ascension chakras and a full opening and activation of all our brain centers, leading to full brain illumination at the seventh initiate level.

We call forth to Archangel Metatron for a 500% Light quotient increase that continues to build all day and all night long.

We call forth to the Great Central Sun, Helios and Vesta, our Solar Logos, to send forth and fully activate our ascension healing modules for full seventh degree activation at the highest possible level of God-realization that is available to us at this time,

We call forth to Helios, Vesta, Djwhal Khul, and Vywamus for the full and complete firing, activation, and integration of all the fire letters and key codes within ourselves and within our ascension healing modules for full realization of all twelve dimensions of reality.

We now call forth Metatron to spin the mini-merkabahs through our entire chakra columns to cleanse, open, and balance our entire four-body systems.

We call forth Lenduce to now magnetically remove all etheric mucus from our four-body systems with his golden hands.

Vywamus, we call you forth to sweep through our energy fields with your golden hands and remove all alien implants, negative elementals, and any and all imbalanced energies that don't belong there.

We also ask that Vywamus and Archangel Michael place a golden dome of permanent protective Light around us at all times to create an impenetrable shield from all negativity. We also ask that this shield be reinforced nightly while we sleep by Archangel Michael and his legions of angels. We ask for this not only for ourselves but also for our family members.

Lord Michael, please cut all cords of negativity and bring forth the Violet Flame of Saint Germain to burn off all dross.

We ask now that our bodies be prepared for the full installation of the seventh-dimensional chakra grid and the full anchoring of our thirty-sixth chakras into our crown chakras.

We call forth at this time the removal of any and all imbalanced matrices in our four-body systems that are preventing us from achieving full God-realization at the seventh initiate level.

We call forth the anchoring of the twelve strands of DNA from our etheric vehicles into our physical vehicles, as God would have it be.

We call forth the mini-tornadoes to now descend to help us fully anchor and blend our higher bodies within our four-body systems.

We call forth the Greater Flame to fully merge with the lesser flame at the 98% Light quotient level by (date).

We call forth the perfect monadic blueprint spinning of all our electrons in their perfect seventh degree orbit.

We call forth a Light shower from Archangel Metatron, the Mahatma, Melchizedek, Lenduce, Vywamus, Sanat Kumara, the Arcturians, and Djwhal Khul to raise our Light quotient to the highest possible level we are capable of integrating at this time so that we may be of the greatest possible service to all sentient beings. We ask that this Light shower continue, twenty-four hours a day, seven days a week, three hundred sixty-five days a year, until our 98% Light quotient levels are stabilized, so we may serve at our highest capacities.

We call forth the spinning of our merkabahs at the 92% to 93% level and the full anchoring, activation, and actualization of our thirty-second chakras in our crown chakras, so we may be of the greatest service as ascended masters.

So be it!

Visiting Djwhal Khul's Ashram

One of the most wonderful places to visit in your meditations is Djwhal

Khul's ashram on the inner plane. Djwhal Khul is Kuthumi's main assistant, and Kuthumi is the Chohan, or Lord, of the Second Ray. Kuthumi is now so busy with more cosmic matters that Djwhal Khul has taken over the second ray ashramic work.

Djwhal is a wonderful, loving, and wise teacher and ascended master. When Caryn and I visit him in our meditations we usually find ourselves in a courtyard in a monastery. In the middle of the courtyard is a three-tiered fountain. There are adobe walls and buildings and wooden gates. There is a large room that serves as the main gathering place for large meetings. In another part of the ashram there is a natural area where there is a stream and lush green vegetation. It is extremely peaceful there. There are many places where you can stop to enjoy and meditate, and there is a beautiful waterfall of a kind of holy water in which you may bathe. There are very tame birds and animals and a picnic area. In the actual building there are what might be called meditation cells to which you can retreat for quiet introspection and meditation.

Djwhal told Caryn and me that he lovingly welcomes students and Lightworkers who come to visit. He offers his services to you as a spiritual counselor in ascension activation work, thought-form clearing, Lightbody activation, karma clearing, Light quotient building, finding golden keys for healing the emotional body in preparation for ascension, removing matrices, relationship counseling, and healing. In truth, he can help with anything you need. Almost all the ascended masters send their students to Djwhal Khul for a period of time for training, for he is one of the best teachers available to Planet Earth at this time. He welcomes new students and old friends and is here to serve. Feel free to take advantage of his most gracious offer, regardless of your particular ray type or affiliation.

World Service Meditations

One of the most important meditations for you to do as an individual, and even more importantly to do in your meditations with friends and in group ceremonial work, is a world service meditation. It can be done in a number of ways.

After doing many of the meditation and ascension techniques suggested here, enormous amounts of Light and energy from very high sources of cosmic, universal, and galactic intelligence will have been created. It would not be right to use that energy just for yourself. That is why, at the end of your meditations, it is good to take a little bit of time for world service work, in that way giving back that which has been so generously and graciously given.

One way you can do it is to call forth the Divine Mother energies and ask that they be sent to trouble spots in the world. Visualize sending violet energy, for example, to the Middle East, Haiti, Cuba, Yugoslavia, Russia, and China, to name just a few. Then send a soothing pink or green Light and then golden Light. You can invoke the rays connected with these colors. As an example, you might invoke, with the help of the masters, the seventh ray violet flame, the fourth ray green, and the twelfth ray gold and send them to the Middle East. You can visualize doing this yourself through your heart, but it might be even better to ask the masters to do it. Visualize them receiving the energy you have gathered and sending it out for healing. It is also a good idea to give the ascended masters free reign in how they use the energy, as their understanding of a given situation and the appropriateness of energy dispersion is, quite likely, much greater than yours. They will collect the excess energies you have created in your meditation and use them for world service if you give them permission to do so.

Another way this can be done is to use the harmonics of sound. Choose a spot in the world that you desire to help and chant the "Om" mantra with the specific intent of sending the Om vibration with the help of the masters. It is always a good idea to ask the masters to coordinate the usage of the Light or sound you are sending forth so they can calibrate the exact amount and proportions of each ray, color, or sound that is being sent.

5

The Core Fear Matrix Removal Program

The opposite of love is fear.

A Course in Miracles

Since taking my ascension, one of the most extraordinary spiritual processes with which I have been working is a new program recently unveiled by the Spiritual Hierarchy called the Matrix Removal Program. It is a new dispensation recently received on Earth to remove core fear.

As has been stated, there are only two emotions in the entire world: love and fear. All other emotions, in their essence, come down to one of these two. Another way of saying it is that there are only two ways of thinking: you think either with your Christ mind or with your negative ego mind; you think either with your lower self or with your higher self; you have either fear-based emotions and reactions or love-based emotions and reactions.

The matrix removal program is a divine dispensation from the Creator that allows the senior members of the Spiritual Hierarchy currently living on inner planes to actually pull your core fear patterns right out of your subconscious mind and four-body system. Clairvoyantly, these can be seen as black roots with many tentacles throughout the body being pulled out in the same way that a gardener would pull a weed from the soil. The roots of that weed from the garden look a lot like the emotional and mental roots of core fear patterns. When these roots are pulled out and removed, as though a vacuum were sucking them right out of your crown chakra, they are completely removed from your soul records.

This work can be done by any one of the masters connected with the seven rays on the inner plane. I might suggest asking Djwhal Khul and Vywamus to help in this work as they are quite proficient at it. This matrix removal program is amazing and has never before been available.

Being a psychologist myself, I find this process to be especially incredible. Most people must be in therapy for many, many years to get rid of their core fear patterns. Only a skilled spiritual psychologist can help them to do it, and even then, there are many tentacles and roots that pervade the subconscious mind from past lives, parallel lives, other soul extensions, and early childhood that no amount of therapy is going to completely remove.

This is no longer the case! The process is so extraordinary that during a workshop that Terri Sue and I hosted on the subject, in one weekend the group of people attending had 45% of their core fear completely removed from their subconscious minds, four-body systems, and soul records. It is the easiest form of therapy known to humanity. Much of the work occurred during sleep. The Spiritual Hierarchy got out their spiritual vacuum cleaners and began pulling and sucking the fear out. This work is not available to you only if you attend our workshops; it is available to you for the asking. You have fear programming or you would not be living on this planet. You would have graduated long ago. Even some of the great masters whom we revere still have some remnants of fear programming.

You can try it right now as you read this. Think of a fear pattern that you have been carrying with you. Now ask Djwhal Khul and Vywamus and your own Mighty I Am Presence to remove it. If you are not clairvoyant and cannot see it actually happening, then you can feel it being subtly removed through your crown chakra.

Any time you feel your buttons are being pushed or you have a negative reaction or emotion, a fear program has been triggered. Immediately call to the ascended masters and have them remove it. Every night before going to bed for the next three to six months, I recommend that you pray that all of your core fear be removed. Also request to be officially signed up for the Spiritual Hierarchy's core fear matrix removal program. Once you have signed up on the inner plane, they will work on you on an ongoing basis without your even having to ask.

There is one extremely important understanding you must have about this process, however: 90% to 95% of your core fear can be removed, but it will return if your conscious, reasoning mind does not hold a philosophy of always trying to think with your Christ mind rather than with your negative ego mind.

The problem is that most people do not know what I am talking about when I say this. In my opinion, this is the single greatest stumbling block for disciples and initiates on the spiritual path, bar none. That is because we are now dealing with a psychological issue, not just a spiritual issue. Most people have not been properly trained in this understanding and there are very few people who really understand it in its full depth. As Sai

Baba said, "God equals man minus ego." You will not recognize God until you learn to transcend the thinking of the negative ego, or lower self. It is your thought that creates your reality. All suffering is self-induced. Sai Baba also has said, "It is your mind that creates bondage and your mind that creates liberation." Through my efforts to fully integrate this understanding, I am learning how to master my mind in the service of soul and spirit. This has freed me.

A lot of sincere spiritual seekers try to get rid of the mind, thinking it is bad. That is a grave mistake that will backfire on them most miserably. All aspects of self need to be integrated into a unified whole. The mind is not bad; it just has to be mastered and used in the service of the soul. Does not the Bible say, "Let this mind be in you that was in Christ Jesus."

As long as you learn to think properly, the core fear that has been removed will not return. Part of the reason the masters are removing core fear so rapidly is, in truth, that it is kind of an experiment. If you are living in core fear, it is like a dark cloud that surrounds you at all times. It reminds me of Pigpen, the character in the "Peanuts" cartoon strip who is always surrounded by a cloud of murky dust. When you are enmeshed in fear, it is hard to make progress or to see yourself clearly.

The rapid removal of the fear eliminates the cloud, and for the first time you can make clear choices. The masters, in truth, are not looking for perfection in the sense of expecting you never to have any negative emotions; that is the ultimate ideal but it is unrealistic. What they are looking for from the higher level initiates and disciples seeking ascension is that you always consciously choose love instead of fear and attack, and that you constantly choose Christ thinking instead of negative ego thinking in every situation in which you find yourself, that you always consciously choose forgiveness instead of holding a grudge. It is intention they are looking for.

If you don't understand the philosophical basis, you don't see that your negative feelings, reactions, and suffering are all coming from your own illusionary negative ego and lower self, from fear-based, separative, selfish programming, from glamour, illusion, and maya. Instead, you blame it on other people, outside situations, and a delusionary philosophy that tells you that having all those negative reactions and emotions is normal and healthy and could not possibly be something you are able to control. You are likely to believe yourself a victim. You might even think you are creating your own reality. However, you are not applying that philosophy to your emotional body, for it does not make logical sense; the negative ego is not logical. As Master Yoda said in *Star Wars*, "Don't underestimate the power of the dark side of the force."

I would recommend that any time you become aware of an area where fear-based programming lives, then immediately call to the masters to remove that specific program. It is very important to be specific and state which fear-based program you want them to remove. You cannot just say one time, "Remove all my fear-based programs" and never ask again. It won't happen. You must continually work with the masters and continually ask them to remove the core fear patterns in different areas. For example, you might be watching a movie on television dealing with the pain of rejection which triggers those feelings within you. Close your eyes while watching the movie and ask the masters to remove all your fear-based programming dealing with the pain of rejection. You might be talking to a friend about death and that stirs up some bad feelings. Again, ask the masters to remove all your fear-based programs on that subject. What I am trying to say here is that there are hundreds if not thousands and even tens of thousands of areas where core fear is stored. For example, you might be watching a television special on tribal circumcision in Africa. You could ask that all fear-based programming be removed from that experience which had traumatized you as a child or in past lives. Are you beginning to see how extensive the subject is?

Sit down with your journal and make a list of all the possible core fears and negative ego programming you can think of. In each meditation, or each night before bed, ask that a particular area be removed from this life and all your past lives. If you would like to do some excellent world service work, ask that it also be removed from the collective consciousness of humanity. This is especially good to do in spiritual group meetings. That way, slowly but surely, the dark cloud in the astral plane of the planet will be lifted.

If you think of all the past lives you have had and recall that you have eleven other soul extensions whose past lives and programming are affecting you, you can see how monumental this job is. Most people take hundreds of lifetimes to do it, so the idea of removing 45% of all core fear in one weekend is extraordinary! That workshop was the first time the program had been used in a large group or for as long as forty-eight hours. Previously, it had been used only for individuals and small groups for two or three hours at a time.

The next important point is the understanding that it is not enough just to remove all the core fear; it must be replaced with core love – this means self-love, love for God, and love for humanity and all other sentient beings. Did not Jesus say that the whole law could be summed up in the words "Love the Lord thy God with all thy heart and soul and mind and might, and love thy neighbor as thyself." This is the whole law. If you follow no other spiritual practice but this you are on the right track and you will ascend. All the other spiritual practices can speed up the process but the essence of it all is unconditional love.

A Course in Miracles is a book that can be of great help in your attitudinal healing. Jerry Jampolsky's book, *Love is Letting Go of Fear*, which is based on *A Course in Miracles*, is also a very helpful book. They will definitely do the trick if this is an area on which you really want to focus.

Positive, loving affirmations can help to replace core fear with love. Doing the workbook lessons in *A Course in Miracles* workbook is highly beneficial even if you never read the whole text. Another helpful method is to do love-focused visualization exercises with your inner child and higher self. Another good book in this regard is John Bradshaw's *Championing Your Inner Child*. A lot of very sincere and high-level spiritual Lightworkers are often weak in the area of developing a proper relationship with the inner child. This is a psychological issue, not a spiritual issue, and it cannot be resolved on a spiritual level but must be resolved at the level of the problem. My book *Soul Psychology* contains twenty-five methods for reprogramming the subconscious mind.

This matrix removal program can also be used with children. I must add here that it is usually used by the masters on disciples and initiates rather than on people who have not even stepped onto the spiritual path.

The main point is that if you just remove core fear and do not replace it with love-based programming, the core fear is going to return. It takes only twenty-one days, however, to cement a new habit, which is not a high price to pay for freedom from fear.

6

The Advanced Light Technologies of the Arcturians

*Arcturus is the highest civilization
in our galaxy.*

Edgar Cayce

My Recent Experiences with the Arcturians

After taking my ascension initiation in March of 1994 with Terri Sue and my two dearest friends, Caryn and Marcia, we all began to work very closely with the Arcturians. I had been working with them previously, but at that time it became one of the main focal points of my spiritual life.

As I look back, I see that the process began when Vywamus kept telling me, over a period of several months, that part of my mission in this lifetime was to be an ambassador for extraterrestrials. I had always been interested in extraterrestrials, but I had never framed it in that manner.

One day Vywamus told me that my monad, or I Am Presence, was considering taking me "off the planet" for a period of time. When he first said this I did not know what he was talking about. At first I thought I was going to die and let go of my physical vehicle. I asked questions and he clarified his statement by saying that my monad was considering taking me to a physical extraterrestrial spacecraft. I asked, "With what group?" and he said, "The Arcturians."

I knew the truth of what he was saying the moment he said it. I immediately told Caryn and Marcia about it and they said they wanted to come too, for they are also ambassadors for extraterrestrials (along with our main focus of work for the Spiritual Hierarchy and Sanat Kumara and for Djwhal Khul's ashram). I was very happy to have my two best friends join me. Of course, I asked Terri Sue to come along as well, but Djwhal

Khul said that she was meant to go spiritually rather than in a physical body. Vywamus told me that it was to occur in 1996. The timing seemed to indicate that it was to occur after we had taken our seventh initiation. Needless to say, I was very excited about the prospect, as were Caryn and Marcia. (Marcia is an anchor for Djwhal Khul's ashram on the East coast, as Terri Sue and I are the anchors on the West Coast. Caryn has cofounded a center in Los Angeles, California, for the facilitation of ascension acceleration.)

The new prospect initiated an intense focus on the Arcturian energies during our meditations. Caryn and I have had an ongoing practice of meditating together every day, usually on the phone but once or twice a week in person. I do the same with Marcia twice a week since she lives in New York and Terri Sue and I currently live in Los Angeles. In our meditations we began to focus on invoking the Arcturians. The results we all got were fabulous! Some of the most profound energy experiences and help in building our Light quotients began to come through the Arcturians and their starships.

To achieve ascension you must have 80% to 83% Light quotient in your energy field. To take the seventh initiation you must have 94% Light quotient in your field. We were interested in raising our Lights quotient to the 94% level. The Arcturians, upon our request, used their advanced technology to run their high-frequency Light energies through our bodies.

I had been working with the ascended masters and even with cosmic masters for a great many years in meditation; however, the energies that began coming from the Arcturian starship had a quality of substantiality totally different from anything I had ever before experienced. Instead of coming in through the crown, the energies seemed to come into my entire body simultaneously. My body would tingle and buzz with energy. The blood in my veins and arteries would flow as though I had just come back from jogging a couple of miles. All the cells in my body felt like they were being fed with the most wonderful flowing energy. Caryn and I would sit, on the phone or in her office, for long periods of time just soaking up these energies. We called it "the spiritual Jacuzzi." I was later to call it, humorously, "the nirvana machine."

We had stumbled upon the Arcturian technology for helping to build the Light quotient. This had been one of the main focuses of our lives for some time, but we had never been exposed to the Arcturian technology for doing it. This technology, in combination with the Light showers we had been receiving for many years from the ascended masters, angels, and cosmic beings, were an incredible "one-two punch." We were having amazing results.

Even after taking the sixth initiation, you must complete all seven levels of the initiation. Caryn and I, in our enthusiasm to complete our ascension and prepare to take the seventh and final initiation, started becoming very chummy with the Arcturians and began requesting that they put us on their computers and run the energies all the time to help us to build our Light quotient to the 94% level within nine months' time. Sanat Kumara agreed to oversee this program.

I began invoking the Arcturians and their starship many, many times during the day. I would certainly do it whenever I meditated, but I would also invoke them while watching television, before bed, even while working at my desk. Immediately, I would begin to feel the energies pour through my body. What I really liked about it was that it was a very physical, full-body feeling. I was not only building my Light quotient, which was one of my main goals in life, but I was also feeling much better physically.

The experience of their technology was, to be perfectly honest, more powerful and substantial than most of the spiritual energies I had been invoking. Djwhal Khul later told me that even the Spiritual Hierarchy uses the advanced technologies from Arcturus. Djwhal said that the Light quotient building program they were using for the second ray each night in the ashram was from Arcturus. The Arcturians worked in perfect harmony and cooperation with Sanat Kumara, Lord Maitreya, and the Spiritual Hierarchy.

Before going any farther, it is important to say that the Arcturians will not help you in any way, shape, or form, unless you ask them to and give them permission. They are not like the Grays, or Zetas, who invade your space. The Arcturians are like ascended masters and are not allowed to help unless you have given permission for them to do so.

I recommend that you request, in your meditations and prayer sessions, to be placed on their computers, and then ask to be placed in their Light quotient building program. They do not do their work in a haphazard manner; everything they do is closely monitored by a team.

This program is set up in two ways, depending on whether you travel to the Light Synthesis Chamber on their starship in your etheric body or whether you keep your etheric body with your physical body and they send the energies to you in your home. For the first six weeks of working with the Arcturians, Caryn and I were receiving the energies from the starship. Caryn was then given an experience of being taken to the Light Synthesis Chamber and shown how, in sleep or in meditation, we could simply go there. The actual experience of going there is even more powerful than the experience of receiving the energies they send.

Being in the chamber is like being in the clouds. The exact machinery they use on my body is concealed. The Arcturians suggest I lie down. I begin to feel my body being filled with the most wonderful Light, love, and joy. I feel myself expanding as though I were a gigantic balloon being filled with beautiful air. Caryn and I were on the phone the first time we did this and I laughingly called it the "euphoria machine." We both are incredibly grateful for their ongoing help in our lives. They are the most wonderful, selfless beings. I recommend reading Norma Milanovich's book, *We, the Arcturians*, to get a more complete sense of their culture.

One of the plans I have set up with the Arcturians, which has already begun in this book, is to write about their culture and this experience of being taken off the planet in 1996. The Arcturian elders are as excited about this arrangement as I am. I would like to write about their civilization, since, in truth, it is the prototype for Earth in the not-too-distant future, and they are our future selves. The information you are receiving now is the beginning stage of this project.

When you ask to be taken to the Light Synthesis Chamber, the Arcturians also recommend that you call in what I would describe as your higher bodies — your monad or spirit, your mayavarupa body, your monadic body of Light, your soul body of Light, your fifteen higher chakras, your solar body of Light, your golden solar angelic body, the three hundred fifty-two levels of the Mahatma, your monadic blueprint body, and your I Am Presence. The Arcturians' technology, with the help of the ascended masters, will help to blend and synthesize all the energies into your being by using their advanced technology.

I have worked out a system with the Arcturians in which I say, "Arcturians, Light Synthesis Chamber, love and joy." Every time I say that I feel myself floating to the chamber and I feel the process begin again. I am now working with the Arcturians all day long. I have also worked it out with them to spend a part of every night on their starship. They said that although I have a very busy schedule at night while I sleep, consisting of service work, meetings, classes, and so on, a certain part of every night could be given to this important work.

The Arcturians want you to know that they are very devoted to your personal upliftment and there is no limit to the number of people with whom they can work. They have an unlimited number of starships available upon request. They want you to feel free to contact them and ask for their assistance.

One of the advantages of going to the ship is that the energies are more refined and of a higher vibration. Do be aware that the Arcturians do not have Adam Kadmon types of bodies, but don't let this stop you from working with them; they are the highest beings in this galaxy and some of the most loving and selfless beings in this entire universe. It is not your physical body that goes to their ship, but your etheric body. They are here to assist and facilitate your personal journey back to God. Their message is one of love, joy, and Light, and they are here only to serve.

They have advanced technologies that can be called forth for personal protection. It is a kind of frequency technology that can protect your energy fields. They are happy to help in this regard but must be asked and given permission to help you before they will do anything.

They have another technology for healing the physical, emotional, mental, or spiritual body. I have been going every night to their Mechanism Chamber for the healing of my physical body. They have said that there is not a physical problem in the entire universe that they have not been able to heal through the use of this chamber. It might not happen instantly, but over time they can help you. If this feels right for you, talk to them in meditation and request to be taken there at night for a specific period of time. If ever you do not feel well, they will run energies using their advanced computers and will clear the blockages.

They have a technology I am going to call their Love and Joy Chamber. Ask to be taken to that chamber and ask them to beam you that energy. When I first experienced it I honestly felt myself filled with the most ecstatic feeling of joy. I found myself smiling and laughing, and I couldn't help myself. Caryn said that she also found herself dancing, singing, and bubbling over with joy and love, kissing her children. Any time you start getting depressed, call to the Arcturians to be taken to this chamber for a treatment. You can do it while seated in meditation, or even better, while lying down.

The Arcturians also have what is called an Information Exchange Chamber. It is here we have been receiving information for our books, classes, and personal upliftment. I anticipate spending a lot of time in this chamber on my trip to the Arcturians' starship. They have said I will probably go for anywhere from one to seven days. I am putting in my request for a seven-day trip. Djwhal said we would probably not actually go to Arcturus but would just stay on the starship.

As Caryn and I were experimenting with these different Arcturian technologies, I would share the information with Marcia and then we, too, would experiment. One day during our regular weekly meeting we went together to Djwhal's ashram to speak with him. Djwhal told us about another bit of Arcturian technology that was called the prana wind-clearing technology.

This amazing machine was anchored into Marcia's and my third chakras with help from Djwhal and the Arcturians. It began to rotate like a fan in a clockwise direction, moving in ever wider concentric circles. What this machine did was to literally clear all the etheric mucus and debris from our etheric meridians, chakras, nadis, veins, arteries, and capillaries. This machine did not add energy, it simply created a wind that cleaned out our entire systems. Djwhal said the effect would be permanent.

Marcia and I both felt fantastic afterwards. Even though we received a permanent clearing, I have been calling it back whenever I have felt myself becoming energetically unclear. It is the most wonderful technology I have ever come across. It takes only two or three minutes to do and, as with all these technologies, is there just for the asking. Say, "Arcturians, please anchor the prana wind-clearing technology." You will immediately feel a warmth in the trunk of your body as it is put into place.

After trying it the first time, then call in the MAP healing team, consisting of the Overlighting Deva of Healing, Pan, the Great White Brotherhood medical unit, and your own higher self to repair any etheric damage, nerve damage, or spinal column leakage. Both Marcia and I had a small amount of nerve damage in our digestive systems and some spinal leakage after being cleaned out, which the MAP healing team immediately worked on and healed. Just tell your healing team to repair anything that needs repairing after you have been cleaned out energetically by this machine.

The Grid Integration Technology

About a month after receiving the information on the Light Synthesis Chamber, Caryn and I were given another useful Light technology that was an offshoot function of the Light Synthesis Chamber. It was called the grid integration technology; you can ask for it after having gone to the Light Synthesis Chamber on the Arcturian starship in your etheric body. What the Arcturians do in this technology is to run the high frequency Light through the grid system in a specific isolated manner rather than through the entire body as they had done previously. Its function is to strengthen, heal, and energize the grid systems of your body.

Experiment with this in your meditations or before sleep. All you have to do is ask the Arcturians to anchor and activate this grid integration technology while you are lying in the Light Synthesis Chamber.

The Arcturian Electronic Plate

In my meditation with Marcia on August 31, 1994, we went to the Light Synthesis Chamber on the Arcturian starship. There we requested the Arcturians' help in building our Light quotient and actualizing our thirty-fifth and thirty-sixth chakras in our crown chakras. I also requested a strengthening of our grids. It was then that Lord Arcturus graciously spoke with us. Lord Arcturus is basically the head of Arcturus, much like Sanat Kumara is the Planetary Logos for Earth.

I asked him if he would help us, with his advanced technology, to actualize the final two chakras in our seventh-dimensional grid. He agreed to do so and added that they had been doing it already, based on our past requests. I then asked him if there were any other advanced Arcturian technologies he could share with us that would be beneficial in our process of completing the seventh initiation. There were, and he, in conjunction with the Arcturian technicians and medical workers, proceeded to anchor an electronic plate into our third eye chakras.

This plate, he said, would reflect Light and help the mind to hone in on the higher mind. It amplifies omnipresence and synthesizes the upper spiritual triad of higher mind, intuition, and spiritual will with the body, heart, monad, and Cosmic Heart. It also has something to do with anchoring a six-pointed star, and would also serve to accelerate the anchoring and actualization of our thirty-fifth and thirty-sixth chakras into our crown chakras. He said it would also help us in our bilocation, teleportation, and telepathic development. This electronic plate seemed to have the effect of bringing all the different spiritual facets of our beings into one unified whole.

I made a personal request to Lord Arcturus to be monitored and placed in the computer banks and mechanism chamber on a full-time basis. I was still experiencing some weakness in my pancreas and third chakra, so I requested that any time that part of my body became out of kilter electrically, the Arcturian technologies would automatically go into play without my having to ask. I was, in essence, giving the Arcturians freedom to work on me without my having to invite them each time. Basically, an automatic feedback loop was being set up for an automatic physical and energetic adjustment every time my pancreas and third chakra went out of balance. Lord Arcturus graciously agreed.

As with all the information in this book, I tell you this so that with your conscious awareness of the existence of it, you have the opportunity to consider doing the same thing if you have any chronic health lessons. Just because you are an ascended master or fully realized seventh-degree initiate does not mean that you will be superman or superwoman and have no physical, emotional, or mental weaknesses. The same tendencies and weaknesses you had prior to ascension will still be there. You will, however, have more energy, Light, consciousness, and techniques with which to deal with their lessons.

In many ways I do not feel particularly different from the way I felt before completion. The only difference is the greater amount of Light, energy, expansiveness, and attunement to spirit. Otherwise, I am very much the same. I also want to emphasize here that more and more people with whom I am in contact have gone through some of these higher initiations (four, five, and six, and even occasionally seventh) without even knowing they had taken them. This may be hard to believe, but it is true.

I also requested of Lord Arcturus help for Marcia and me in building our Light quotient from the 94% to the 97% level over the three and a half months leading up to the 12:12. I was requesting one Light quotient point a month, which seemed to me to be a reasonable request, and it was granted by Lord Arcturus. I felt very honored that he had taken the time to speak with us. Marcia later told me that we had spoken with him before, but I had not realized that he was basically the Planetary Logos for Arcturus.

Marcia and I ended our meditation by going to the Golden Chamber of Melchizedek with greetings and doing a Huna prayer for the same timetable of Light quotient building to Melchizedek, Mahatma, Metatron, the Arcturians, and Djwhal Khul. I have included this Huna prayer here. You can change the numbers to make it appropriate for yourself.

Huna Prayer

Beloved Presence of God, Melchizedek, Mahatma, Metatron, Mighty I Am Presence, Vywamus, Sanat Kumara, Arcturians, and Djwhal Khul,

We hereby pray with all heart and soul and mind and might for a divine dispensation to take the beginning of the twelfth initiation (seventh level of the seventh) at the Wesak festival of 1995.

We also ask to be fully stabilized at the 96% Light quotient by Wesak of 1995.

We also request to go to the Atomic Accelerator in the third-dimensional sense in June or July of 1995.

We also request a divine dispensation for the actualization of our thirty-sixth chakras in our crown chakras in the month of September. Djwhal Khul has told us that these things are within our potentiality and we are hereby invoking them in the name of the fully realized Christ, so that we may be of greater service! Amen.

(Repeat three times.)

Our beloved subconscious minds,

We hereby ask and command that you take this thought-form prayer, with all the mana and vital force that are needed and necessary to manifest and demonstrate this prayer, to the Source of our being. Amen.

(Repeat once; then visualize it going straight to the Godforce like a beautiful fountain for 15 to 20 seconds before closing the prayer with the following statement.)

Beloved Presence of God, Sanat Kumara, Melchizedek, Arcturians, and Godforce, let the rain of blessings fall. Amen.

(Experience the rain of blessings.)

The Arcturian Plating System

Three or four years ago I visited a woman in Sedona, Arizona, who was an Arcturian. At that time she installed a complex plating system which she said was an advanced technology from Arcturus and was the future replacement system for the chakras. She used a metaphor to describe it: "If you were to mail a letter, the chakras could deliver in three months, and the new plating system could get the same letter to its destination in eighteen seconds." It is the next four-thousand-year dispensation.

I bring this up because the two new plates that the Arcturians installed were very similar to part of the plating system the woman had installed. It was part of a program called the A Project that I am involved in. As I was going for my afternoon ascension walk I got to thinking that people did not have to go through an intermediary to have this whole system installed; they could just ask for it themselves. In meditation, call forth Lord Arcturus, Sanat Kumara, and Djwhal Khul. (It is essential that you call forth all three of these masters.) Request as a divine dispensation to accelerate your own personal evolution so that you can fulfill your spiritual mission on Earth.

I cannot promise you that they will install the entire system; however, my intuition tells me that it is a possibility. It certainly could not hurt to ask. They might install part of it, such as the electronic plates I mentioned, and see how you fare. In future meditations more plates can be added. I highly recommend doing this, for the plating system is truly four thousand years ahead of Earth's evolution. If you request this you will probably not be able to see it unless your clairvoyance is developed, but this does not matter. Just request it in meditation or in a Huna prayer, accept it as done, and move forward.

Light Packages from Arcturus

During meditation call to the Lord of Sirius, Sanat Kumara, and the Arcturian technicians, temple workers, and healing team for an anchoring during sleeptime of all Light packets, or Light envelopes, of information from the higher universities on Sirius. Request that this Light information be programmed into your subconscious mind and four-body system for your future mission on Earth and for Light quotient building and ascension acceleration.

The Arcturians and the Twelve Strands of DNA

Call to the Arcturians in meditation and request their assistance in helping you to create your twelve strands of DNA and also in transferring them from your etheric vehicle to your physical body. With their advanced technology they can do just about anything you can possibly think of that is of a positive, spiritually uplifting nature.

In Summary

I cannot recommend highly enough that you call to the Arcturians in your meditations and prayer sessions and take advantage of their wonderfully advanced spiritual technologies. The Arcturians, in conjunction with the Spiritual Hierarchy and the ascended masters, are an unbeatable team. You have the best of the spiritual world and the best of the extraterrestrial technologies. It is time for the world to recognize more fully the unity of the loving and wise extraterrestrial forces with the spiritual forces that govern our planet. The Arcturians are not allowed even to enter our sphere of influence without getting permission from Sanat Kumara and the Spiritual Hierarchy. They work together as one team in conjunction with the Ashtar Command and other positive extraterrestrial groups for the upliftment of humanity.

7

The Golden Key to Accelerating Your Spiritual Evolution

*The true golden key
to the spiritual path is love.*

Dr. Joshua David Stone

The golden key to accelerating your evolution is to develop a lifestyle that lets you live within the current of spiritual energies 100% of the time. This golden key needs some explanation. Let me use my personal lifestyle as an example of what I am trying to say.

Every night before bed I ask to be taken to one of the spiritual retreats to be worked on by the masters. This ensures that I am in the spiritual current all night while I sleep. I also meditate or read something spiritual or do Light quotient building every night before going to sleep which automatically sends me to higher dimensions.

Upon awakening I try to remember my dreams and interpret them. I jump into the shower and call on Metatron or the Arcturians to begin the Light quotient building. I then either begin my formal meditation or immediately start doing my desk work and working on my books. This begins the more masculine mode of running the spiritual current. The methods before this were the more feminine modes of receiving the spiritual current. All through my day I switch back and forth between these two modes.

Sometimes in the mornings I do my phone meditations with Marcia or Caryn. Around ten or eleven o'clock I stop working after having drunk about three or four glasses of water every hour. Then I have some breakfast. If the breakfast takes time to cook I will watch some news and sit in the ascension seat in Shamballa, Lenduce's ashram, or the Golden

Chamber of Melchizedek. I often do this while watching TV.

If my physical body does not feel well I send my spiritual body to the Mechanism Chamber on the Arcturian starship to get rejuvenated and balanced. I then pray over my food to bless and energize it and eat a healthful breakfast. Then I usually go for my ascension walk for an hour to an hour and a half. I begin by calling in Metatron or the Arcturians for Light quotient building or by sending my spiritual body to one of the ascension seats while I walk. I also use the walks for processing and integration. I could sometimes call my walks "journal walks," depending on my need, but I prefer the focus of "ascension walks."

I come home and return phone calls or run errands. When I run errands I usually call on Metatron or the Arcturians to continue running the energies while I am driving or standing in line at the market and bank. This errand time and walking time can also be used for chanting the name of God, singing devotional songs, and doing spiritual affirmations and visualizations.

Are you beginning to see what I am talking about here? There is never a time when the spiritual current is not running through me in either a yin or a yang manner. I come home, have a healthful lunch, then go and meditate. It might be a silent meditation to enjoy the stillness, or another type of meditation. Then I take a little catnap and request to go to one of the ascension retreats again for spiritual acceleration.

Upon waking I go back to work on my books or do other service work. Currently, my focus has been writing lectures, seminars, and workshops, so I am not seeing individual clients as I did for many years. One of the best ways to run the spiritual current is to do your service work, regardless of the kind of job you have. Being of service is an attitude.

After dinner I might call a friend and meditate or just talk while sitting in the ascension seats. You might want to do some spiritual reading or write in your journal. It does not matter what form your spiritual practice takes, as long as attention is focused on God and your spiritual path and you are always moving up the mountain. The idea is to constantly move toward increasing your frequency, energies, and health in all areas.

At night I enjoy watching some television. Again, I call in the energies and just soak them in as I am enjoying the television show. Other evenings I hold classes, lectures, or workshops. The key is to just move creatively in an ongoing, flowing manner from one spiritual practice to the next, depending on the need.

The key to raising your vibration and accelerating your evolution is never to give in to your lower self and negative ego and always to remain attuned to your soul and spirit. Perfection does not mean never making a mistake; it means never making a conscious mistake. Make a vow to yourself and to God never to leave or step back from your attunement to God, no matter what. Close the door on your lower self and negative ego and lock it for eternity. That is the way to really accelerate your spiritual evolution.

Make a vow to remain joyous, loving, forgiving, and peaceful at all times, regardless of outer circumstances. Remain in evenmindedness and equanimity whether you have profit or loss, pleasure or pain, sickness or health, victory or defeat, whether people praise you or criticize you. This is the consciousness of the Godself.

When things do not go according to your preferences, immediately do a positive affirmation and a prayer to your Mighty I Am Presence to heal and balance the situation. This keeps your mind always on God, perfection, and abundance. The key is to keep your mind steady in the Light at all times and to stay focused at all times on ascension and service — and nothing else. I, personally, make tons of mistakes; however, I do not make conscious mistakes. When you do make an error in judgment, learn from it and move forward. The golden nugget you have gained has raised your vibration. Have fun, be happy, take recreation time, stay in balance.

The key is never to waste a single moment, a single second, or a single bit of energy. Every thought, every word, every deed, every moment, every piece of energy you use is moving you either toward ascension or away from it. Since I made my ultimate vow never to become disconnected from my soul and spirit ever again, my life has become much easier and my evolution has increased a thousandfold.

Recently I have actually gone through the equivalent of three major initiations in less than two years' time. This is mind-boggling! Every single thing I have done to achieve this growth is in this or another of my books. I have shared with you every insight and tool I've used. There is no reason, if you apply the same methods, you will not get similar results.

All the practices mentioned can be done on your job and with family and friends, no matter what your circumstances. Your job, your spouse, your children, your extended family, and your friends are all part of your spiritual path, not separate from it. Let your every thought, word, and deed be in alignment with your soul and spirit, and you will continue to raise your frequency and vibration.

Never give up, even for an instant. This incarnation is too precious. You will never have a better opportunity to ascend and complete your seven levels of initiation than you have right now. "Be about the Father's business," for there is no other reason for living on Earth. If you think there is, you are living in glamour, illusion, and maya. Earth is a school to realize God and to be of service.

When you learn your lessons and graduate from this school you will then break the wheel of reincarnation and continue your schooling at a higher university. Do not allow yourself to be over-identified with matter. Do not invest in the impermanent. "Seek ye first the kingdom of God and all things shall be added unto thee."

Can the pleasures of your lower self and the hedonism of the negative ego and desire body compare with the glories of God-realization, becoming an ascended master, completing the seven levels of initiation, and liberation from the wheel of rebirth? It is like comparing infinity with one grain of sand; yet, remarkably enough, some people choose the grain of sand over infinity. This is the delusionary nature of the lower self and the negative ego. As the great Sai Baba has said, "God equals man minus ego." It is your choice.

This kind of ascension thinking to which I have been referring could also be called choiceless awareness. As a child, then an adolescent and an adult, you come to the understanding that you have free choice. As you progress along your spiritual path and move to the level of becoming a high-degree initiate you learn that, in a sense, you do *not* have free choice; there is no longer a free choice about whether or not you are going to choose negative ego, separation, or fear as opposed to God, Christ consciousness, and love.

There is only God and it is virtually inconceivable to consciously choose anything else. In this sense you have moved into choiceless awareness. Being in this state of consciousness actually makes life much easier, for there is no more conflict or battle between the lower and higher selves. There is no longer any choice, because the door to the lower self has been locked and bolted shut and the key has been thrown away forever.

It is ironic that choiceless awareness would be the key to true freedom. Choiceless awareness removes temptation, for temptation is seductive only if you allow yourself the freedom to choose it. This state of consciousness takes total commitment. The question I ask is this: How much do you want to achieve liberation, ascension, and completion of your seven levels of initiation? As Yogananda said, "The only way to realize God is to want God as much as a drowning man wants air." If you want God that much and can move into a choiceless awareness in which God is your only choice and nothing else exists, in which nothing can detour you from your appointed union, then you will certainly find God.

To accelerate your spiritual evolution, constantly run the spiritual current in either a yin or yang manner and move into choiceless awareness in which God is your only reality, and lower self, worldly over-identification with matter, and separative, selfish, fear-based temptations hold no possible sway over your consciousness because it is locked onto the Mighty I Am Presence for eternity. Your choiceless awareness prevents it from ever being pulled away consciously. It might be pulled away unconsciously but as soon as the conscious mind becomes aware of it, your choiceless awareness automatically looks back to God because that is your only choice.

In truth it is not really even a choice, for the negative ego, separation, glamour, illusion, and maya do not really exist. As *A Course in Miracles* says, "The fall never really happened; we just think it did."

8

More Ascension Tools and Information

Spend as much time as you can sitting in the
Golden Chamber of Melchizedek.
Melchizedek and Djwhal Khul

O ne of the most extraordinary developments that has occurred since
we recently took our seventh initiation deals with the understanding
of the antakarana, or rainbow bridge. The antakarana is the bridge of
Light you build from your personality on Earth to your soul and then to
your monad. It was Djwhal Khul who brought this teaching forth in the
Alice Bailey books. The silver cord is the bridge from God and your monad
to you, the personality. To ascend you must build your bridge of Light,
which serves to connect the three aspects of self — personality, soul, and
monad. Once connected by the antakarana these three aspects of self can
then merge together in that bridge, which is what ascension really is.

Djwhal Khul, in the Alice Bailey books, focused most of his attention
on helping humanity to create the antakarana from the personality to the
soul, or higher self. He spoke of the need to create the bridge to the
monad, too, but most of humanity was not at a high enough level to begin
to do that. Fifty years later, things have changed dramatically and there is
a great need now for the masses of humanity to begin creating the
antakarana to the monad.

In the past year, however, I have often worked in my meditations to
bridge my antakarana beyond my monad and all the way back to Source.
Although not guided by any of the masters to do this, I intuitively felt that
it was right. I would often call on the Mahatma for help since the Mahatma
is the embodiment of all three hundred fifty-two levels to the Godhead. I
would ask for help in widening my cosmic antakarana to allow more God-

current to flow through. Even though I was doing this, I never really knew how effective it was. On a ten-inch ruler the normal antakarana goes up only about two-thirds of one inch, according to Vywamus. I was attempting to go nine and one-third inches up the ten-inch ruler.

Approximately three and a half months after our completion, Djwhal spoke of the need to blend the antakarana with the ascension column. It was at that time that he gave Marcia and me a prayer invocation to achieve it:

> We call forth the radiance of all seven rays and the combined full power of all seven ray masters to shine through our third eye centers and connect the force of the rainbow bridge into the Light of the ascension column, through all chakras and to the monad.

Marcia and I began doing this in our meditations together with fabulous results. Not only was my antakarana becoming my ascension column, but my chakra column was also merging with my ascension column and antakarana as well as with my soul and monad.

About five months after our completion I was scheduled to do an hour-long ascension meditation at our regular Wednesday night class. I gave a wonderful ascension meditation using all the new material I had been working with in recent months. At one point in the meditation I felt really creative and, after giving the invocation quoted above, I then called to the Mahatma, the Cosmic Consultant, Melchizedek, and Sanat Kumara to help the group in creating their cosmic antakaranas all the way back to the Godhead. I asked the Mahatma's help in widening the cosmic antakarana to allow in more God-current and to connect it to the personal antakarana.

Although I do not know the full effect of my inspiration, it seemed to be a good idea. I love to travel in the cosmic realms as much as possible and consider a big part of my mission to be making those realms more understandable and easier to access for everyone. In any case, the meditation seemed to be a hit and was much appreciated by the participants and the masters. Leading meditations seems to have become one of my more important as well as pleasurable tasks.

The results of this spontaneous creativity came back to me three days later during an advanced ascension workshop Terri Sue and I were holding at our home. During part of the seminar it was again my job to assist in the alignment of our antakaranas with our ascension columns. This time I led a very powerful meditation to the Golden Chamber of Melchizedek at the universal level. Sanat Kumara chimed in at the end of the meditation through Terri Sue and established what had been invoked the previous Wednesday night.

He set up our cosmic antakaranas all the way back to Source, all the way up to the top of the ten-inch ruler. Our ascension columns were now being set up with our antakaranas on a cosmic level. I think you can see the profundity of this. Our antakaranas and our ascension columns were now established all the way from the Godhead down through our monads and souls, through our chakra columns, and through our legs to approximately six feet below the surface of the Earth.

Given that we had just completed initiations, our chakras were also no longer separate but rather one elongated chakra tube from way above the head all the way down. In addition, for each of us, the kundalini was fully raised and also a part of the antakarana, ascension column, and chakra column. I was really struck by the tremendous leap we had made and by the leap humanity had made since the time when the Alice Bailey books were written.

Djwhal later chimed in during the workshop, very pleased that we were serving as a prototype, or blueprint, for humanity in doing this work. What we had done was simultaneously sent around the globe for the rest of humanity. Sanat Kumara said it was being placed in certain key grids and was being multiplied. Djwhal seemed excited about this and I sensed that we were part of an evolutionary step for humanity. I do not mean to suggest that there were not others who might have done this before, but they had not done it in the exact manner in which we were now doing it. We were blending the ascension column, the chakra column, and the kundalini, and grounding all of it to the core. It is not something I had ever read about in any book and I was very happy to be a participant in such a forward step for the group and for humanity.

Sanat Kumara reiterated the importance of continuing to ask and invoke, no matter how silly it might seem. I had the feeling that he was talking to me because I am always asking questions and continually trying to extrapolate my present understanding to the cosmic levels and then integrate them into myself. That is why some of my friends call me "the Sherlock Holmes of the spiritual world."

I bring this information to your attention for the obvious reason that it is something that you should perhaps invoke for yourself and for the spiritual groups with which you are involved. I honestly feel that it is something that can accelerate all of our paths manyfold. These cosmic levels were not available to us in this way until after the Harmonic Convergence in 1987. It is because of their availability now that things are accelerating as fast as they are.

In a later meditation after the workshop, Marcia and I checked with Djwhal to find out if the work had been completed, and he said it had. The work we had been doing the previous year had laid the groundwork for the full completion of the process.

The Third-Dimensional Atomic Accelerator

Earlier in this book I spoke of the atomic accelerator ascension seats that exist in Mt. Shasta and Table Mountain, Wyoming, under the auspices of Saint Germain. They were spoken of in Saint Germain's wonderful books, *The "I Am" Discourses*. In my meditations with Marcia and Caryn we often went to visit these ascension seats in our spiritual bodies, but I wanted very much to know if it would be possible for us to experience these ascension seats in a third-dimensional way.

Marcia and I went to Table Mountain with Djwhal Khul to visit Saint Germain and ask him about this possibility. After a couple of months and a number of meditations we were told that we had been given the divine dispensation to actually sit in an ascension seat with our physical vehicles, not just with our spiritual or etheric bodies. We were told that before we would be allowed to do so we would have to fully complete our seventh initiation, and the timetable for that is anticipated to be Wesak of 1995, so we were told that sometime during the summer of 1995 the trip was a distinct possibility. We were also told that there was no way you could ever find it by searching for it. It is mystically protected and a master would have to guide you to it.

Over the next couple of months, I continued asking about it. It was hinted that quite likely the way it would work would be that we would be teleported there by the Arcturians or possibly by the Ashtar Command. Djwhal said it would have a most amazing effect on our whole program to actually do it in a physical sense.

I have been somewhat reluctant to speak of this subject here for a number of reasons, the first being that I was not sure it was even permissible. However, I have decided to share the information, for I thought you might find it of interest. We were told that our physical trip on an Arcturian starship for one to seven days was also very much on line, probably to occur closer to 1996. We would be teleported onto their ship for that adventure. If we do actually go, and I very much hope we do, I will probably share the experiences in a new book. I am thinking that these two excursions would make fascinating reading and have made a request to serve as scribe for the Arcturians.

A Spiritual Post Office

Within a few days after our taking our seventh initiation, Djwhal Khul suggested to Terri Sue that she put out the "treasure chest" that we use in the prosperity workshops. She was to put it into the ascension column in the living room. He did not say much, but the message seemed clearly to be that there was the distinct possibility of the masters' being able to manifest physical objects, letters, or perhaps even monies for us out of the ethers. This may sound strange to some of you, but if you have ever studied Theosophy and the story of Madam Blavatsky, you know that this is exactly what occurred at the beginning of this century.

Madam Blavatsky set up a particular cabinet as her astral post office for communicating with the ascended masters. She would put letters in the cabinet and minutes later they would disappear. Minutes, hours, or days later, new letters would appear from the Master Kuthumi, El Morya, Saint Germain, or Djwhal Khul. These masters were physically embodied at the time and living in the Himalaya Mountains, yet the letters appeared in that particular cabinet. That astral post office went on for years.

When Djwhal first told us to put out the treasure chest, Terri Sue was a little skeptical. I, however, jumped at the idea and immediately wrote a Huna prayer about setting up our own post office in the ascension column. If it worked a hundred years ago for Madam Blavatsky, or Lady Helena as she now likes to be called, why could it not work now?

Physical Immortality and Cellular Rejuvenation

An issue I have begun to address seriously is that of physical immortality. One of the newest techniques in this field is the Light synthesis cellular rejuvenation process. Basically, the way it works is that you call to your monad or Mighty I Am Presence for the Light synthesis cellular rejuvenation process to begin. Then a rainbow of spiraling energy will begin moving up and down your body. It feels wonderful and has a tremendously rejuvenating effect. I suggest then doing a few affirmations such as "I am rejuvenating now" or "My physical body is in perfect radiant health" or "My physical body now manifests the health and perfection of Christ!" Lastly, call to your Mighty I Am Presence and ask for a "body wrap" of green, liquid gold, and pink. This serves as a sort of spiritual blanket that soaks into every cell of your body.

Mystic Vision and Occultist Vision

Djwhal Khul has spoken of two paths back to Source: the path of the mystic and the path of the occultist. What I have recently come to understand on a much deeper level is that the mystic and the occultist hold different kinds of spiritual vision. Terri Sue and I share these complementary aspects. She has been much more on the path of the mystic and I on the path of the occultist; she is more the emotional type and I more the mental type; she is the clairvoyant channel and healer and I the spiritual psychologist, scholar, teacher, and human encyclopedia. I think you get the point and I am sure you can relate to it in respect to your friends or mate. I would venture to guess that there are more occultists than mystics.

The important understanding here is that people access Source differently. One is not better than the other, they are simply different. Caryn is also more the mystic and has awesome clairvoyant and clairaudient abilities. She came into this life with these abilities. Although I am not clairvoyant or clairaudient in the way Caryn, Terri Sue and Marcia are, Caryn was kind enough to say that I had been instrumental in lifting veils for her. She has done the same for me and I know I have done the same for Marcia and Terri Sue, as well.

I recently asked Djwhal whether or not I should try to develop more mystic vision in addition to my occultist vision. His answer surprised me: he said no. He said that I was here to bring forth another type of spiritual vision which was equal in every way to the mystic vision. He said my vision was more an intuitive knowingness. I bring this up because I know it is likely that you might wish to have "psychic abilities" like some of your friends or people you have seen. You want to channel or see clairvoyantly. I am here to tell you that it might not be your destiny to access God in that specific way. After Djwhal gave me that feedback I took a nap and had a dream that really pushed the point home.

In the dream, Terri Sue and I were in a large classroom and we were getting back the test scores on our spiritual IQ tests which had to do with our aptitude for achieving liberation. Terri Sue got her scores and there were about twenty pages stapled together. We were told by the teacher that the scores were based on a numerical scale and to achieve liberation you had to receive a score of three or lower. It seemed there was a one-to-ten scale and the lower the score, the better the grade. Terri Sue, in the dream, received a score of three on one part of the test and two on another part of the test which was excellent, and the teacher called out congratulations, for she had achieved liberation.

I then received my test scores back and was very nervous and worried in the dream that maybe I had not achieved liberation. All of a sudden there was an earthquake and the building started shaking. I said, "Let's run outside." We ran outside and then Terri Sue and I sat on a park bench and returned to looking at my test scores. My scores were based on a different scoring system which used letters instead of numbers to grade my intelligence and aptitude for achieving liberation. All of a sudden Terri Sue pointed to my grade and said, "See? There was no need to worry or be concerned. You received an A plus."

I channel all the time in a way that is naturally integrated into my being, and in some ways my vision exceeds Terri Sue's while in other ways hers far exceeds mine.

I have formed a simpler complementation with Caryn and Marcia and they with me. It is no accident we have been drawn to each other as occultist and mystics. In truth, we are all a blend of both, but there is usually a tendency toward one more than the other and it is subtly apparent. I bring this up so that whether you are a mystic or an occultist, you will acknowledge yourself and honor each other as essential to the whole picture.

There is the tendency on the spiritual path to give too much power to voice channeling or to psychic awareness as opposed to such things as spiritual knowingness, spiritual intelligence, intuition, and spiritual understanding. There are many people who are quite psychically developed yet not very spiritually developed. There is a glamour around psychic abilities that you must watch out for. If, however, they can be used in service of the soul and monad and in true service to humanity, they can be a great addition to your spiritual path.

Zipping the Chakras

The following is a very simple energy tool which Djwhal Khul has taught us and which I find absolutely invaluable and use every day, often many times a day. Take your right hand and place it below your first chakra about one inch from your physical body. While breathing in, move your hand upward through all the chakras and over the top of your head all the way to the back of your head. Do this movement three times in a row, exactly the same way.

The act of doing this has the effect of spinning open all the chakras. If ever you feel out of sorts or low in energy, do this. It really helps. It is a quick and effective tool to instantly open your chakras, balance them, and give you more energy.

When You Are Not Feeling Well

Whenever I am not feeling well, I immediately ask to be taken to the Mechanism Chamber on the Arcturian starship and I ask them to heal the problem. They will immediately begin running the energies to correct the imbalance.

The second thing I do is call to the MAP healing team, the Overlighting Deva of Healing, Pan, the Great White Brotherhood Medical Unit, and my monad to correct the energy flow in the area that is having the problem. Then I ask that all the etheric mucus be removed from that area. Thirdly, I ask for a complete balancing and opening of all my chakras.

The zipping of the chakras is the first step. Sometimes, however, there is lesson going on and the chakra might be blocked or too out of alignment for the zip to work completely. The MAP healing team will go in energetically and make the energy corrections in a most miraculous way.

This little section could be the most important in this entire book. I cannot tell you how many times my physical, etheric, emotional, and/or mental body has been out of balance and I have asked them to come in. Within five to twenty minutes I have felt great again. The Arcturians and the MAP healing team have been literally a Godsend. I cannot recommend strongly enough that you take advantage of their wonderful service.

Crossing Your Legs

One of the worst things you can do to your energy body is to cross your legs. If you take a pendulum or dowsing rod and check your chakras and energy flow when your legs are crossed, you will find that they completely shut down. Make it a spiritual practice: any time you find yourself crossing your legs, immediately uncross them. It is okay to have them touching. This is a very difficult habit to break; women in particular are socially trained to cross their legs, which is very symbolic. Keeping your legs uncrossed will allow energy to flow through your foot chakras and grounding cord and through all your chakras unimpeded, from both Heaven and Earth. It will keep your vitality up and ensure that your four-body system is being fed the energy it needs.

It is also important when you sleep and it applies to the arms as well. Illness stems from a blockage in the flow of energy. Health and vitality occur when there is an unimpeded flow of energy; this small but important insight can help greatly to maintain the flow. At lectures or classes, people often get tired because of the prolonged practice of avoiding leg-crossing, especially when they are unused to it, but in the long run they will feel much better and the energy flow through their bodies as well as through the entire group will be greatly improved.

The Importance of Calling for Protection Every Day

I cannot emphasize strongly enough the importance of praying and asking for protection every day, as well as creating it yourself. Even after you have had all your alien implants removed, you can be totally implanted again. I used to be under the assumption that once they were removed you did not have to be concerned about them. This is not true, however. (Terri Sue and Marcia can remove them for you.) Once they are removed, if you do not ask for protection every day and every night, they can get back in.

The protection you ask for is not just against alien implants but is also against all other forms of negativity. There is so much negativity in this world. I suggest that you call to Vywamus and Archangel Michael every day to place a golden dome of protection around you, especially upon getting up in the morning and even more importantly, before going to bed. If you are having problems with dark forces, I suggest reading my book *Soul Psychology*, especially the chapter on psychic self-defense, which contains some of the best information available about how to protect yourself. You can shortstop many, many problems in your life by taking the time to do these simple spiritual exercises. It is when you get lazy and don't do them that you become vulnerable and, in a sense, a victim.

You are not naturally a victim of negative extraterrestrials or any other form of negativity on the astral plane or on this plane or of people on this plane or even of your own subconscious mind. You are only a victim if you allow yourself to be. If you own your power and create your protection then, in truth, you have nothing to be concerned about. I speak from personal experience. I suggest you learn by grace instead of by karma; that is the purpose of this book. Learning from other people's mistakes and successes will save you many lifetimes of trying to do it all on your own.

Vywamus' Prophecy for the Economy

During one of our regular Wednesday night classes I asked Vywamus about the world economy for the next five to ten years. The reason I asked this question is that there are a lot of doom-and-gloom prophecies floating around that are similar to many of the false Earth change prophecies. I know most of the Earth change prophecies are now inaccurate, but I had not asked about the economy in a long time.

Vywamus confirmed that the economy, although having problems, is no longer in danger of collapsing in any way, shape, or form. Those who believe that are holding on to a past thought form and are not tuned in to the profound transformation that has taken place on this planet in recent times. Humanity is now invoking transformation through grace instead of transformation through karma. In the past this was not the case; it is the reality now.

My advice to you is to avoid getting caught up in all the doom-and-gloom prophecies that are floating around. They are no longer accurate and are another glamour trap of the negative ego in which many Lightworkers are unfortunately getting caught. It often happens when you focus on channelings and writings from the past instead of listening to material from the present time or paying more attention to the guidance of your own inner I Am Presence. Just because Edgar Cayce said something fifty years ago does not mean it is accurate now. I am Edgar Cayce's biggest fan, but the whole reason he and others like him gave their prophecies was so that we would use our free will to change the future. We have!

The Pleiadian Healing Center

Any time you are not feeling well physically or on any other level, call forth your own Mighty I Am Presence and the Pleiadians and ask to be taken to the healing center in the Pleiades. The first couple of times you go you might ask one of the ascended masters to join you to make sure you get to the right place, for, in truth, there are many healing centers around the universe. I have gone there and bathed in the most beautiful blue healing waters. Tell the Pleiadians what ails you and ask them to help you heal. They have teams of healers specializing in all areas of healing who are honored to serve.

Zenith Healing

Call to the Pleiadians for a Zenith healing. It is a special form of energy healing that has been brought forth by the Pleiadians and can be requested in meditation. When invoked, it serves to clear the meridians and meridian points throughout the body. It helps to integrate Light and provides a polarity balancing and overall healing of the physical body.

Ancestral Mass Karma Clearing

Ancestral mass karma clearing is a particular meditation process to be done on the inner plane that, I believe, everyone should do at least once. My suggestion is to ask to be taken to Djwhal Khul's ashram on the inner plane. With the help of Djwhal Khul and Vywamus, ask that all your ancestral connections with all the people in this life, in past lives, and in lives on other planets be called forth into a sort of stadium connected with Djwhal's ashram. Once all are gathered, pray to Djwhal Khul, Vywamus, Sanat Kumara, and Lenduce that all karma be cleared and all imbalanced matrices and fear-based programming be removed. Give permission that this be done and ask that all memories and karma be completely cleared from the soul records. Give yourself at least twenty minutes for this process.

While doing this, state your forgiveness of and unconditional love for all present and ask for their forgiveness. The most important part is your forgiving them! While this process is going on, also call for the Violet Flame to transmute all negativity into the purity and perfection of God. At the end of the meditation, call forth the cosmic fire to pour down under the guidance of Sanat Kumara to burn away all dross for all involved.

Also call in the MAP healing team for all involved to help balance out the energies. Have a giant mass hug and lovefest at the end and ask the masters to complete this work if need be, even after your meditation is over.

Light Packets of Information from Sirius

In meditation, call to Vywamus, Djwhal Khul, and the Lord of Sirius for an anchoring of all Light packets of information from Sirius over a one-year period. Request that a cylinder of Light directly to the Lord of Sirius, or an information superhighway, or spaceway, be set up between the ascension column you have created in your home and the Lord of Sirius and the higher university on Sirius. Also request that this information superhighway be permanently connected with your crown chakra so you are receiving a constant flow of Sirian Light information over a year's time.

I am suggesting a year because that is approximately how long it will take to fully anchor all the Light information that is available. Also realize that this particular ascension acceleration tool is one that connects with the etheric Sirius, not the physical Sirius. The etheric Sirius is the Great White Lodge for which Shamballa (humanity's "capital" on the etheric plane) is an outpost. In a sense, the Great White Lodge on Sirius is the real galactic capital. If you do not have an ascension column in your home, request of the masters that one be built for you. Hold classes and spiritual gatherings there and meditate in it if possible.

In your personal meditations, call forth these Light packets and energies and bathe in them as you would when sitting in the ascension seats or receiving Light quotient building from Metatron. Once this information superhighway, or tube of Light, is established, the Light packets will be anchored while you sleep. It is a good idea, however, to initiate the reception of them consciously. The masters Vywamus and Djwhal Khul and the Egyptian masters Isis, Horus, Osiris, and Thoth can help to activate the Light packets as you receive them. They are like little stars bursting open. Sit and bathe in these energies as much as you can.

Melchizedek also told us that it was appropriate to request to sit in the ascension seat in the Great White Lodge on Sirius by invoking the Lord of Sirius. Once in the ascension seat, the new Light packets of information can be invoked. Just say, "Lord of Sirius, ascension seats, new Light packets!"

Triple Overlighting

Triple Overlighting is a new dispensation that has been received from the Creator for Planet Earth. There are three levels, or stages, to the process. In the first stage you are overlighted by a particular ascended master who is in charge of the inner plane ashram with which you are involved. The second stage, once ascension is achieved, is to be overlighted by the Lord Maitreya who is the head of the entire Spiritual Hierarchy and all the ascended masters. The third tier of this overlighting process, upon completion of your ascension, is to invoke the overlighting of the Universal Logos and Grand Master Melchizedek. Move through these stages and add tiers as you progress spiritually. This is an extremely profound process.

The Anchoring of the Five Christ Universes

This ascension technique is one of the most powerful and profound in this book. To invoke it, call forth the Lord Maitreya and Melchizedek. Then request that the Christ energy from the five Christ universes be anchored into your four-body system. The experience of this is truly a divine dispensation from the Creator.

When we first did this in class, the energy was so profound as we were immersed in the God-energy that we almost felt we did not even have to breathe. This dispensation comes through the order of Melchizedek with his and Lord Maitreya's facilitation.

A Christ Tidbit

Lord Maitreya revealed to us in class that of the full universal Christ energy on cosmic levels, he is anchoring 10% on Earth as the Planetary Christ, which might also be considered the Galactic Christ. He further revealed that His Holiness, the Lord Sai Baba, who is now living on this planet in India, is the Cosmic or Universal Christ. He is anchoring 30% to 31% of the Universal Christ energy. It is quite extraordinary to have two beings such as this on Earth at the same time – or at all!

The Anchoring of the Universal Chakra Pattern

Call forth to Melchizedek and request that the universal chakra blueprint be anchored and imprinted onto your existing chakra system. I do not claim to fully understand the significance of this divine dispensation, but it was another gift our ashram received and I share it with you, for I intuit its great value even though I can not explain it. Ask Melchizedek and/or Djwhal Khul for further information if you should so desire.

Identifying with God

One of the confusions you might founder in as a Lightworker has to do with the polarities of identifying with God versus identifying with humans. You fall into the trap of excusing your inappropriate behavior and emotional reactions by telling yourself you are human and hence cannot avoid it. This is an illusion. What will manifest in your life stems first from who you think you are: who you are is God! It is true you live in a physical body, but a physical body is completely neutral. It is your instrument for communicating on Earth. See yourself as God living in a physical body. In truth, it would be more accurate to say that your physical body lives in you. Identify yourself as the Eternal Self, as the Christ, and let all thinking, all emotional reactions, and all behavior stem from that identification. The negative ego can be very tricky in this regard and will use any rationalization possible to take control. As Sai Baba says, "God equals man minus ego." Don't let the negative ego run you under the false belief that you are human and hence do not truly cause your own reality!

The Photon Belt

There has been a lot of discussion about the effect of the photon energy that is coming in around 1995. The information I have received quite emphatically is that it will not be traumatic in any way, as many of the prophecies are suggesting. It will have a very gradual effect and will be almost unnoticeable even to the high-level Lightworkers. It will have a very strong spiritual effect; however, it will not physically affect the Earth as some of the channelings have suggested.

The Issue of Desire

If you study Hinduism, Buddhism, the teachings of Sai Baba, or the teachings of Djwhal Khul through Alice Bailey, you know that one of the main principles is the complete relinquishment of desire. This often presents a great deal of confusion for seekers on the path. For example, if Sai Baba and Buddha say to get rid of desire, then is it all right to desire liberation and ascension? Is it all right to desire to go to the movies on Friday night? Is it all right to desire to make love to your spouse? Is it all right to desire to have a particular type of food for dinner? Is it all right to desire to have a new car or make a lot of money? Is it all right to desire to get well if you have been sick? I remember a quote from Sai Baba that says, "My only desire is to make you desireless." Buddha and Djwhal have said almost the same thing in other words. What is the truth?

Some people, to clarify this, have substituted the words "material desire" for the word desire. This, however, is still not quite right. I have tons of material desires. I want to be a millionaire. I want to build a five-million-dollar retreat in Arizona. I want to make a certain amount of money every month. Is this wrong? Clearly not. It is not that the great masters and Vedas and Upanishads and Buddhist texts are wrong. It is an issue of semantics, of needing to be a little more precise. The key lesson here is not to get rid of all desire but rather to get rid of the desires of the lower self.

Lower-self desire is what needs to be completely abnegated to realize God. Higher-self desire, or soul and spiritual desire, is good. For example, there is no way you are going to achieve liberation, ascension, and God-realization if you do not desire it. Sai Baba has clearly stated this. What you are doing here is substituting lower-self desire with higher-self desire. When that is done you are no longer attached to material things and your happiness is not dependent on them. That is why Buddha said that all suffering comes from your attachments.

The soul and monad still guide us to be involved with material things and to be financially prosperous. However, it is no longer idol worship. Material things are gained and used to create Heaven on Earth. This is essential to understand, for one of the biggest lessons you must learn as a Lightworker is the ability to manifest your vision and ground it into physical reality. This is the energy of the seventh ray which is now coming in on a planetary level.

The former sixth ray planetary energy kept the vision too much on spiritual, mental, and emotional levels. It is now time for Lightworkers all to become millionaires so you can manifest God's divine plan in the material world. Abdicate negative ego desire and cultivate soul and spiritual desire. This is the airplane ticket to God!

Psychic versus Psychological Development

One small insight I have had in the past couple of days has to do with a distinction among Lightworkers between those who are psychically developed and those who are psychologically developed. Those who are psychically developed (are clairvoyant, clairaudient, clairsentient) seem much more likely to have emotional and psychological problems. Those who are psychologically and emotionally developed seem to be less psychic. I am not saying that this is a hard and fast rule, but it is an observation I have been making. It makes sense, for psychic development has to do with developing the subconscious senses, and being more identified with the subconscious mind tends to leave you open to emotional and psychological victimization. Psychological development tends to let you identify more with the conscious mind and leads you toward mastery of the thinking process. This is a little bit like the path of the mystic versus that of the occultist. The lesson here is that it is best to develop both simultaneously.

Eliminating Viruses and Bacteria

Vywamus told us that a fantastic way to get rid of all virus energy in the body is to call forth the golden twelfth ray through the crown chakra and flood it through the physical body, the etheric body, and the entire four-body system. To get rid of bacteria, Vywamus recommended calling forth the emerald green fourth ray which will have the same cleansing effect on the bacterial level.

The Desensitization Dispensation

If you are psychically sensitive to the point of discomfort, you have recently received a dispensation. Your sensitivity can now be smoothed out and adjusted so that it is easier and less traumatic for you to live on the Earth. If you want your sensitivity toned down a bit to allow for a greater barrier, then request this in meditation from Ascended Master Djwhal Khul and Sanat Kumara and it will be done for you. Some people are too sensitive and some are not sensitive enough. Neither extreme is good. It is the middle path you are looking for. This ascended master dispensation can help to bring this ability into balance upon your free will request.

The Cosmic Consultant

The Cosmic Consultant is a being of the most vast nature. I have just recently been made aware of the existence of this being and that he is available to humanity. The Cosmic Consultant is beyond even Lenduce in evolution and is merged at the highest Source of Sources level — the three hundred fifty-second level of the Mahatma. (Remember, when you ascend, you are at only the sixth level.) It is amazing to me that a being at such a high level is now readily available to the Earth. The Cosmic Consultant is apparently interested in Earth now because of its recent movement forward into sacred status and into the fourth dimension.

Recently, we have been calling in the Cosmic Consultant in meditation and asking him to blend his frequency and Lightbody with ours to help us get used to the higher frequencies. He has been happy to do this for us, even though he must lower his energy way down to a seventh-dimensional focus. It feels marvelous when he steps in! The Cosmic Consultant has said he will help us during this next year of transformational acceleration we are in.

The Elohim Computers

During my continuing research I have become interested in the firing of the elohim computers. Supposedly, the firing of the first elohim computer took place in April 1994. Djwhal Khul told us that there would be a firing of three in 1994. The rest, equaling a total of twelve, would be fired within a two- to four-year period. Archangel Michael is overseeing this project.

The effects are manyfold. One is to link humanity and the Earth. These firings serve to create a mutation toward higher evolution which is accomplished through the angels, through a kind of coding of the elohim. The firing causes an activation of the crystalline DNA structure on a planetary level. Caryn and I, in some of our meditation work together, energetically connected with the first three firings on a personal level as a means for personal ascension activation. This can be done in meditation with the help of the masters.

Vywamus' Heaven on Earth Mantra

Vywamus has suggested that Lightworkers say a mantra that begins by your making the sound "eeeee" in the high-pitched tone that resonates in your roof of your mouth. Then lower your voice and say "Om" so it resonates in your throat chakra. Do this sequence three times. Vywamus and Djwhal Khul have said that it serves to manifest Heaven on Earth. It also balances the feminine and masculine energies and builds an enormous amount of Light. We have begun doing this on a regular basis to end our Wednesday night classes.

A Personal Council of Twelve

Djwhal Khul recently told us another fascinating piece of information during class. He said that you have twelve guides when you come into incarnation. These guides, I sensed, are at different levels of consciousness. If you are not very evolved you might contact only two of these guides during your incarnation. If you are a more advanced soul, you will contact all of them at some point in your evolution. When you die and pass on to the inner plane you meet with your personal Council of Twelve before reincarnating in order to discuss plans and lessons for the next incarnation. Call on your personal council in times of great decision-making or need and they are sure to help you.

Death for a Seventh-Degree Initiate

Death for a fully realized seventh-degree initiate can occur in two ways; there are two levels of mahasamadhi, the conscious exiting of the physical vehicle. In other words, when you are ready to leave the physical body as a fully realized seventh-degree initiate, you just exit the body from the crown chakra and go. The most advanced and ideal way to do this is to dematerialize the body and then transfer it, or teleport it, to the inner plane ashram in which you are working. Death, in essence, is the ultimate teleportation experience. The only difference between death and teleporting is that you do not return.

Hypertime

One of the most extraordinary experiences I have been having in going through this whole ascension process is the experience of hypertime. By going through two major initiations in only one year it often feels like two or three months have been two or three years. When I wrote this particular section it was five and a half months after my completion; now it feels like a lifetime ago even though chronologically, five and a half months is not really that much time.

Hypertime has to do with the understanding that it is not the linear time that matters, but the amount of energy, Light, and information you are processing. Djwhal gave us a most excellent example of this after the major earthquake in Los Angeles in January of 1994. Only three days after the earthquake I felt as if I had lived a month, for there was so much extra processing I had to do, given the severity of the crisis. For this reason, Djwhal said, the earthquake had actually greatly accelerated our ascension process. This was quite an extraordinary insight!

It is not only a personal acceleration but also a planetary phenomenon which all are being swept into.

Running the Energies

One of the most important spiritual exercises you need to learn if you are on the spiritual path is how to run the spiritual current, or spiritual energies. In the beginning it requires a little bit of practice to become more sensitive to the energies. Even if initially you are not as sensitive as others, you can easily learn to be.

There are many different healing systems such as Johrei (channeling divine Light), Reiki, and so on, which are all very good; however, you do not have to learn such a system to run energies. You can just channel the energy through your body, particularly your hands. All you really have to do is call in the spiritual energy, the love aspect. If you want to be specific, you can call in a color, one of the twelve rays, the Mahatma energy, or the energy of Metatron, Melchizedek, or one of the other masters. You can also call in a Light shower from many of the great ascended masters.

If you are in the earlier initiations, it is likely that you are aware of much information but not necessarily aware of the full energies of that information. There are many ways to tap into God — by thinking and reading, through intuition, feeling, knowing, inner seeing (clairvoyance), inner hearing (clairaudience), or inner sensing (clairsentience), or inner smell. Most people are more highly developed in some of these faculties than in others, and that is fine. No matter how you do it, a real acceleration will occur on your path to ascension when you really feel, energetically, the experience of the God force. All you have to do is to begin to call in these different energies through your crown chakra and learn to become sensitive to them. You should try to differentiate the qualities of each one. This can easily be done in the beginning by trying the various ascension seats recommended herein. Each one has energy of a different quality.

Call for a Light shower from Metatron, then from the Mahatma, then from Melchizedek and experience the subtle differences. The same will be true if you choose to study some of the different healing modalities such as Reiki, Seichim, Laochi, or Johrei. Each has a different quality of energy. I like to call it spiritual current, and I enjoy running different spiritual currents, depending on the need and my mood. Running only one type of energy can get boring. That is one reason the masters have provided many different ascension seats. It is fun to work with different energies and various masters.

Running the spiritual current through your body just for yourself, for Light quotient building and for personal healing, feels wonderful. Once you get comfortable running the spiritual current, then send it to other people through your hands or through your heart. You do not have to be clairvoyant or clairaudient or a voice channel to do it. This is a different type of channeling that you can easily do just by invoking the particular type of energy you want.

For example, as you live your day, invoke the twelve rays, letting your need determine which one. When you want power, invoke the first ray; love, the second; cleansing, the eighth; transmuting, the seventh; precise thinking, the fifth ray. When you want Light quotient building, call Metatron or the Arcturians. When you want ascension integration, ask to be taken to the ascension seats. When you are doing healing, call forth the Mahatma energy. This will energize you. You will feel unbelievably good and it will accelerate your ascension! You will be enabled to fully experience God, rather than just thinking about God.

Thinking is important, much more important than people realize. For, as Sai Baba says, it is your mind that creates bondage and your mind that creates liberation. The key is to learn to switch into the different faculties to experience God. Don't get stuck in just one mode. Think God, feel God, intuit God, know God, hear God, actually see God, smell God (such as in a rose or with your inner sense of smell), sense God, energetically touch God. When all these faculties are working in balance, you are a fully self-realized being.

You do not necessarily have to be proficient in all of these ways of knowing God to achieve your ascension. However, you do need to be energetically connected for the transformation to come about. This is so incredibly simple and enjoyable to achieve that even children can learn to do it with a simple request.

Vertical and Horizontal Aspects

Carl Jung, the great Swiss psychologist, made reference to what he called the vertical and the horizontal aspects of life. The vertical is the focus on the spiritual aspect of life, the horizontal being the more Earthly relationships – children, family, jobs, and so forth. Jung postulated that most people spend their initial forty or forty-five years focusing on the horizontal plane, including schooling, establishing a profession, getting married, raising kids, maintaining a social life, and so forth. He said it is usually after the children have left home that the vertical side has the opportunity to come in. There is no hard and fast rule about this, and fifty years after Jung's writings the world has changed a great deal. However, I believe there is some truth to what he said.

Once you get hooked on God and the path of liberation and ascension, there is the tendency to want to spend all of your time focusing on the vertical — meditating, praying, reading spiritual books, doing service work, chanting the name of God, visiting ascension seats, building your Light quotient, attending spiritual workshops and lectures, and so on. There is nothing wrong with this as long as you maintain some recognition of the necessity for balance between the vertical and horizontal.

The correct vertical-horizontal balance is unique to each person. It depends on your chronological age, whether you are single, married, or in a relationship, whether or not you have children and how old they are, how you make your money, and the social group with which you are involved. There are bound to be times in your life as a Lightworker when you will be vertically focused, just as there will be times when you will be more horizontally focused. The real lesson is to avoid trying to be vertical when your lesson is to be horizontal and trying to be horizontal when it is time to be vertical.

Terri Sue is a great channel and has been for many, many years. Sanat Kumara told her before we met that she needed to be in a relationship with a man. I probably had a similar need. The spiritual pull is often so very strong that it can take you away from life. That might be okay for a certain period but it can actually be very detrimental to your growth if it goes on for too long. Stay in the Tao in terms of this important vertical-horizontal balance. Both are important, and both must be mastered and integrated to achieve ascension. Jesus lived in the marketplace, not in a cave.

In the reincarnation process, you might occasionally need a vertical life in the Himalayas or in a monastery, but true mastery and self-realization require coming back to the horizontal. You can create karma for yourself by not meeting your horizontal responsibilities. Marriages can end, children are affected. The key lesson is balance and moderation. Buddha said, "Follow the middle path." For short periods of time a singular focus might be totally appropriate; however, do it in the context of achieving balance in the big picture.

Heaven must ultimately be manifested on Earth. Learn how to be God in a romantic relationship or in raising children. If you can be God in a relationship, in your family, on your job, then you truly are a master. Easier said than done! This lesson forces you, as a Lightworker, not only to be right with God and the ascended masters, but also to be right with the yourself which is the most important relationship of all. Meditate on this vertical and horizontal balance for yourself and see how your present path fits into this important ideal.

The Nine Insights of *The Celestine Prophecy*

There is a bestselling book on the market called *The Celestine Prophecy* by James Redfield. It is a very interesting book that many people are reading now. Alan Atkisson has condensed the nine key insights upon which it is based, and as I have always enjoyed a condensed, golden-nugget version of things, I share with you Alan Atkisson's condensation of James Redfield's wisdom. I am quoting directly from Alan's article in the August 1994 issue of *New Age Journal,* page 65:

1. Feeling restless? You're not alone. Everybody's starting to look for more meaning in life. Start paying closer attention to those seemingly chance coincidences – strange occurrences that feel like they were meant to happen. They are actually synchronistic events, and following them will start you on your path to spiritual truth.

2. Observe our culture within its proper historical context. The first half of the past millennium was spent under the thumb of the church; in the second half we became preoccupied with material comfort. Now, at the end of the twentieth century, we've exhausted that preoccupation. We're ready to discover life's ultimate purpose.

3. Start to get acquainted with the subtle energy that infuses all things. With practice, you can learn to see the aura around any living being and to project your own energy around it to give it strength.

4. An unconscious competition for energy underlies all conflicts. By dominating or manipulating others, we get the extra energy we think we need. Sure, it feels good – but both parties are damaged in the conflict.

5. The key to overcoming conflict in the world is the mystical experience, which is available to everyone. To nurture the mystical and build your energy, allow yourself to be filled with a sense of love.

6. Childhood traumas block our ability to fully experience the mystical. All humans, because of their upbringing, tend toward one of four control dramas: Intimidators steal energy from others by threat; interrogators steal it by judging and questioning; aloof people attract attention (and energy) to themselves by playing coy; and "poor me's" make us feel guilty and responsible for them. Become aware of the family dynamics that created your control drama and you can focus on your essential question, which is how to make of your life a higher-level synthesis of your parents' lives.

7. Once cleared of traumas, you can build energy through contemplation and meditation, focus on your basic life question, and start riding a steady stream of intuitions, dreams, and synchronistic coincidences, all guiding you in the direction of your own evolution and transformation.

8. That evolution can't be done alone, so begin to practice the new Interpersonal Ethic by uplifting those who cross your path. Talk to people who make spontaneous eye contact with you. Avoid codependent relationships. Be there for people. Call attention to other people's control dramas. In groups, speak when the spirit (instead of the ego) moves you.

9. Our purpose here is to evolve beyond this plane. Fewer people (a result of reproductive abstinence) and more old-growth forests will help us to sustain our energy and accelerate our evolution. Technology will do most of our work for us. As we begin to value spiritual insight more and more, we will pay those who bring it to us, and this will eventually replace the market economy and our need for paid employment. We can connect to God's energy in such a way that we will eventually become beings of Light, and walk straight into Heaven.

— A.A.

Futureplex Homeopathics

What I am going to share with you here is one of the most important golden nuggets in this entire book. There is a man by the name of Roy Martina who has developed a line of homeopathics called Futureplex that, in my opinion, are the best homeopathics on the market. I have no financial investment in telling you this, only concern for your good health. I do suggest that you try some of these products.

Specifically, he has a product in this Futureplex line called Bacterotox. In my experience it has knocked out 90% of all bacterial infections. He has another set of products called Acute Virotox and Post Virotox. These remedies have annihilated 90% of all viruses I have encountered the past five years.

After I had hepatitis and developed a chronic weakness of the pancreas, I was constantly getting bacterial infections and low-grade viruses. I began taking these two remedies on a preventive basis and now I hardly ever get sick any more. I attribute this, to a large extent, to these remedies.

Other remedies I use a lot are Lymphtox for clearing out my lymph system when it gets clogged; Enviroprotect for protection against environmental pollutants; Adrenal Ped and Revitalization for extra energy; and Immune Energy to bolster my immune system. You might take these rememdies on a preventive basis, using a pendulum or muscle testing to determine which ones you need each day. They are not widely available but can be ordered by mail:

Capitol Drugs
4454 Van Nuys Blvd.
Sherman Oaks, CA
(818) 905-8338

Sanat Kumara on Groups

The following is an excerpt from a channeling by Sanat Kumara through Terri Sue Stone on April 24, 1994, during an ascension workshop:

As you know, you are pioneers, or travelers and explorers, who are working the kinks out of a system that will become the blueprint for humanity; thus, it is essential that you understand group dynamics. Consider, if you will, within your microcosm here, twenty-eight physical bodies present and several other energetic ones, which I might add are also influencing the group dynamics, but just let's take the physical count for a moment. That is an extremely tiny microcosm compared to billions called humanity as one whole group.

With your understanding, with your enlightenment, with your psychological self-studies, with your experiences of having had many contacts with groups and meditations and so forth, this is where you have finally evolved. It is my humble desire to see the rest of humanity finally make it to this point. So please do not feel as though you've fallen short of a desired goal today. This is the underlying purpose for all work being done within the ranks of the Spiritual Hierarchy — to create group consciousness in a design that can move forward with one focus, depending upon what that focus is. So what attracted each of you here today was the focus on ascension and perhaps also the focus on the astrological doorway — twofold. Thus, this group is, in essence, not purely, singularly, focused on ascension. That makes a little bit of a difference in the dynamics. Do you understand what I am saying?

Each group that gathers produces something energetically and the idea is to eventually, by the conclusion of your time, produce something that was valuable or enjoyable to all involved, no matter what your role was.

There will be a new group of world servers coming forth specifically to teach these occurrences within a group. Because this specific focus, this group that I am addressing now, had the dual focus, it is a little bit different. But for instance, tomorrow night all will be focused upon Wesak; that is a singular purpose. It does make it a bit easier in any group situation if there is a singular focus, which is why topics are channeled for group meetings or a title is given to the name of the workshop or a group names themselves, usually after much debate. But it's important to have a focus or an intent to move the group forward, otherwise it does flounder.

So let us be clear about this group focus right now. Right now, the work with the Sirius doorway has been done, so your focus right now is clearly to invoke ascension energy for yourselves personally and as a group for the benefit of humanity. You're not here solely for your own personal benefit. You are here to take that personal benefit and then find a way, at least energetically, to share it with humanity — if not literally, in a teaching focus or what have you, then through the transcendence of your personal relationships.

So let us all focus our attention on the ascension process. Take a moment to hold that. Now each of you will probably define that a little differently. That's all right, as long as you're all focusing on the same outcome, which is ascension. You can define it any way you want. So let's take a moment to align your being with that purpose for this time frame. Now that may include, you know, "I fully focus on ascension right now, even with my little voice telling me I should resist it, or that it won't work out anyway," but that you, as a conscious being, are claiming the predominant energy is ascension, period. Your resistances will always be there and you'll move forward, but you're going to have a certain element of darkness or resistance in your consciousness for quite a long time in your whole evolutionary cycle. So it's your choice to focus intent on ascension and not be concerned with these other things except for the purpose of clearing them or noticing them.

I would further say the best service to humanity and the ashram in general on the inner planes, in any group gathering, would be to have a clear intent. In other words, you may come to the group with a clear intent to learn to meditate. Even though your mind chatters and you have resistance and your body won't relax, if you are there because you want to learn to meditate, you will eventually overcome the resistances. That's a pure intent, and by all means follow the higher self's direction in that intent. However, if you're really not certain whether or not you really want to focus on meditation, then your decision-making process may be to want to sample it and then decide that a sampling is sufficient.

What is currently impacting the abundance-realization and the movement into the higher levels of initiation is this lack of focus — just sort of floating around, not really defining what you are here to do, and also in life, sort of floating day by day, not really sure of what purpose you want to fulfill.

So I would encourage you to design your purpose, even it if is moment to moment: my purpose right now is to go out into the garden and pull some weeds; my purpose right now is to clean the bathroom and do the dishes; my purpose right now is to work on a new class format; my purpose right now is to get my degree; my purpose right now is to raise my child. Focus on your exact purpose, which always will be rotating. No one can live with only one purpose — it's out of balance.

So claim the purpose and the focus and the direction of what you are doing rather than having a kind of nonchalance: "Well, I'll just put one foot forward and see what I stumble into." It won't work right now in this time period and I know that all of the masters have been conveying that message.

This is the year of decision-making, of having focus and following it through, of being firm in what you intend to create. You might not know how you are going to create it, but you must define what you will create or what you are focused upon right now. Maybe your focus is personal growth. That is a very broad spectrum. Then also within that, carry your intent for personal growth as your individual focus as well as the group focus. Actually, your whole participation in the group is for the group focus primarily and then your personal agenda secondarily. The group focus will coincide with your personal focus.

For instance, if you want personal growth, and you want to learn it through Eastern teachings, why would you go through Catholicism to learn it? Certainly you will have personal growth, but you're in the wrong place to get it through Eastern thought. So work now very consciously, now and for this year period, with consciously aligning where you are and whether or not it is sitting with your purpose. Usually, you're guided to places that fit in with your purposes anyway. You would not have to be working at it, but occasionally you will place yourself somewhere or find yourself placed somewhere that really does not resonate, or perhaps with an individual in a relationship that doesn't resonate, or whatever. When that occurs, take necessary action as soon as possible. In other words, honor your sacred path. Bring honor to your own self.

So, ascension — back to this group focus — is not yet understood in your consciousness even if you have begun the sixth initiation. It is not yet understood. There are concepts, there are preconceptions, there are expectations, there are things that are not particularly true but they have guided you to this point, in which case you understand they were misconceptions. Drop them away and keep focusing on — what is this? Do I need to give it another name? Everyone else calls it ascension. I'm going to call it completion, or graduation.

[There is a question from a group member about having three purposes and being unable to do one to the exclusion of the others.]

They will intertwine. You really have a multipurpose but there is an order of primary, secondary, tertiary and you understand that like a braid, they will be woven together; but one focus will keep you focused on all three, whereas if you focus on the third you will get distracted from the first two.

There is a special ceremony for you as a closing but until we come to that point in time I want to stay with this concept of what it is like to be in a group. What we have as a formation here is each of you individually, the core coming up from the heart focus to the actual group entity, which is above you.

And occasionally you've brought the energy down to that diamond and pointed it into the Earth and then when that doesn't quite focus anymore, it becomes too melded, you push it upward. So you're moving the group entity about. Let's bring it down again and let it be all around you. Think of the group as a pool of water and each of you as an individual in it, that you will not run together, but stay as individual dots or drops. Or could I say you are like a beautiful lawn and each one of you is a blade of grass. But when you look at the lawn you see all of the grass, you don't see one blade until you inspect more closely. So look at your group entity. Don't be afraid to contribute to it. Spill your heart over into it. That's what makes it a group. Your group joy or your group sincerity or your group laughter or any other emotional force is what brings the group together in one bond. In this focus it is the cosmic love.

Since you have physical bodies, it seems to be the most simple way of explaining the fact that you cannot lose your individuality. That would be like saying two of you could really blend together and only one body would be left. It is physically impossible. So think of your body as that assurance that you won't lose your individuality; even if you want emotionally to get it lost, you can't. That's the beauty of your physical structure.

To return to singular focus of ascension: I prefer the word ascension, although individually some of you may hold it as mastery or whatever other term you want. I personally like the vibration of the word ascension, so let's focus on that intent, on personally reaching that point in consciousness which is inevitable, choosing to do it sooner rather than later. You can take eternity to get there if you want to, or you can do it in four years or five years or two years or twelve months or whatever. You are choosing to do it sooner rather than later on your personal time scale for the benefit of serving humanity so that the whole world will be raised up another vibration and become a world of peace, eventually, where people are not hurting one another in any way, where it is safe to be a member of humanity, to be part of that group without any pain, where you can trust the Light in every other being all the time. That's where Earth is going. And you are the ones who are focusing this intent to help it move forward because the group of humanity, just like any other group, cannot move forward unless there is a focus or intent.

Now, let yourself leap into Light, just leap fully into it. Again, it's like jumping into that pool of water. You're in the water, you're surrounded by the water, your skin is absorbing some water, yet you are individual. Your spark brightens the whole group of Light, but yet you remain individually lit. This is a very important concept for you to get energetically.

If you merge mindlessly into the rest of the Light and lose your sense of self then you're not holding the group focus. Each one of you must hold the group focus while you bask in the Light of it. So perhaps you might imprint ascension into the third eye or into the heart or maybe bridge the two, but hold your intent. Make no mistake about it, if you are sitting here right now, if you made it here, then your focus is ascension, or your whole being would not have let you come. You would not have been physically able to arrive if this were not your purpose in life.

Good. We are going to continue our work focused in this room while you enjoy the Valley of Wesak and you may want to send that bilocation to Telos, to the beautiful city underground there and view various things, and then you may want to go on, perhaps to Luxor and a variety of other things in that level in the dimension of being. You can set an agenda there so that the work will continue to filter into this particular location. But rather than moving somewhere else where you can once again feel like you are off wandering around by yourself or in your own private healing room, I'm going to bring you back to this group awareness and see if, again, you can practice this energy as you come out of your meditation and you hold that ascension focus. Can you look about the room and know, even if you just met yesterday, or if you haven't even spoken to each other and formally met, and see that you are old friends? See that familiarity and likeness in each other. I would like for the group to produce a toning so that this effect is given to symbolize the singular focus of ascension and that melding and blending, yet holding your own individual flame, or voice. Then when you come from the toning, really focus on the divineness. Namaste; greet the divine being in each one from your own divine being, from that equal status.

Group Consciousness

One profound insight that has very much deepened for me is the understanding of group consciousness. It was brought to a very clear focus in our weekend ascension workshop on April 23 and 24 in 1994. So often when you go to a workshop, you go with an attitude of "what is in this for me?" and identify yourself as an individual in a group.

As you move into the higher levels of initiation, you begin to deal much more with the group identity, letting it be of primary importance and the individual of secondary importance, although still important. It is essential that you understand that any group of people with which you are involved forms a group body. It is an entity in and of itself. It is almost as if you could imagine expanding your physical body to include, let's say, thirty people in a given workshop you are attending. You have an individual body and identity; however, you also have a larger group body.

The idea is to be able to shift back and forth between these two states of consciousness. In doing that, you are no longer focused only on how you feel personally, but also on how the group body is feeling. If someone in the group body is having a problem, then, in truth, it is like having a severe pain in your own body.

In truth, you have many group bodies. You have a personal family body. You have bodies of all the different groups and organizations with which you are involved. You have a planetary group body called humanity. You have a solar body. You have a galactic body. You have a universal body. The incredible job someone like Sanat Kumara has now becomes evident, for his job is to unify the consciousness of the planetary body, just as you have been trying to unify and integrate your personal four-body system. If you are going to move into the higher initiations, you must begin to see life through Sanat Kumara's eyes — in other words, see your body as Sanat Kumara's body which is all kingdoms of life, including mineral, plant, animal, human, and spiritual. You can do that when you see all forms of life in all kingdoms as incarnations or embodiments of God. Every rock, plant, animal, and human is the Eternal Self embodied in physical form.

As a human, you are inclined to put a little mental fence around your personal physical body and say, "This is me." Well, that is an illusion. With each initiation into which you expand, you identify changes. Ascension and the seventh initiation deal with identifying yourself as a planetary, solar, and galactic body. The job of Melchizedek, the Universal Logos, is to unify the universal body. Eventually, you move through the three hundred fifty-two levels of initiation into even larger states of consciousness, identification, and responsibility. Before you expand to a larger level, you must demonstrate your mastery of the current one. This is the Path of Initiation.

You cannot go from A to Z in an instant, but must go through the entire alphabet, one letter at a time, and prove your mastery over each letter. Each letter is a further expansion.

At the workshop, I gained a deeper understanding of identifying with the group body. It was a difficult process for the group to get there, but by the end of the workshop we had all merged into one unified group being while at the same time honoring the diversity of the individual members.

It is so easy to go the extremes of this polarity, either staying stuck in your individual identity and refusing to surrender your personal fence at all, or going to the other extreme and losing your individual identity in the group. The lesson is to maintain both simultaneously: unity in diversity. You can have the best of both worlds. It is absolutely crucial to understand this spiritual insight.

One of the keys to achieving identity with a group body is to maintain that ideal as a focus. If all the members of the group don't hold the focus, there will be resistance and fragmentation in the group body. Each person's individual "stuff" is a part of the group process.

It reminds me a little bit of my early training in family counseling. In family systems theory, the focus is on the family rather than on the individual psyches of the family members. I, personally, do not agree with this theory, for in my opinion you have to deal with both. The pendulum swing they were doing, however, was important. In focusing on the family group rather than on the individuals, they were working with the group identity, and adjustments in the group identity did have a transformative effect on the individuals. The entire infinite universe is just one intricate family system. There is only one being in the infinite universe and that is God; everything in existence is a part or incarnation of Him. I am God writing this book, you are God reading this book. Your pet is God keeping you company in your home. Your plants are God doing their thing. The insect flying around your room is, again, God.

Each incarnation of God has its specific part to play in God's grand design. God is the grand orchestra leader of the universe. There are infinite numbers of mini-Gods. Melchizedek is the mini-God who is in charge of the universe. Sanat Kumara is the mini-God orchestrating this planet. When Sanat Kumara finishes this job, he will expand to an even greater position with even more expansive responsibilities as an orchestra leader in God's symphony.

Eventually, when you move to the three hundred fifty-second level of initiation, your responsibility will be the infinite universe and that will be your body and your focus. That is too big to focus on now, at this level of understanding, so you start by focusing on harmonizing your four-body system. Once you gain mastery of that, you focus on a planetary level.

Tune in to this when you are in a group. Don't focus only on how you, personally, are doing, but also feel how the group body is doing. For example, right now, tune in and feel how the planetary body of humanity is doing. I, personally, am feeling very peaceful and blissful; however, when I tune into my planetary body I sense a lot of suffering.

One of the important principles of this process is to develop compassion rather than empathy. Compassion has an ingredient of detachment; empathy takes on the energy without detachment, which is not good. Play with this in your consciousness. It is just a matter of your attitudinal focus.

If you tune in to the group consciousness, or humanity's body, as your identity as well as tuning in to your individual identity, then you would never hurt another person, for to hurt another person would be, literally, to hurt your own group body. If someone in the group body were suffering, you would automatically help him as if you had a severe pain in your own body. Do you see how beautiful this state of consciousness is? You are still taking Shakespeare's advice that says, "This above all, to thine own self be true," but now that self includes every member of the group.

The state of ascension and the seventh initiation is one of having mastery over your personal self and energies so your entire point of focus can be that of service to the greater body. The personal self is so whole, complete, unified, fulfilled, and clear of negative ego and separative consciousness that your entire focus can be that of helping the greater whole to live in that state of consciousness, too.

Group consciousness is similar to a marriage. Upon making the commitment, two people move from being two separate I's to being also a we. Each of you maintains your individual consciousness, but the problems, pains, and concerns of your partner become yours and yours become his or hers. The same is true of a parent-child relationship. As a mother, you see your child literally as an extension of yourself, and one of the lessons of the mother is to allow the adolescent to have an individual focus, an I, while maintaining the we. The ultimate goal is for your I to identify all of humanity — and the galaxy and the universe — as we.

More on Group Consciousness

The understanding of group consciousness is, in my opinion, one of the real keys to moving into the higher initiations. This has been pointed out to me in a most extraordinary manner during the past fourteen months of my own evolutionary process. In forming the ascension buddy system with Terri Sue, Marcia, and Caryn and later expanding it to an even larger core group, I have seen that group consciousness works in a most wondrous manner.

The Findhorn community perfectly exemplifies what occurred within my own core group. At its inception, Findhorn had a core group of people. Dorothy Maclean had the ability to speak to the plant kingdom. Oliver Crombie was able to speak to the animal kingdom. Eileen Caddy was the channel of the higher self and God. Peter Caddy was the Earthly worker and manifester. Later David Spangler joined the group and added yet another dimension. It was the group consciousness that made Findhorn so unusual. Any one of the people working on his or her own would not have been significant; all of them working together made Findhorn the most extraordinary spiritual community on the planet. Later, more people joined the core group and added still other dimensions.

Just as it happened with the group at Findhorn, in our group, Terri Sue brought her extraordinary clairaudient channeling abilities, Caryn brought her amazing clairvoyance and ascension activation abilities, Marcia brought her well-rounded spiritual, psychic, mystic, channeling abilities, and I brought clarity of mind, intuition, knowingness, and telepathic and investigative abilities. Each of us contributed a quarter of the pie. Because we were working together as a group consciousness, exceptional things began to develop.

Moving through three major initiations could never have occurred so quickly unless we had formed the group. The level of information in this book is a product of that group mind; no one person could have brought it all forward. The evolution of each of us occurred literally four times as fast as it would have if we had worked separately.

Melchizedek told us that there is a six-pointed star on the planet with each point being an ashram or group that is bringing in the highest energy to the planet. One of these points is Terri Sue's and my center which is Djwhal Khul's ashram. Marcia's center in New York is also Djwhal Khul's ashram and, in truth, one with our ashram even though there is a three-thousand-mile-distance between them. The third shall remain nameless at this time and the other three were not revealed to us, although one seemed to be in the United States. These are groups or ashrams that are now anchoring galactic and universal energy and information in a manner that has never before occurred on this planet.

Each of us, in our own right, has a lot on the ball, but it is only because we pooled our resources and became a larger body of four, then of twelve, then of fifty, that the divine dispensations from galactic, universal, and cosmic sources have come through as they have. Imagine what would happen if all of humanity took on a group consciousness, working together and pooling talents and resources. The entire planet and all of humanity would instantly ascend! Arcturus is an example of a place where this has occurred. Begin practicing this on a microcosmic level and slowly but surely let it expand and become larger. I assure you that most miraculous things will begin to occur.

The Purple Positive Energy Plate

One of the most extraordinary tools I have found to raise my overall energy and even my Light quotient is the purple Positive Energy Plate. I am not one to go for gadgets. I have seen them all and I use almost none of them. My style is to rely on my own natural energy and my own resources for everything. The one exception I make is the use of the purple Plate, which I am sure many of you have seen. It is actually a free-energy plate. I pretty much pooh-poohed it when I first saw it about ten years ago. However, a very good friend of mine who is an expert in the Hanna Kroeger work, radionics, and using the pendulum, told me about it. She said that she had been scientifically testing its effectiveness with her pendulum, and she was amazed. Even though she sold the Soma Boards created by Hanna Kroeger to protect and clear food, she said the plate worked one hundred times better. (Hanna's Soma Board has special herbs and crystals in it; you place your food upon it and it automatically clears the food of all negative energies.) To my amazement, when Terri Sue and I checked it with our pendulum, the Positive Energy Plate worked far better. Within seven minutes of food's being placed on the plate, it became amazingly energized, much more so than when placed on the Soma Board. Almost every food we tested before putting it on the purple plate made the pendulum rotate backwards, indicating that the food had negative energy or no energy at all. This was true for all vegetables and other forms of food considered healthful.

The purple Plate not only cleared the food of all negative energy and negative residues such as pesticides, but also energized the food. Now I religiously put all my food on it and continue to be amazed.

Regardless of your diet, if you use the purple Positive Energy Plate it will guarantee that you get the positive energy you need, even if the actual food you eat is not that good. It is like the difference between eating a fresh apple you pick directly from the tree and one that has been picked before it is ripe, sprayed with pesticides, shipped to market, handled by two or three different people, left to sit in the market for three or four days, put through the grocery scanner and irradiated, handled by a cashier, and has then sat in your house or refrigerator for a few more days. After two weeks that apple does not have nearly the vitality and God-energy it originally had, and in addition, the negative energies of people and pesticides have been added. This is an example of a healthful food; frozen foods, canned foods, and processed foods are much worse.

I put a large Positive Energy Plate under my drinking water stand and use the plate to energize the crystal I keep in my water jug. I store my homeopathic remedies on one. I also have a purple Plate on which I have placed a picture of myself. The picture is energized and cleared and has a radionic effect on my four-body system! A friend put them into the walls of the house she was having built. Terri Sue sits on one every day while she channels, and she swears by their effectiveness. They might also be put under your mattress or pillow, although you must be careful about this as it might cause too much energy for restful sleep. Some people wear them as necklaces or earrings and carry them around in their purses or pockets. How can you afford not to get one?

Please don't just believe me; check them out yourself with your own pendulum. I do not own stock in the company, nor do I know the person who invented them. I am just very excited about all the ways this Positive Energy Plate can be used. The plates come in different sizes: the largest plate, which is 12" square, is approximately $40 (at the time of this printing), and the smaller plates are about $10. As far as I know, they last forever. If they do not have them in your neighborhood homeopathic pharmacy or metaphysical bookstore, then I suggest you order them from:

Capitol Drugs
4454 Van Nuys Blvd., Sherman Oaks, CA 91403
(818) 905-8338

or

Susan Bryant and Sandy Burns
P.O. Box 31149, Flagstaff, AZ 86003-1149
(520) 527-1128

Archangel Michael's Blue Flame Armor Shield

One of the most important factors on the spiritual path is the issue of protection. In Soul Psychology, a chapter is dedicated to learning how to defend yourself against the negativity you can be exposed to on the spiritual path. Here are some new tools I have found. You can never have too much shielding. When your shielding needs bolstering or just to start your day, call forth Archangel Michael to place his blue flame armor shield around you. Some refer to it as his blue flame armor ball. It serves to dissolve all negative thought forms that are not of the Light of God.

The Crystalline Ankh

Call to Isis, Horus, Osiris, and Thoth for a crystalline ankh that you will wear around your neck. This will serve to energize your entire aura and seal in your existing Light to make sure there is no leakage.

Sanat Kumara's Shield of the Sun

For those of you who are having a lot of trouble with negative energies and forces, call to Sanat Kumara and request a gift of one of his Shields of the Sun. This shield will enlarge upon insertion and protect all of the chakras.

Djwhal Khul's Golden Orb

In meditation, call to Ascended Master Djwhal Khul and ask for a gift of his golden orb necklace. Continuous wearing of this necklace will automatically keep all of the etheric nadis and energy meridians sealed and will also prevent you from losing Light.

Arcturian Protection

With their advanced technology, the Arcturians are able to send protective energies to surround you if you request them. They also have an advanced Arcturian technology that you wear on a chain around your neck. It looks like a circular golden pill box. When the pill box is opened it provides extra protection.

The Arcturians gave them to Caryn and me to wear on the fronts and backs of our bodies. They said if we wanted to we could leave them open all the time.

There are many different necklaces that are worn over the chakras. Let the Arcturians or masters place them wherever they feel the necklaces would help you the most. All of these spiritual amulets work together and there is no danger of wearing too many, as there would be if you were wearing physical jewelry of this kind.

Some of them need to be activated each day. As you are dressing, also put on and activate your spiritual amulets. Just think of them and say, "Activate."

Jesus' Necklace of Rejuvenation

In meditation, call to the Master Jesus and request that he place around your neck his Necklace of Rejuvenation. It is pink, green, and gold in color and serves to help the physical body rejuvenate in conjunction with health affirmations. It also helps to build the Light quotient.

Heaven on Earth Seal of Protection

Phase I

Call forth in meditation Melchizedek, Metatron, and Thoth for their special protective seal to be placed around you in conjunction with your normal tube of Light. This seal is made up of sacred geometries that are all packed together, such as triangles, circles, diamonds, merkabahs, fire letters, and key codes. Once they place this seal around you it is automatically and permanently activated for your protection. This permanent activation is unusual; most techniques must be requested every day in order for them to work. Melchizedek told me that this seal could be called the Heaven on Earth Seal for the Children of Light.

Phase II

The second part of the sealing system is a most extraordinary process that I highly recommend you request. In this phase Melchizedek, Thoth, Metatron, and Djwhal Khul place, through your chakras, spinal column, skin, and any organs and/or glands that need support, a kind of sealing that contains geometric shapes, forms, and colors. What this sealing substance does is to automatically heal the chakra, organ, or gland if it begins to get out of balance. If that happens, the geometric forms begin to light up and spin like mini-merkabahs and they eject any energies that do not conform to the perfected ideal. This system will remain dormant as long as your body and chakras are in balance. The moment any organ, gland, or chakra goes out of balance, the system kicks into action. This program will work automatically for the rest of your incarnation, once it is installed.

Each of my organs was coated and then filled with these geometric forms by the above-mentioned masters. The whole process is extremely gentle and, in truth, barely noticeable. It takes about an hour to fully install the whole program. I was also guided to call on the higher Light quotient to come in and to say the words "Heaven on Earth" as a type of additional programming process. Once installed, the program works automatically, but it can also be consciously invoked to kick into action. The system works in conjunction with the process of sitting on the ascension seats and calling in the higher Light quotient from Metatron, the Arcturians, Melchizedek, or other masters.

One of the major benefits to having this program installed is that the masters go through your chakras, organs, glands, spinal column, brain, and entire four-body system and clear out all the etheric mucus and imbalanced energies before they cover each area with the geometric shapes. When I had it done, all my chakras were cleaned out, and many energy adjustments were made. Imbalanced matrices were removed. Energy repairs were made to my brain, liver, pancreas, bladder, and spine. In actuality, it was one of the best healings and clearings I have ever received.

They can put this sealing and automatic healing program in place only after all the chakras and organs and glands have been cleared out. When they install the program, they will go through one chakra at a time and one organ at a time to make sure you are feeling comfortable. I would recommend lying down on your bed for one full hour the first time you invoke this process. It feels very much like sessions I have had with the MAP healing team.

You can feel very subtle energy sensations and tingling going on in the parts of your four-body system they are working on. Do not invoke this particular process unless you have a full hour to meditate. We were also told that the process would stabilize our physical, emotional, and mental health to a great degree. It would also allow us to carry a much greater Light quotient and in general to feel more comfortable. It is truly a gift from the Creator!

The Healing Modules

The healing modules are a special dispensation from the Great Central Sun that can be called forth and that are disseminated by Helios, the Solar Logos. The healing modules look like two geodesic domes put together in the same way that two pyramids can be put together to form a merkabah.

The healing modules are a specific type of merkabah. They contain within them all information for the full completion of all initiations and for your specifically designated mission. They are specifically designed and programmed for your unique gifts, challenges, and lessons. They can help work on your physical, emotional, mental, and spiritual lessons. They also help with building the Light quotient.

They can be spun like a regular merkabah. As a matter of fact, your personal merkabah and healing modules can be blended or overlaid to work together. You can also travel in your healing module. There are many types of merkabahs and the healing module is one design that has been programmed by the Great Central Sun for healing and for the completion of your mission.

Fire letters seemed to surround the entire healing module, and Light seemed to emanate from the triangular pieces of the geodesic form to the grid points in the body. Your healing modules can be programmed for any use you might have for them. I recommend calling your healing module in from the Great Central Sun and Helios during every meditation. Ask Helios to help you and work with you.

Light Quotient Building and Healing

This particular technique is one that I have used a great deal. I call forth Metatron and request a 100% Light quotient increase. I then follow that by saying, "Heal my pancreas, liver, digestive system, and/or third chakra." Metatron or any other master you choose will channel to you the higher Light quotient while simultaneously running the spiritual current through the physical body part that needs healing.

This way you are killing two birds with one stone — building your

Light quotient and healing and strengthening your physical body. Nearly everyone has some part of the physical body, be it an organ, gland, chakra, or structural problem, that needs some healing. Thus, both your spirit and physical body will be provided for.

More Guidance from Djwhal Khul

Djwhal gave us two interesting pieces of spiritual guidance. One was the importance of not swearing. If you have to say something, then think of a word that is not a curse word. I am not one to be angry very much, but occasionally when I stub my toe or something of that kind, there is an automatic tendency to exclaim some sort of expletive. Since Djwhal's statement I have been working on not letting it happen at all.

The second bit of guidance Djwhal gave us had to do with euthanasia. Djwhal said that suicide is not spiritually correct; however, in some cases, even for humans, euthanasia is a spiritual principle and is appropriate.

Djwhal also said that in terms of taking the higher initiations, you do not necessarily have to transcend all negativity, but rather you must have chosen, on a conscious level, always to intend to manifest love instead of fear and attack.

One little side note that Caryn passed on to me was that whenever Sanat Kumara wanted to speak with her, in meditation or during one of her sessions, she would see a purple dot to the right side of her head. The purple dot acted like a beeper such as a doctor might have for emergency phone calls. This dot would "beep" and she would know Sanat Kumara was asking permission to come through. For some reason, I find that rather interesting. Modern technology is often more like spiritual technology than you realize.

The Physicalization of Shamballa

At a recent workshop Terri Sue and I hosted, Djwhal told us that Shamballa, the home of Sanat Kumara and the "White House" for this planet, is now in the process of becoming more solidified. Shamballa resides above the Gobi Desert in etheric form. Djwhal said that, because of the speeded-up process of evolution with which everyone on this planet is now involved, Shamballa can occasionally be seen with third-dimensional eyes. He went on to say that even satellites are beginning to pick it up with their scientific apparatus. The only problem is that the United States government then sends spy planes to check out the phenomenon and they can't find anything, for it has again moved back into etheric form. This is not that different from the manner in which UFOs operate in their interdimensional traveling.

Ascension and Normal Living

Another thing I want to make clear about my personal ascension process is that Terri Sue and I are both ascended masters but we love to go to the movies, and we watch television – sometimes even too much. I like sports and love to watch a good football game. She has a sweet tooth. She can also be very moody at times. We are totally committed to God and the Spiritual Hierarchy, and that is our main focus and what we put first in our lives. However, we are also into pleasure and having fun!

My friend Caryn, who has also ascended, has two children and a husband, and my friend Marcia is married to a lovely man named Tom. What I am trying to say is that you do not have to be ascetic or put yourself through painful contortions to prove yourself worthy. The important thing to remember is that you already are God, the Eternal Self, and the monad, and that you are just, in truth, letting your true identity unfold and bloom forth. The spiritual path is a path of integration and balance and moderation. I do not believe you will achieve your ascension if you do not cultivate joy and happiness and fun in your life.

Descension

Ascension is really the wrong word. One of the keys to my own ascension process was to realize that it is really a matter of descension. I was not to go up, but rather I was to invoke and allow the soul and monad to descend into me on Earth. My job is to stay grounded and bring God to Earth and into my body. That is why the ascension meditations and techniques in my books call the energies down into you rather than having you going up to them.

Ascension

Most of my life, ascension seemed like an impossible and unreachable goal. I am here to tell you, from direct experience, that it is very reachable for humanity, as will be demonstrated on a large scale in the next twenty years.

Part of my reason for writing books is to reach the masses. Ascension is a very natural experience, just like learning to write a book, getting a college degree, or finishing any big project you have been working on. Ascension is just a natural byproduct of being on the spiritual path for an extended period of time. The consistent, focused attention on living according to spiritual ideals in a consistent manner over time leads you, step by step, through initiation after initiation. The outcome is inevitable. Everyone on this planet will eventually ascend. Maybe not everyone will do it in this lifetime, but everyone will do it. It is just a matter of time. If you want to shorten the time, then be more focused on reaching ascension and realizing God, love, joy, and service. It is your only reason for being alive.

Sanat Kumara's Golden Medallion

Request in meditation, from Sanat Kumara, a gift of one of his most sublime Golden Medallions of the Sun. It will be placed around your neck as a necklace. It will connect you directly with the Great Central Sun and will also serve as a protective amulet. Just as humans on Earth wear physical jewelry, it is important to wear certain spiritual jewelry on your spiritual bodies. Each kind of jewelry has a specific function in the acceleration of your spiritual evolution.

Ascension and the Practice of Channeling

In retrospect, as I look on my path of completion, I see that one of the other important keys was the practice of channeling. Channeling your own soul, your monad, or the ascended masters will accelerate your path of ascension as will no other spiritual practice.

What you are trying to do in achieving your ascension is to merge with the fifth kingdom, which is the spiritual kingdom. When you channel, you are channeling the fifth kingdom; the human kingdom is the fourth kingdom. When you are channeling you are, hence, healing the separation between the two kingdoms and bridging the gap.

I want to emphasize the importance of practicing. Take a channeling class; in fact, I suggest that you take many of them. They give you a chance to practice with people in the group. Practice with your friends, on the phone, or with a small tape recorder by yourself.

Visualize a tube of Light moving from the top of your head to the spiritual plane of the ascended masters and your higher self and monad. Then call in your soul, monad, or the ascended master with whom you wish to speak. That energy will move down the tube. All you have to do is begin talking and it will glide in on the initial words that you must speak yourself. It is just that easy. The key to doing it is role-playing. In the beginning, you might just pretend you are doing it. Pretend you are the Master Jesus and soon more and more of Master Jesus will speak through you.

Do this also when you write in your journal. Let your I Am Presence speak through your pen or your typewriter. Many of you who do not think you are channeling are, in truth, channeling profoundly but are just not aware of it. Everyone channels; often it is just a matter of understanding that you are channeling. You will find that different people channel in different ways. I am not suggesting only conscious voice channeling, although that is a most excellent form of it. You can also channel art, music, poetry, writing, dance, or cooking. The list is endless. Allow yourself to be a vehicle for spirit. This is another one of the golden keys for accelerating your ascension.

Melchizedek Transmitting Station

Ask to be taken to Melchizedek's Golden Chamber. Ask Melchizedek in meditation for installation through the third chakra and into all your chakras of Melchizedek's specialized transmitting station to allow you to receive the sacred elohim scriptures at night while you sleep and in meditation. This specialized Melchizedek transmitting station looks like Tesla coils that have been installed in each chakra in a conic, or spiral, fashion.

This installation of the universal core technology allows you to increase one thousandfold the lens of inner sight and the ability to receive knowledge. It is installed at whatever frequency you can handle. It also helps to serve as a transmitting station for the Spiritual Hierarchy. It helps to anchor the five higher bodies and facilitates the transfer of the DNA into the etheric and then the physical vehicle.

The elohim scriptures come in a series of twelve Light packets. This transmitting station allows dispensation from the highest cosmic levels through Melchizedek at the Universal Core and thence to Earth. It also helps greatly to facilitate the building of the Light quotient. This level of Light transmission has never before been made available to Earth. It is a brand new dispensation from the Creator. Make the request to Sanat Kumara and Melchizedek in meditation or in some kind of formalized prayer form. This will all take place during sleeptime.

I further suggest asking Melchizedek to upgrade the above-mentioned transmitting station. Every couple of months ask that he turn it up so you may carry more spiritual wattage.

Melchizedek's Information Disk

In a separate meditation ask to be taken to Melchizedek's Golden Chamber and ask Melchizedek to place the Melchizedek information disk in your brain. This information disk is much like the Arcturian technology, but it is coming directly from the Universal Core and is an even more advanced technology.

The purpose of this disk, or medallion, is to serve as a translation orb. It helps your consciousness translate the Light packets of information coming in from the seven mighty elohim, Sirius, and Arcturus, as well as from the Keys of Enoch in all five sacred languages and all fire letters and key codes of the twenty-four dimensions of reality.

This, again, is a universal technology that has rarely, if ever before, been given to Earth. Only since 1987 has Earth had direct access to the Galactic Core, let alone to the Universal Core. These last two dispensations are quite sacred and should not be asked for lightly. I would not recommend asking for this level of Light and understanding unless you are totally committed to your spiritual path. As Djwhal Khul said recently to Marcia and me, "Much is given and much is now expected." If you are not prepared to take the full responsibility of the mantle of the Christ, I would not yet invoke this level of Light energy, understanding, and quickening of vibration, frequency, and karmic return.

Anchoring the Golden Chamber of Melchizedek

This ascension technique is one of the most extraordinary to come forth yet. After you have worked with the Golden Chamber of Melchizedek for a good period of time and the energies have been built up to a sufficient level, it is possible to request that Melchizedek, the Universal Logos, actually anchor his ascension seat into your physical home through the ascension column you have previously established there.

What this means is that you will actually be living in an ascension seat all the time, and anyone who walks into your home will enter this ascension seat. Everyone will receive the ascension seat energies at his or her own level of development. I would recommend going to the Golden Chamber of Melchizedek and working in the ascension seat for some time before this request is made, however, as it is what might be termed an advanced ascension technique.

The Cosmic Pulse

Here is another extraordinary meditation we recently received from Melchizedek. In this meditation, go to the Golden Chamber of Melchizedek and tune in and listen to the cosmic pulse of the universe. Just as you can get in touch with the pulse of the Earth, the solar system, the galaxy, it is also possible to experience the pulse of the universe.

Meditation for Imprinting Humanity

This is a meditation process Djwhal Khul taught us which is used for world service work. Do this particular meditation under the guidance of one of the ascended masters and Sanat Kumara. The idea is that any time you have a very advanced discussion or do advanced world service work, the image of that prototype can be imprinted, with the help of the masters, into the information banks of humanity.

In doing this, you are not forcing your information on humanity; rather, you are placing the prototype you have just manifested in your group consciousness into the collective unconscious for humanity to have at its disposal for use as another potential idea. Use this technique when you feel humanity can benefit from the world service work you are doing in your small groups. Ask the masters to aid in this process, which is simply one of breathing and focusing it into place with a prayer to the masters.

Melchizedek's Golden Rod

Call to Melchizedek, while sitting in the Golden Chamber, to anchor and place in your heart the Golden Rod of Melchizedek for Light quotient building and ascension expansion.

Traveling to Sai Baba's Ashram

One of the greatest blessings you can possibly receive in this life is a blessing from His Holiness, the Lord Sai Baba, the Cosmic Christ and Universal Avatar, now physically embodied in Putaparti, India. In meditation, ask for permission to travel to India and visit Sai Baba in your spiritual body. Ask for Sai Baba's blessing and help in your ascension process and for help in your service work. Once touched by Sai Baba, you will never be the same!

More on Sai Baba

I have recently learned a few more tidbits about the glory of Sai Baba. The aura of his physical body extends one thousand miles. His astral body is the entire Earth; his causal body, the solar system; his mental body, the galaxy; and his spiritual body, the universe. He has said that he is a seventeen-point avatar. There has never before been a seventeen-point avatar incarnated on Earth. He has also said that there are sixteen facets to achieving God-realization; fifteen of them you can achieve through spiritual practice, while the sixteenth can occur only with the descent of one who is a God-realized avatar at birth. This sixteenth quality is absolute omniscience, omnipresence, and omnipotence. Sai Baba said that Krishna was a fifteen-point avatar who was a past life of Lord Maitreya.

The Love Seat of Sai Baba

While I was talking to Sai Baba, I asked him if he had an ascension seat we might come and sit in as we do in some of the other ashrams around the universe. Sai Baba told me that he did not have an ascension seat, but that he had a love seat we could come and sit in. His exact words were that we could "come and sit in the love seat and experience the love, the sweetness, and the succor of Sai Baba." To go there all you have to say in meditation is, "Sai Baba's ashram, love seat!"

The Seat of Immortal Bliss in Babaji's Cave

Marcia and I, in one of our meditations, figured that if Sai Baba had a love seat, maybe Babaji had a seat of some sort too. We traveled to Babaji's cave and were warmly greeted. Babaji told us that he had a seat which I am going to call the Seat of Immortal Bliss. If your devotion is pure and you are drawn to the energies of Babaji, then I suggest that you ask to go to this seat where you can bathe in his holy presence and experience his immortal bliss.

The Chakras of Planet Earth

In another meditation, Marcia and I asked Djwhal Khul about the chakras of Earth herself and where they were located. The crown chakra, amazingly enough, is now located in the middle of the United States, possibly leaning a little bit toward the Southwest. He said this was connected to the concept of the New Jerusalem. The United States' divine mission is now to lead the people of Earth back to God. Djwhal then told us that the third eye of the planet is in Egypt, connected to the Great Pyramid. The heart chakra is in Africa.

More on Mass Ascension

I asked both Vywamus and Melchizedek how often mass ascension has occurred or does occur on Planet Earth. Vywamus replied that it usually occurs during the descent of an avatar. Melchizedek told us that it usually occurs once every hundred years, although in the past it has included incredibly small numbers of people, nothing like what is about to happen as of May 14, 1995, when mass ascension officially begins during the Wesak Festival of the full moon.

Ascension Seat in the New Jerusalem

I have discovered another wondrous ascension seat. This one is in the etheric city above the middle of the United States and is called the New Jerusalem. Have you ever really looked at the spelling of "Jerusalem"? Notice the letters "usa" in the middle of the word! Serapis Bey is in charge of the Old Jerusalem energies with his connection to Egypt. Melchizedek told us that he and Jesus were two of the masters connected with this energy. I believe Saint Germain might also be connected with it. Anyway, there is an ascension seat to which you can travel in your spiritual body and work with for a change of pace. It might be a most appropriate one for people living in the United States.

Ascension Lineage and Support System

Every person has a certain ascension lineage and ascended master support system. For each person it is different. It will evolve and change as you evolve. As you close in upon your ascension, however, it will begin to become more refined and focused.

The best way I can explain this is to use myself as an example. My ascension lineage begins with Djwhal Khul as my planetary teacher, moves to Lord Maitreya and Vywamus as my galactic-level teachers, and then moves to Melchizedek as my universal teacher. There are other ascended master teachers with whom I work almost as closely. So there is a direct ascension lineage and a group of ascended masters who all work together on the inner plane.

For example, even though Djwhal Khul is my main planetary teacher and I work out of his ashram, I spend a lot of time talking to other teachers as well. Another teacher in my ascension support system who is helping me in my planetary service work is the Lord of Sirius who runs the Great White Lodge on Sirius. I also work with the Lord of Arcturus, Metatron, Sai Baba, Mahatma, Kuthumi, Lady Helena (Madam Blavatsky), the Master Jesus (Sananda), and Sanat Kumara. These beings are my main teachers.

Ascension lineage refers to the teachers by whom I am being over-lighted. However, that does not mean they are the only teachers I spend time talking with or receiving guidance from. Also, I use different teachers for different purposes. I often go to Metatron for Light quotient building, to Archangel Michael for protection, and to Melchizedek for his vast knowledge as the Grand Master of the Universe.

It is important to narrow your focus as you come closer to your ascension. One of the keys is knowing the ray of your soul and monad. If you don't know your ray, have a ray and initiation reading done by someone who is able to do that kind of reading. Knowing what your ray is will give you some insight as to which of the seven chohans and ashrams you are connected with. This is important information. Even though you might be connected, for example, to El Morya's first ray ashram because of your monadic ray, your ascension lineage still could be Djwhal Khul's ashram or Sananda's or Saint Germain's.

I was not always focused in Djwhal's ashram. I spent much time earlier in my life in Jesus' ashram and in Saint Germain's. The most important thing is that you attune to the master or masters whom your intuition and emotional body tell you are right at the time. It really does not matter which teachers you work with, for all take you to the same place. Some ascension lineages are more connected to Serapis Bey, some to Hilarion, some to Paul the Venetian, some to Commander Ashtar. Everyone has some connection to Lord Maitreya, Sanat Kumara, Helios, Melchior, and Melchizedek, because Lord Maitreya is the head of the entire Hierarchy, and the other above-mentioned masters are the Planetary Logos, Solar Logos, Galactic Logos, and Universal Logos, so everyone falls under their auspices.

This issue of the ascension lineage is, in truth, not really all that important. I bring it up only so you can avoid the danger of becoming too scattered in terms of how many different teachers you work with. It is fine to do that for a while, but in your later stages of evolution you will want to narrow your focus. You know the adages about becoming a Jack of all trades and a master of none and about too many cooks spoiling the broth. In later stages of evolution it is better to let one group of teachers work with you and help you to move along. Even though this is the case, I remain eclectic and universalist in my orientation and philosophy.

9

The Ultimate Ascension Meditation

Meditation is listening to God.

Edgar Cayce

Of all the ascension meditations I have done in my life, I find the
following meditation to be the most profound. In previous chapters I
have spoken of the ascension seats in Shamballa, in Lenduce's ashram, and
in the Golden Chamber of Melchizedek. To me, these three ascension seats
are clearly the most powerful.

For the ultimate ascension meditation, ask to be taken to the ascension seat in Shamballa. Then call forth Sanat Kumara, Vywamus, Lenduce,
and Melchizedek. Request a triple overlay and activation of the ascension
seats in Shamballa, Lenduce's ashram, and the Golden Chamber of Melchizedek. It can be visualized as a triangle with yourself in the middle. On
top is the Golden Chamber of Melchizedek, on the left is the ascension seat
in Shamballa, and on the right is the ascension seat in Lenduce's ashram.
The ascension seat in Shamballa is a pure white Light. The ascension seat
in Lenduce's ashram is a very pure blue-white Light. These three ascension
seats form a trinity representing the planetary core, the galactic core, and
the universal core. To invoke in meditation a blending of all three provides
a merging of all the energies and frequencies necessary for full completion
of the ascension process.

The following is a shortened invocation that Marcia and I began using
upon the completion of our sixth initiation and ascension. Added to the
three ascension seats are the key anchorings and activations needed for full
completion of the seventh initiation.

As with all the information in this book, please use it as it resonates
best for you. You can even change it or add to it if it feels appropriate to

do so. I have termed this the ultimate ascension meditation because that is what it has been for me. I would feel greatly honored if you find this meditation beneficial to your growth, for this is why I have shared it.

The Ultimate Ascension Meditation

Melchizedek, Lenduce, Vywamus, Sanat Kumara, Djwhal Khul, Kuthumi, Lord Maitreya, Arcturians, Metatron, Mahatma:

I, (we), (name or names), hereby call forth a triple ascension seat activation of the Golden Chamber of Melchizedek, Lenduce's ashram, and Shamballa in conjunction with the Arcturians and Lord Metatron.

I (we) call forth
> a full anchoring and activation of the three hundred fifty-two levels of the Mahatma,
> all fire letters and key codes,
> the Microtron,
> axiatonal alignment,
> brain illumination,
> Light quotient building,
> seventh degree activation,
> teleportation activity,
> mayavarupa energization,
> thirty-sixth chakra actualization in the crown chakra,
> full antakarana merger with the ascension column,
> chakra balancing and strengthening,
> physicalization of the twelve strands of DNA,
> seventh degree completion merger,
> the twelve Christed universes,
> the opening of all chakra chambers and facets,
> Light packets from the Great White Lodge on Sirius,
> the anchoring of the Cosmic Heart,
> the anchoring of the twelve bodies of Light,
> the anchoring of the twelve cosmic stations,
> the opening of the alpha and omega chakras,
> the opening of the ascension chakra,
> the merger of the Greater Flame with the lesser flame,
> and ascension activation and blessings from the
>> twelve mighty elohim and the twelve
>> mighty archangels so we may be of greater service.

Amen.

I would like to add one more technique to this meditation. After all the energies are anchored and while sitting in the triangular formation, call forth your double merkabah. Call to your Mighty I Am Presence to spin the inner merkabah to the right, and then ask that the outer merkabah spin to the left, or counterclockwise. If the merkabahs start to slow down, spin them as you would a top, with your hands. Remember to breathe while doing this. Spinning the merkabahs in this manner will serve to stabilize and solidify all the energies you have called forth and anchored.

10

The Twenty-four Dimensions of Reality

*In my Father's house
there are many mansions.*

Master Jesus

One of the most confusing subjects for any seeker on the spiritual path is the subject of the dimensions of reality and planes of consciousness. Djwhal Khul, in his writing through Alice Bailey, has spoken of the seven subplanes of the cosmic physical through which all are evolving: the physical, astral, mental, Buddhic, atmic, monadic, and logoic. Once you evolve through these seven subplanes of the cosmic physical plane you must then evolve through the seven cosmic planes, which have the exact same names as the seven subplanes, but they are cosmic in nature instead of just subplanes of the first cosmic physical plane. Each of the seven major initiations through which all must evolve on this plane are associated with the seven subplanes of the cosmic physical plane:

> First initiation . . . . Mastery of the physical plane
> Second initiation . . Mastery of the astral plane
> Third initiation . . Mastery of the mental plane
> Fourth initiation . . Anchoring of the Buddhic plane
> Fifth initiation. . . . Anchoring of the atmic Plane
> Sixth initiation. . . . Full anchoring of the monadic plane
> Seventh initiation. . Full anchoring of the logoic plane.

What gets very confusing now is that there are not only these seven planes of consciousness and seven cosmic planes of consciousness that make up the three hundred fifty-two levels of the Mahatma; they also make up the three hundred fifty-two levels of initiation needed to return completely to the Godhead at the highest level. There are also ten dimensions of reality that all human beings are working with which are different from these seven planes. It wasn't until very recently that I have finally been able to understand the difference. I am sure this chapter will be of great value for I know how confused I have been when terms such as fourth, fifth, and sixth dimensions have been thrown around. For example, at ascension, you merge with the monadic plane which is also merged with the fifth dimension. The dimensions do not coincide with the seven subplanes.

It was really Vywamus who finally helped me to understand the dimensions. This understanding began to come forth in the process of many long conversations I had with him. Vywamus also guided me to read his book *Scopes of Dimensions*, channeled by Janet McClure, which was invaluable. The only problem was that after reading it I still didn't understand the dimensions completely so I had to go back to Vywamus to have him explain them further and answer all my questions, which he was kind enough and patient enough to do. Vywamus, the higher self, or soul, of Sanat Kumara, has brought forth some of the most profound information ever given to humanity on this subject. I am going to attempt here to explain it in the most simple terms possible. My profound thank-you to Vywamus for all his help on this subject and to Janet McClure for her groundbreaking work in this area.

The First Dimension

The key term for the first dimension is completion. It is a passageway or a corridor that leads to some kind of completion. Any time you complete a project in your life you are accessing the first dimension. This feeling of completion stimulates a flow of energy that leads to the second dimension.

The Second Dimension

The key word for the second dimension is *new beginnings*. Once you complete something, it leads to an automatic desire to begin something new, sometimes even before fully completing the previous project. An example of this might be the initiation process. You might be in the process of completing your fifth initiation, but you are already thinking about beginning your sixth initiation and ascension. The example could also be more mundane, such as finishing up high school but already beginning to take a few college courses.

It is the first dimension and a person's response to it that stimulates a connection to the second dimension. I am sure you can relate to this process. As soon as I complete a project or a certain phase of my life I automatically begin thinking about what I am going to focus on next. This process is accessing the first two dimensions of reality.

The Third Dimension

You are more familiar with the third dimension. The key term here, according to Vywamus, is *magnification*. Magnification is like densification. The third dimension vibrates at literally one-tenth the frequency of Source, or God. That is why, after completing the seven levels of initiation and fully ascending, you are still only one-tenth of the way up a ten-inch ruler in terms of the total scope of your spiritual path back to the Godhead. The slow rate of vibration explains why everything looks solid in the third dimension when, in truth, nothing is solid but merely looks so to your physical eyes which perceive a very narrow frequency band. The reason God and the creator gods (elohim) have slowed the material universe ten-fold is so that it can be taken apart, studied, and then put back together. The third dimension is a slowed creative flow that allows you to see all of creation through a type of mirroring process. It is, in a sense, a practice area for apprentice gods.

Once humanity has shown itself to be responsible in this slow dimension, it then will be allowed to create in the more rarefied dimensions of reality. The interesting thing is that Planet Earth, as of the Harmonic Convergence in 1987, has moved into the fourth dimension. Vywamus and Djwhal Khul have said that each dimension has a scale from one to one hundred. Planet Earth is now at level one or two — the very beginning stages of the fourth dimension. That is why Planet Earth is now considered a sacred planet, esoterically speaking.

The Fourth Dimension

The key term for the fourth dimension is *flow*. Everything flows more smoothly and evenly and in a deeper fashion than in the third dimension. The third dimension has a type of flow, but it does not have depth and gets stuck and jammed up very easily. The fourth-dimensional flow has a stability that allows it to flow easily even during the storms of life. This flow operates on physical, emotional, mental, and spiritual levels.

An example of the increased flow, Vywamus said, is that professional athletes will begin to break all records that existed when Earth functioned as a planet in the third dimension because of the way the fourth dimension allows a greater flow, even at the physical level. This flow will operate on the emotional, mental, and spiritual levels in the same way. There will be greater flow among people on the planet as a whole, which is already evidenced by the downfall of Communism in the Soviet Union and Germany, greater cooperation in the United Nations, and the end of apartheid in South Africa.

It is also occurring in our personal lives. The fourth dimension is more continuous and more like a circle. The emotional body is the resident guide for the fourth dimension. The resident guide for the third dimension is the physical body, for the fifth dimension, the mental body, for the sixth dimension, the spiritual body. Even though this is true, it is essential for all the bodies to be able to access all the dimensions, despite having a dimension or dimensions to which they relate the best.

Humanity is now beginning to learn to create its base, its foundation, in the fourth dimension instead of in the third dimension. Obviously, this process is not complete yet, but it is beginning to happen.

The Fifth Dimension

The key term for the fifth dimension is *divine structure* or *ideal structure*. It is the structural blueprinting system. The fifth dimension is the dimension with which you merge at your sixth initiation and ascension. An example of this structural blueprinting system is that at ascension, the mayavarupa body, or monadic blueprint body, is fully anchored into your physical vehicle. In other words, you are then operating entirely out of the monadic blueprint and not out of a blueprint tainted by all your past incarnations. At ascension you are totally merged with your ideal structure forevermore.

The resident expert, again, is the mental body. The fifth dimension deals with divine order and with the building blocks with which creation takes place. The sixth dimension bring forth the concept, but it is the fifth dimension that executes the plans.

The Sixth Dimension

The key term for the sixth dimension is *complete understanding*. You merge with the sixth dimension when you take your seventh initiation which is the full completion of the seven levels of initiation that can be taken on this Earthly plane. The sixth initiation brings the first major contact with the Galactic Core, which is fully realized in the seventh dimension.

The sixth dimension is also the circuitry system that ensures there is enough divine current to meet all of the dimensional structures' needs. The sixth dimension also has a connection with the ninth dimension from where, Vywamus told me, this whole process is programmed. The Galactic Core inputs into the sixth dimension in a way that allows beings on Earth to begin a more complete usage of the dimensions. There is also a restimulation of energy on the sixth dimension from the ninth, eighth, and seventh dimensions of reality so that that energy can flow directly into dimensions one through five. The electrical flow of the energy the fifth dimension uses in its blueprinting system is generated from the sixth dimension.

The Seventh Dimension

The key term for the seventh dimension is *expansion*. The seventh dimension is a turnaround point for inner and outer experiences. It is a corridor that allows you to reframe the way you experience the dimensional structures. It allows for experiential objectivity. The seventh dimension is a dimensional reality you can go to to take a look at how well you have manifested the ideal. The experiential objectivity you gain from this perspective will stimulate new ideas upon which you can then expand in other-dimensional realities.

The Eighth Dimension

The key term for the eighth dimension is *potentiality*. The eighth dimension is the area that contains all potentialities. Potentialities are tried out and experimented with in the eighth dimension. This brings up the fascinating subject of cosmic days. A cosmic day is a conceptual framework within which the Source may completely explore a particular theme.

The theme of Planet Earth's cosmic day is courage. A cosmic day lasts for 4.3 billion years; 3.1 billion years of this cosmic day have already passed, so there are still 1.1 billion years left. Humanity has been on Earth for only about 18.5 million years. When a cosmic day is completed, the particular Source who is in charge of that cosmic day pulls it back in. This has been referred to as a cosmic night. It could last for another 4.3 billion years or not, depending on the Source.

Humanity's Source is in charge currently of fifty-one different cosmic days. What sometimes happens is that a cosmic day based on a particular theme in a particular universe does not work out as planned. It is like a book you are reading but after having read a quarter of it you find it is boring and not going anywhere. Then the Source ends the cosmic day prematurely and sends it back to the "laboratory" in the eighth dimension in a sort of miniaturized form. That particular cosmic day is reworked and then brought to completion.

The eighth dimension is a kind of cosmic laboratory in which ideas coming from the ninth dimension are first tried out to see if they will work. When cosmic days are brought to completion and proper resolution in miniaturized form, it is possible for humans and for the Earth as a whole to access this divine knowledge.

It must be stated here that most of the accessing of the seventh, eighth, and ninth dimensions of reality occurs during sleeptime. It is possible to request, before bed, the retention of this information for your own personal evolution and also for service to others.

In Janet McClure's book *Scopes of Dimensions,* Vywamus tells of a most extraordinary recent occurrence in regard to the Source that Earth's Source is merging with. If I am not mistaken, these two Sources are referred to as Melchizedek and Kalmelchizedek. During a sixteen-day period from July 25 to August 10, 1988, no fewer than ten cosmic days were pulled back prematurely because they were not working. All ten were put into a miniaturized state in the eighth-dimensional laboratory and brought to proper resolution. This, to me, seems absolutely extraordinary. This all occurred fairly close to the Harmonic Convergence and this planet's movement into the fourth dimension. It is beginning to become clear now what an amazing time that really was. The themes and withdrawal dates of those ten cosmic days were:

1.	Unlimited Energy	July 25, 1988
2.	Parallels of Love	July 26, 1988
3.	Joyous Beginnings	July 26, 1988
4.	Balancing of Oppositions	July 28, 1988
5.	Integration	July 30, 1988
6.	Unlimited Communication	July 31, 1988
7.	Surrender to the Plan	August 3, 1988
8.	Sacrifice	August 6, 1988
9.	Unconditional Love	August 7, 1988
10.	Joyous Movement	August 10, 1988

I find it absolutely fascinating to note the themes of other cosmic days. My understanding is that this cosmic day of courage is not in danger of being called back to Source prematurely. Even if it were, there is nothing to fear, for a cosmic night is like an incubation period before a new expansion. It is expanding and contracting or is, in truth, the "inbreath and outbreath of Brahma."

The key point here is that you are able to use the strengths that are developed in the cosmic laboratories in the eighth dimension even when a cosmic day is prematurely closed down. It makes a lot of sense when you think about it. Why continue a cosmic day if it is not really working out? God, in a sense, is stopping unnecessary suffering and unfulfillment. Life is eternal, as there is always another cosmic day. There are infinite numbers of cosmic days and Sources who are in charge of them.

The ending of the ten cosmic days affected not only the Earth, but also the entire cosmos. The eighth-dimensional laboratory also tries out cosmic day ideas from the ninth dimension to see if they will allow the theme ascribed to them to flow creatively and expand. One of the key lessons here is to see that even God learns from His mistakes and is constantly creating, expanding, and adjusting His creations in a most unlimited fashion. Vywamus has provided a glimpse of the true nature of reality at the cosmic levels. I think you will agree it is quite mind-boggling, especially given the fact that there is no time and space at these levels so everything is happening multidimensionally and simultaneously.

The goal of creation is to expand whatever theme is being explored. If it is not working, close it down, fix it in miniaturized form in the eighth dimension, and try something new. It feels to me like God is having a lot of fun. You get a sense here of the unlimitedness and the creativity of the Godforce. Vywamus has said that the full purpose of creation is simply joyous expression, a loving exercise in creativity.

The eighth dimension is the most expansive of the dimensions, as you can see from all the potentialities that are experimented with there. I am personally very taken with how God is so creative on these cosmic levels and obviously not fearful in the slightest of making mistakes. The traditional view of God in most religions is that God, being perfect, is incapable of anything but perfection. I have a feeling that God does not even look at closing down cosmic days prematurely as being mistakes. It feels more like unlimited creativity and having fun. Life is eternal, so what does it matter?

When cosmic days are ended and brought back to the eighth-dimensional laboratory, they are often played out in miniaturized form to see where they would have gone if allowed to continue. God learns more about Himself and then appropriate adjustments can be made for future cosmic days. The resolution of cosmic days in this miniaturized form is a cosmic substitute for the actual physical experience that humans can tap into and use. Vywamus said that the Source will always finish and compile all cosmic days and bring them to proper resolution. It is just a question of whether it is done in actual experience or is completed in the eighth-dimensional laboratory. So you could say it is not really a mistake, it is just a transfer of dimensions for the completion of God's Divine Plan.

The Ninth Dimension

The key word for the ninth dimension is *cocreation*. The ninth dimension is the administration level for all the dimensions. It is also the think tank for the cocreator level where the conception of existence takes place; that is, the experiential side of existence. True divine beingness lies far beyond any dimensional structure. Vywamus told me that at the very highest level there is the Creator level; then comes the cocreator level where there are twelve cocreator gods. You usually end up working for one of these cocreator gods, although you are not limited, by any means.

The ninth dimension is the Source's overall viewing level and the home territory of the cocreator levels. Each of you has a part that lives at each of these levels and at all three hundred fifty-two levels of the Mahatma, all the way back to Source. The ninth dimension is the entrance to your full cosmic evolution. It is the last stage before leaving the cosmic physical universe, you might say. It is the entrance to the full scope of the three hundred fifty-two levels of the Mahatma. The understanding that a part of you already exists on all the higher levels, even back up to the Creator level, means that in one sense, you have already achieved full completion and reunion with the Godhead. You are, in truth, already there. The problem is that you haven't fully realized it yet — that is the process of initiation and evolution.

Vywamus has told me that at higher levels of evolution you will not look at the initiation process in the same linear way you are seeing it now. Since there is no time and space and you are multidimensional, you will be working on all initiations simultaneously. (I, personally, don't claim to understand this. I am just kind of probing it with my right brain.)

The ninth dimension is the basic point of Creator contact. The idea is for you to learn to merge with the higher aspects of yourself in the same way that you have learned to merge with your soul and then your monad at ascension. It is a process of merging with higher and higher levels of your true Godself. The Mahatma is the group-consciousness being that is the amalgamation of all aspects of self all the way back to the Godhead. The Mahatma would literally be your self, not yet fully realized.

The image that Vywamus gave through Janet McClure for tuning into this energy (again in her book *Scopes of Dimensions)* was to imagine sitting on top of a mountain at the perfect temperature and allowing yourself to receive, with the intent of tuning into the ninth dimension. In truth, most of these dimensions are only truly available during sleep, but a subtle or stepped-down experience might be available to meditate upon.

I asked Vywamus if there is any limit or "ring pass not" beyond which you could not soul travel. He told me that at this level the limit is the tenth dimension. It is a built-in system of protection because you are not at a level to comprehend the cosmic planes. That does not mean that you are not totally connected to the Godhead and the cosmic planes, for you are; however, you will probably not soul travel there very much until you expand your level of evolution and initiatory status.

The Earth experience is about dealing primarily with the first six dimensions of reality. After ascension, seven, eight, and nine become more readily available. My intuition tells me that there might be exceptions to this; I am thinking of certain revelations of God people on the Earth plane have had that go beyond, I believe, soul and monad. What Vywamus said does ring true, however, because it can clearly be seen that progress in service and in the initiation process occurs gradually. You first work on yourself, then on the soul level, then on the monadic level serving the planet, then the solar system, then the galaxy, and then the universe.

Why would you be traveling to the highest cosmic planes when you haven't even mastered the first seven planes? I think you travel to the level you can integrate and use; otherwise, what would be the purpose? There are some who, in meditation, can tap directly into the ninth dimension. Others receive it more subtly. Still others can tap in during sleep. The ninth dimension interacts with all the other dimensions.

I asked Vywamus if it was possible to manifest a ninth-dimensional focus on Earth. He said it was possible, but that it has not happened very often in the history of the Earth. He said it was a good goal to aim for, but it must be remembered that the seventh initiation is the highest initiation that can be taken on this plane, and that is merger with the sixth dimension. Even seventh-degree initiates, hence sixth-dimensional beings, are somewhat rare, especially given the fact that in the past, most people have physically died after ascending. You would have to merge with your eighth- and ninth-dimensional selves while still remaining a seventh-degree initiate to do this. Vywamus said that a being at that level would be a luminescent Light, constantly changing. It would be invisible. (I was unclear whether he meant all the time or just some of the time.) The metaphor he used was that of ice, water, and steam: a ninth-dimensional being would be beyond steam.

The Tenth Dimension

The tenth dimension, Vywamus told me, marks the movement beyond physicality. The ninth initiation is the last initiation that can be taken in the cosmic physical universe. After that the master leaves the cosmic physical universe altogether and begins the progression through the next six cosmic planes — the cosmic astral, cosmic mental, cosmic Buddhic, cosmic atmic, cosmic monadic, and cosmic logoic planes.

Dimensions Nine through Twelve

Dimensions nine through twelve, especially — and actually, dimensions seven through twelve — deal with the galactic level of consciousness. Dimensions nine through twelve also deal with the higher university on Sirius: when you request to go to Lenduce's ashram and visit the ascension seats you are accessing this level, as you are when you travel to Sirius while you sleep to attend classes and when you go to the ascension seat in the Galactic Core.

Dimensions Twelve through Twenty-four

Dimensions twelve through twenty-four deal with the universal levels of consciousness. This is the domain of Melchizedek, the Universal Logos. When you request to be taken to the Golden Chamber of Melchizedek, you are beginning to access these levels. Vywamus told me that Sai Baba is a universal avatar who is accessing dimensions twelve through twenty-four.

The Kabbalah and the Ten Dimensions

The Kabbalah and the Tree of Life are wonderful multidimensional tools. The ten sephiroth could be associated with the ten dimensions. The three pillars of the Tree of Life represent the third dimension of reality, the dimension in which humans are anchored and which they call home.

Music, Art, and Other Dimensions

Vywamus has brought forth some fascinating information on music and the dimensions. The music you listen to often carries you into the third, fourth, fifth, and sixth dimensions of reality. "The Star-Spangled Banner" is quite unusual in this regard, for it allows you to access the sixth dimension. Its focus is the fourth dimension, but it is able to integrate all the levels. This dimensional shifting is affected not only by the sound, but also by the words and by the person or persons playing the piece of music.

The greatest musicians are those who can travel interdimensionally. The angelic kingdom harvests a great deal of the energy that is created by people listening to concerts. Djwhal Khul has told me the same thing about sports events and other gatherings of all kinds. The energy is gathered and used for the purposes of Sanat Kumara and the Spiritual Hierarchy.

Vywamus told me that Beethoven takes people to the fourth, fifth, and sixth dimensions. Rock concerts usually remain in the third, unless the group is focused on brotherhood in its music, as an occasional group is. Mozart has an occasional piece of music that takes people to the experience of the seventh dimension, along with the fourth, fifth, and sixth. No piece of music is one-dimensional.

I asked similar questions of Vywamus about the arts. He told me that the Sistine Chapel takes people to the fifth and sixth dimensions. He said certain modern paintings occasionally take people into the seventh dimension. Which dimension you move into is dependent upon two factors: the creator and the experiencer. The more highly evolved you are, the more likely you are to be able to allow yourself to experience the higher dimensions through the catalyzation of a work of art or music.

Watching television, Vywamus said, is usually a third-, fourth- or fifth-dimensional experience; being in nature is a fourth-, fifth-, or sixth-dimensional experience, as is attending lectures.

Sports and Other Dimensions

I was surprised to hear that even sports events can take people into different dimensions. Vywamus said that football unites the third, fourth, and fifth dimensions. Achieving a goal brings forth a feeling of freedom, self-confidence, and accomplishment for both players and fans. The losers create a reality of not achieving a goal and they feel the opposite way.

Dimensions and Vortexes

Another very interesting discussion I had with Vywamus was about vortexes. There are certain vortexes on the planet that could be likened to major and minor chakras. Some of these vortexes have higher-dimensional relationships, such as those in Sedona (Arizona), Egypt, Tibet, Siberia, India, Kenya, and South America, particularly Machu Picchu and Brazil, to name a few. Many of them are seventh-dimensional in nature. One of the most famous is the Bermuda Triangle, which Vywamus said was actually an aberration, or imbalance, caused by the great crystal from Atlantis. Vywamus said this vortex has a seventh- and eighth-dimensional relationship. He likened it to the wormhole described in *Star Trek*. People, planes, and ships are actually dematerialized and transported through a type of wormhole to another place. I asked Vywamus where, and he said, "Sometimes outside of the solar system." I asked him if they were all alive in a physical sense. He said sometimes they are, and other times they lose their physical bodies.

Vywamus told me there is an eighth-dimensional vortex at the polar ice caps near the entrance to the Hollow Earth. This particular vortex takes you out of the galaxy and is used a great deal by extraterrestrials. It is natural and is not caused by an aberration as is the Bermuda Triangle.

The vortexes in Sedona, he told me, are mostly of the fourth, fifth, and sixth dimensions, although one of them is a seventh-dimensional vortex. Most of them are protected by Native Americans. Just as there are major and minor chakras in the human body, so there are the same in the Earth.

More Information on the Ten Dimensions of Reality

The ability to teleport occurs in the fifth and sixth dimensions, with knowledge about it coming from the ninth dimension. It is essential to be able to access all of the dimensions with your physical, emotional, mental, and spiritual bodies. Not to access all dimensions would be like moving into a ten-bedroom house and never entering seven of the rooms. Each dimension gives you the opportunity to access certain strengths. Life mirrors certain inconsistencies to you when dimensions are left out. The key word here is integration. Each of the four bodies speaks, in a sense, a different language, and each relates to the dimensions differently. Each body has an affinity and a lack of affinity for certain dimensions, and that is fine as long as there is an open flow of communication. Your consciousness needs the information from all four bodies to fully understand and use all ten dimensions.

Earth is now moving into the fourth dimension, which will allow everything on the planet to flow more smoothly and easily. Communication will be more consistent and reach deeper levels of understanding. Transportation will be less problematic; people will learn to teleport. (Teleportation is an example of the physical body's learning to contact the fourth dimension and not stay stuck in the third dimension.) All forms of athletics will be more graceful. There will be a greater link between Earth and the Galactic Core, especially with Melchior who is the Galactic Logos.

Vywamus has said that there is another Earth in the fourth dimension, one in the fifth dimension, and so on, all the way up through all the dimensions. This makes sense because as I have already stated, you have a self that already exists and functions in those higher dimensions, so why shouldn't the entire Earth have the same? The idea is to merge the fourth-dimensional, fully realized Earth with the Earth that has just entered the fourth dimension. This process, as you can see, has already begun to happen.

Within the ideal grid system, Vywamus says, the emotional body's home base will be the fourth dimension, the mental body's, the fifth dimension. That doesn't mean they won't visit, merge with, and access the other dimensions, just that these are their ideal home bases and their areas of greatest expertise.

The fourth-dimensional Earth will be free of all pollution, for pollution comes from a third-dimensional, stuck perspective. The heating up of the Earth's atmosphere, the greenhouse effect, is another example of that perspective; so is the cellulite so many people carry around in their bodies. Merger with the fourth dimension on planetary and personal levels will allow the energy to flow more freely and clear away the debris caused by holding onto the third-dimensional perspective. Life is mirroring the resistance and signaling the need to move into the fourth dimension with the four-body system.

Each of the four bodies will always be affected by the other bodies' perspectives: It is as though each of the bodies takes parts of the other bodies with it when it attunes to another dimension. The ideal is to create clarity of communication within the four-body system.

If there were no dimensions or dimensional structure, there would never be a way to contact one another or to differentiate parts in any way. The dimensions that God has created are the tools by which you are allowed to use your five senses and four bodies to make contact with each other and with the different aspects of life. In Janet McClure's *Scopes of Dimensions*, Vywamus says that "Source talks to Itself through the dimensions." Without the dimensions, life would be just a kaleidoscope of light and sound with no contact whatsoever. True reality is beyond the dimensions, but the dimensions are used as a way of outpicturing God's Divine Plan.

Vywamus also says that the clearest way to attract a relationship partner is by going to the spiritual level on which the divine blueprint lives. It is there you can make the first contact. That will create a magnetic attraction that can build and extend onto other levels. I can't help thinking of my first meeting with Terri Sue. I met her at a workshop about anchoring the monad. The monad is the fifth dimension, which is the divine structure and blueprinting system. Given that Terri and I come from the same monad, I believe we met each other in the exact way Vywamus is speaking of. It was our spiritual, or monadic, attraction that caused us first to meet in a monadic anchoring seminar; then the attraction flowed downward to the other levels.

I have always said that the best way to meet your spiritual mate is to focus completely on your spiritual path and on service to humanity. When you are totally right with self, right with God, and fulfilled in your spiritual path, that special person will just show up at your doorstep without your even trying. A great many people bond on the sexual level first and then often find they don't blend on all four body levels or on higher-dimensional levels, so connecting on a higher level first is preferable.

I also had a discussion with Vywamus about the parallel Earth realities in other dimensions. It might be said that there are nine different Earths, one in each of the nine dimensions of reality. They are like nine rooms in a house with walls that separate them; you can't see from one to the other. The ideal, ultimately, is for the nine Earths from the nine dimensions of reality to become one Earth. The same could be said for the nine aspects of the self.

When people on Earth occasionally have an experience of revelation, they are usually accessing the galactic or universal plane. They are still only about two inches up the ten-inch ruler of the Source's full creation, but for the Earth, it is a very profound contact. Sai Baba is a walking revelation, for he is a universal avatar.

I asked Vywamus if it is possible to travel all the way back to the Source of all Sources on the highest cosmic plane. He said it is possible if there is an important purpose for doing so, although you might not remember it. It would, however, have an effect on your energy matrix. For the most part, you travel to no higher a level than you can comfortably integrate.

You are not going to have a revelation of the Godhead at the highest cosmic plane because you are not at a level where you can integrate or even resonate with that experience. The galactic or universal level would be a big enough stretch. I also asked about the next aspect of self beyond the soul and monad in the communication link with Source. He said it is the Creator level.

I also asked Vywamus about the status of the cosmic day in which Earth is now involved. I wanted to know if there is any possibility that this cosmic day will be closed down and returned to the eighth dimension for completion. Vywamus said that this cosmic day of courage is working magnificently and there is no reason for it to be ended. He also told me that when a cosmic day is closed down and miniaturized, it does not necessarily affect the physical universe, although sometimes it does. Sometimes the closing down and miniaturizing occurs only on an energetic level. Other times there is a complete deactivation of even the physical level. That would lead to a full cosmic night, or what Vywamus referred to as a "cosmic pause." A cosmic night might or might not last as long as a cosmic day. During a cosmic night you still exist, but you live in more of a "being" state, a state of reflection and passiveness. Evolvement does not occur in the same way.

I asked Vywamus if the cosmic day and cosmic night applied only to the nine dimensions of reality or to God's entire infinite universe. He said it was applied to all of creation. He ended the discussion by saying that the macrocosm could be understood by focusing on the microcosm of my physical body and four-body system. As I can focus on certain organs, glands, cells, molecules, atoms, and electrons in my body, so God and the infinite numbers of Sources and cosmic days that make up all of creation can do the same thing on a much grander scale. As you learn to master yourself, you are being prepared to work on the much larger scale of a planet, star system, galaxy, or universe, which are nothing more than organs, molecules, atoms and electrons in God's body.

People on Earth often feel an energy drain because they are spending too much time concentrating on one dimension to the exclusion of the other dimensions. In this society, it is usually the mental dimension that is overemphasized, although sometimes people also lose energy by focusing too much on the emotional body.

Another way of understanding the dimensions as they relate to the Earth is to look at the ley lines, or grid system, of the Earth. Most of you, I am sure, are familiar with this concept. What most people don't understand is that there are grid lines on all nine levels of Earth, in each of the nine dimensions of reality.

Vywamus says the soul level is required in order to reach the sixth dimension. If you are not attuned to your soul or higher self, you will not be able to access the sixth dimension. A person who has died or ascended and who is living in the seventh dimension will utilize the sixth dimension as the connecting link or relay station to channel to humans on Earth. The angels, in particular, use this system. The angels can actually speak from the fourth dimension, even though they come from dimensions six, seven, and nine.

Conclusion

Once more, I want to acknowledge Janet McClure's wonderful book, *Scopes of Dimensions,* which provided me with a framework upon which to build my discussions with Vywamus. I highly recommend reading this book. It too is published by Light Technology Publishing in Sedona.

11

Huna Prayers

Prayer is talking to God.
Edgar Cayce

O ne of the ways I greatly accelerated our collective path of ascension
was through the use of Huna prayers. When I communicated with
Marcia telepathically when she was in Bali and told her that I had made a
deal with the masters to ascend earlier than we had previously expected, I
did it through the use of Huna prayers. (*Hidden Mysteries* provides a more
complete explanation of Huna.)

The Huna method of prayer as taught by the Kahunas of Hawaii is to
write out on paper in very clear and precise language exactly what you want
to manifest. Address the prayer to exactly the being or beings you are
asking to respond to it. Then say your prayer three times out loud. Then
command your subconscious mind to take the prayer to your soul or
monad with all the mana, or vital force, that is needed and necessary to
manifest your prayer. Wait about fifteen seconds to allow time for the
subconscious mind to do that. Finally, to complete the prayer process, say
the phrase, "Lord, let the rain of blessings fall!"

Before performing the prayer, it is recommended that you do some
deep breathing or physical exercise to build your vital force and that you
forgive anyone who needs your forgiveness, so that the path to the higher
self is clear. Huna belief also recommends praying from full personal
power and not from weakness or lack of self-worth.

I first learned about the Huna teachings from Paul Solomon in his
channelings of the Universal Mind. The Universal Mind said that the
clearest form of psychology and religion on the planet was the Huna
teachings of Hawaii. It was through the study of the Huna teachings that I

learned this method of prayer. I have used it hundreds and hundreds of times, particularly whenever something of major importance was occurring in my life. I think I can honestly say that every single Huna prayer I have ever said has been answered.

In my personal ascension process I have used Huna prayers frequently. There were about ten of them I said at different times concerning different aspects of our group ascension process. The overall theme of all my Huna prayers was the supreme acceleration of the process. God, Sanat Kumara, and the ascended masters have clearly responded to my prayers.

Below, you will find a Huna prayer you can use for the acceleration of your personal ascension. I recommend using the same basic format in your future prayers. The power and effectiveness of this particular technique will amaze you. You can use it for any area of your life, of course; it is not meant only for ascension.

If you want to increase the power of your prayer, say it in unison with your core ascension group. We do them often in our Wednesday night classes and the power is unbelievable. The first night we did this, Sanat Kumara responded and suggested we continue doing it. You are assured of getting God's attention as well as the attention of the ascended masters when you use this method.

Sometimes I say the prayers alone, sometimes with Terri Sue, and sometimes with certain friends. Other times I do them in large groups. As Edgar Cayce said, "Why worry when you can pray?" I might add that the use of the Huna prayer is not necessarily for everyone. Occasionally, someone feels an aversion to this style of working because of some deep difficulty from his past. As with everything, you must use your discernment to determine what is appropriate for you. Try it out and if it rings true for you and feels right, then use it. It is truly a powerful tool and can work wonders.

The Lords of Karma

I also recommend you work with the Lords of Karma, also known as the Karmic Board. Their names can be added to all Huna prayers, or you can pray to them specifically. The members of the Karmic Board are as follows:

> The Great Divine Director, representing the first ray;
> The Goddess of Liberty, representing the second ray;
> Lady Nada, representing the third ray;
> Pallas Athena, the Goddess of Truth, representing the fourth ray;
> Elohim Vista, representing the fifth ray;
> Quan Yin, representing the sixth ray; and
> Portia, the spokesperson for the Karmic Board, Goddess of
>   Justice, representing the seventh ray.

Twice each year the ascended masters and students attend a meeting on the inner plane in the Royal Teton retreat for the purpose of presenting the Lords of Karma with their prayers, plans, and petitions for the service of humanity. These meetings are held each year from June 15 to July 14 and from December 15 to January 14; these are especially good times to address your Huna prayers to the Lords of Karma. Although you can add them to your regular Huna prayers at any time, during these windows of opportunity it is especially beneficial to do so.

The prayers, specifically those to the Karmic Board during these periods of time, should be written or typed and read on several succeeding nights before bed. They should be stated so as to benefit humankind as well as yourself. You must also be willing to put out the energy needed to manifest the prayer. It might also be of benefit to add the name of the Keeper of the Scrolls to the list of ascended beings to whom you are addressing your prayer. He is the being on the inner plane who records all prayers for the Lords of Karma. The prayers should be burned in a special burning pot of some kind after the end of the Lords of Karma invocation. Examples of some of the major dispensations that have been granted by the Karmic Board include the dispensation to allow Djwhal Khul to work with Alice Bailey, the dispensation to allow Saint Germain to work with and through Guy Ballard in bringing forth the *I Am Discourses*, and the dispensation to allow El Morya to work with Geraldine Innocente in a later phase of the *I Am Discourses*.

Your prayer requests can also be of a personal nature. I want to emphasize here that this particular focus on the Lords of Karma is really separate from the Huna prayer method, but I have added it because it seemed to be appropriate information.

Huna Prayer I

Beloved Presence of God, Mahatma, my Mighty I Am Presence, my monad, beloved Sanat Kumara, Lord Maitreya, Vywamus, Sai Baba, Jesus, Saint Germain, El Morya, Kuthumi, Serapis Bey, Djwhal Khul, and beloved Spiritual Hierarchy:

I hereby ask and pray with all my heart and soul and mind and might for your divine help, guidance, direction, and divine intervention in helping me to accelerate on my path of ascension.

I ask and pray to be worked on by the ascended masters and by my own I Am Presence every night while I sleep, in Serapis Bey's ascension retreat in Luxor.

I am hereby calling forth a thousandfold acceleration of this process and I ask for the building of my Light quotient to the 83% level needed for ascension.

I ask and pray that this preparation and training continue twenty-four hours a day, seven days a week, and three hundred sixty-five days a year until I ascend.

I thank you and accept this as being done according to God's will.

Amen.

Repeat aloud three times.

My beloved subconscious mind, I hereby ask and command that you take this thought form prayer, with all the mana and vital force needed and necessary to manifest and demonstrate this prayer, to the Source of my being through my beloved monad.

Amen.

Wait fifteen seconds and visualize the prayer shooting up through your crown chakra like the geyser, Old Faithful.

Lord, let the Rain of Blessings fall!

Amazing Effectiveness

This is one possible example of a Huna prayer. Just say the first part three times out loud. Then make the command to the subconscious mind once, also out loud. Wait ten or fifteen seconds to allow the subconscious mind to do its work. Then make the final statement.

You do not have to address your prayer to all of the ascended beings I mentioned. If you want, you can address it only to God or, if you prefer, to God and just one master. This is up to you and your own creativity. Make up your own prayers and then fit them into this basic format.

I could tell you stories that would amaze you about the effectiveness and power of these prayers. Make your own deal with God and the ascended masters. Never forget, you create your own reality. The Godforce responds to your free will choice and to the power of your spoken word. You are God, and your word is law!

These prayers are sacred, so make sure that it is your higher self writing them and not your negative ego. Your soul or monad will not respond to any prayer that would hurt another person or yourself. Pray for those things you really need help with. It is all right to pray for material things as long as you really need them.

I have included some other examples of Huna prayers with which I am working in my movement toward completion. These Huna prayers are so important that I want to give you plenty of examples with which to work. You may use the ones I have made or you can alter the wording to suit your own particular focus at any specific time.

Huna Prayer II

Beloved Presence of God, my Mighty I Am Presence, my monad, beloved Mahatma, Melchizedek, Universal Logos, Melchior, Helios, beloved Sanat Kumara, masters of Shamballa, and beloved Spiritual Hierarchy:

I ask and pray with all my heart and soul and mind and might for the full divine intervention of the Godforce to now fully end the war in Yugoslavia.

I ask and pray for the divine miracle that a peace plan be developed that all parties involved will sign and fully implement.

I hereby call forth with all my heart and soul and mind and might that peace and God's Divine Plan now manifest and anchor into this region.

I call forth now, in the name of the Christ, an absolute, complete cessation and ending of all violence and warring consciousness in the former Yugoslavia.

I thank you and accept this as being done according to your will.

Amen.

Repeat aloud three times.

My beloved subconscious mind, I hereby ask and command that you take this thought form prayer, with all the mana and vital force needed and necessary to manifest and demonstrate this prayer, to the Source of my being through my beloved monad.

Amen.

Wait fifteen seconds and visualize the prayer shooting up through your crown chakra like a geyser.

Lord, let the Rain of Blessings fall!

Huna Prayer III

Beloved Presence of God, my Mighty I Am Presence, my monad, beloved Mahatma, Melchizedek, Universal Logos, Melchior, Helios, beloved Sanat Kumara, masters of Shamballa, and beloved Spiritual Hierarchy:

I ask and pray with all my heart and soul and mind and might for your guidance, help, direction, and divine intervention in helping the Israelis and the Palestinians to resolve the differences that are preventing them from fully implementing the peace plan that was agreed to this past year. I am hereby calling forth the divine intervention of the full Godforce to help this peaceful resolution and divine implementation of the peace agreement come about. I thank you and accept this as being done according to God's will. Amen.

Repeat aloud three times.

My beloved subconscious mind, I hereby ask and command that you take this thought form prayer, with all the mana and vital force needed and necessary to manifest and demonstrate this prayer, to the Source of my being through my beloved monad.

Amen.

Wait fifteen seconds and visualize the prayer shooting up through your crown chakra like a geyser.

Lord, let the Rain of Blessings fall!

Huna Prayer IV

Beloved Presence of God, Mahatma, my Mighty I Am Presence, my monad, Sanat Kumara, Vywamus, Lord Maitreya, Master Kuthumi, Djwhal Khul, Serapis Bey, Metatron, and Jesus:

I hereby pray with all my heart and soul and mind and might for your divine help, guidance, direction, and divine intervention in my life to help me now to unfold and develop fully the ascended master abilities that go along with being a fully realized initiate and ascended master,

I ask and pray for your help in fully opening my psychic abilities of conscious telepathy, bilocation, teleportation, transfiguration, shapeshifting, dematerialization, materializing objects, physical immortality, and all the other ones I have not mentioned.

I also ask to be intensively prepared now to take my final initiation with my core ascension group.

Amen.

Repeat aloud three times.

My beloved subconscious mind, I hereby ask and command that you take this thought form prayer, with all the mana and vital force needed and necessary to manifest and demonstrate this prayer, to the Source of my being through my beloved monad.

Amen.
Wait fifteen seconds and visualize the prayer shooting up through your crown chakra like a geyser.

Lord, let the Rain of Blessings fall!

Huna Prayer V

Beloved Presence of God, Mahatma, my Mighty I Am Presence, my monad, beloved Melchior, beloved masters from the Galactic Core:

Beloved Melchior, I hereby pray with all my heart and soul and mind and might to be overshadowed by masters from the Galactic Core to help me in my mission on Earth.

I also humbly request your assistance, combined and collectively, in helping our core ascension group prepare ourselves to take our seventh initiation. Any help you can provide would be greatly appreciated.

I thank you and accept these things as being done in the name of the Christ.

Amen.
Repeat aloud three times.

My beloved subconscious mind, I hereby ask and command that you take this thought form prayer, with all the mana and vital force needed and necessary to manifest and demonstrate this prayer, to the Source of my being through my beloved monad.

Amen.

Wait fifteen seconds and visualize the prayer shooting up through your crown chakra like a geyser.

Lord, let the Rain of Blessings fall!

Huna Prayer VI

Beloved Presence of God, Mahatma, my Mighty I Am Presence, my monad, beloved Sanat Kumara, Lord Maitreya, Master Kuthumi, Vywamus, Sai Baba, Sananda, and Djwhal Khul:

I hereby ask and pray with all my heart and soul and mind and might for your divine intervention in helping me now to open fully to my clairvoyance and clairaudience and to fully open my channel so I may speak with the masters directly.

I hereby make my request as an initiate of the Spiritual Hierarchy and as an ascended master for the divine, miraculous intervention of the Godforce and my own monad to open these faculties within me.

I wish now to be able to spiritually see, to spiritually hear, to allow the masters to speak through me, and to write books authored by Djwhal Khul, Vywamus, Master Sananda, and Sanat Kumara.

I hereby give my complete permission for you to do whatever you have to do to accomplish this task.

I ask for these things so I can expand my ability to seve.

I thank you and accept these things as being done in the name of the Christ.

Amen.

Repeat aloud three times.

My beloved subconscious mind, I hereby ask and command that you take this thought form prayer, with all the mana and vital force needed and necessary to manifest and demonstrate this prayer, to the Source of my being through my beloved monad.

Amen.

Wait fifteen seconds and visualize the prayer shooting up through your crown chakra like a geyser.

Lord, let the Rain of Blessings fall!

Huna Prayer VII

Beloved Presence of God, Lord of Sirius, Vywamus, Sanat Kumara, and Djwhal Khul:

(Name) and I hereby pray with all our hearts and souls and minds and might for a divine dispensation from the Lord of Sirius and Sanat Kumara to be allowed to serve as direct anchor points on Earth for the Lord of Sirius and the Great White Lodge on Sirius.

We are calling forth to be your channels and instruments to bring forth your galactic and universal knowledge, wisdom, and love to Earth in any way you see fit to use us.

We are also now calling forth your direct guidance and intervention to teach us how to fully actualize and utilize all the Light information that is now pouring in.

We are calling forth direct consciousness during our meditations, sleeptimes, and conscious waking lives to accelerate the manifestation of the Divine Plan on Earth.

We thank you and accept this as being done according to your will.

Amen.

Repeat aloud three times.

Our beloved subconscious minds, we hereby ask and command that you take this thought form prayer, with all the mana and vital force needed and necessary to manifest and demonstrate this prayer, to the Lord of Sirius and Sanat Kumara.

Amen.

Wait fifteen seconds and visualize the prayer shooting up through your crown chakra like a geyser.

Lord of Sirius, Sanat Kumara, and Vywamus, let the Rain of Blessings fall!

Amen.

Huna Prayer VIII

Beloved Presence of God, we hereby call forth His Holiness, the Lord Sai Baba. Om Sri Sai Ram, Om Sri Sai Ram, Om Sri Sai Ram.

Beloved Sai Baba, our cosmic guru, we call you forth.

We hereby pray with all our hearts and souls and minds and might for your divine aid in helping us to raise our Light quotient to the (*appropriate number, such as 94*)% level within (*period of time*).

We also ask for your specific divine help in assisting our core ascension group of (*names*) to achieve our seventh initiation (within Djwhal Khul's system of initiation, as described in the Alice Bailey books) within (_____) months' to one year's time. (*Use whatever period of time is appropriate to you and your group.*)

We ask and pray for a divine dispensation in this regard from you, Sai Baba, our beloved cosmic guru.

We ask for these things so we may be of greater service to humanity.

We thank you and accept this as being done according to your will, beloved Baba.

Amen.

Repeat aloud three times.

Our beloved subconscious minds, we hereby ask and command that you take this thought form prayer, with all the mana and vital force needed and necessary to manifest and demonstrate this prayer, to the Lord of Sirius and Sanat Kumara.

Amen.

Wait fifteen seconds and visualize the prayer shooting up through your crown chakra like a geyser.

Beloved Baba, let the Rain of Blessings fall!

Huna Prayer IX

Beloved Presence of God, Sanat Kumara, Vywamus, Lenduce, Lord Maitreya, Kuthumi, Djwhal Khul, Lady Helena, Saint Germain, and Melchior:

We hereby call forth a divine dispensation, if this prayer be in harmony with your will.

We hereby call forth an anchoring of all inner plane Light packets of information from the Alice Bailey material, from the Theosophical materials written by Madam Blavatsky, from the material of the Tibetan Foundation, and from the three dispensations of *The "I Am" Discourses* of Saint Germain.

We ask for this so we are fully grounded in the four ascended master dispensations for Light quotient building.

Secondly, we request a full and complete anchoring of all Light packets of information from the hierarchical archives and from the Shamballa archives that would help us in our planetary, solar, and galactic missions on Earth and beyond.

Thirdly, we also request all Light packets of information from the Galactic Core and Melchior that would also be beneficial to our overall development, service work, and Light quotient building program.

Lastly, we request that this vast amount of Light information we have now officially invoked also be connected to our ascension columns in a vast information highway so all may benefit.

We thank you and accept this as being done in the name of the Christ.

Repeat aloud three times.

Our beloved subconscious minds, we hereby ask and command that you take this thought form prayer with all the mana and vital force needed and necessary to manifest and demonstrate this prayer to Sanat Kumara and the Source of our being.

Amen.

Wait fifteen seconds and visualize the prayer shooting up through your crown chakra like a geyser.

Beloved Sanat Kumara, beloved Godforce, let the Rain of Blessings fall!

Huna Prayer from Djwhal Khul for Money

The following is a Huna prayer Terri Sue channeled from Djwhal Khul for the manifestation of money for the Lightworkers on the planet. It is quite powerful and I suggest you share it with the spiritual communities you are involved in as well as using it for yourself. It was suggested by Djwhal that you say this prayer once a day for thirty days to clear blocks and manifest your divine inheritance of full abundance on all levels so you can do the service work you came here to do.

Beloved Presence of God:

We hereby ask and humbly pray with all our hearts and souls and minds and might for divine abundance made manifest through personal fortune and success.

We are willing to move beyond fear in order to fulfill God's Plan on Earth and beyond.

I personally pledge to open myself to financial wealth in order to fulfill my group and individual service commitments.

In God's name, we accept our divine heritage *right now*, and thank Thee for the timely answer to this prayer. God's will be done!

Amen.

Repeat aloud three times.

Our beloved subconscious minds, we hereby ask and lovingly command that you take this thought form prayer to God, along with all the mana and vital force needed and necessary to manifest and demonstrate this prayer.

Amen.

Breathe the prayer to God. Wait ten to fifteen seconds.

Lord, let the Rain of Blessings fall!

Amen!

Feel energy coming from God back to you. Soak it in.

Om. Om. Om. (*Sing peacefully and with devotion.*)

12

The Seven Paths to Higher Evolution

*The completion of the seven levels of
initiation on this plane moves you only one
inch up a ten-inch ruler in terms of your
entire cosmic evolution.*

Vywamus

At the time of taking your sixth initiation and ascension, you must
make a decision as to which of the seven paths of higher evolution
you will follow. As I have stated previously, the completion of the seven
levels of initiation means that you are, in truth, only one inch up a ten-inch
ruler, with nine inches to go. At that point you have completed the seven
subplanes of the cosmic physical plane but have not yet even entered the
cosmic astral plane, the cosmic mental plane, the cosmic Buddhic plane,
the cosmic atmic plane, the cosmic monadic plane, or the cosmic logoic
plane.

One of the seven paths to higher evolution will serve as a focus on
your journey. God is too infinitely vast for you to evolve without some kind
of focus. All seven paths ultimately lead to the same place; even so, if you
want to, it is possible to transfer from one path to another at a later time.

The Path to Sirius seems to serve as a preliminary training ground for
some of the other paths that are more advanced. You must go on record as
to which path you choose at the time of your ascension. It is a good idea to
familiarize yourself with these seven paths now, even before you ascend,
and to begin meditating upon them. The seven paths are the following:

1. The Path of Earth Service
2. The Path of Magnetic Work
3. The Path of Training to become a Planetary Logos

4. The Path to Sirius
5. The Ray Path
6. The Path on which the Solar Logos Himself is Found
7. The Path of Absolute Sonship

I believe that Djwhal Khul, in his writings through Alice Bailey (particularly *Initiation, Human and Solar*), is the only ascended master who has ever written about these paths in any detail on the Earth plane. He has done humanity a tremendous service by doing so. The only problem is that some of the material is very technical and esoteric and difficult for the average person to understand.

With Djwhal's blessing I have attempted to expand upon his writings to make the information a little easier to understand and a little more accessible by humanity. It has taken a good deal of spiritual research to do this, and I consider this particular project one of the most important I have ever been involved with. It is my prayer that my efforts in this regard will be of value to you.

One: The Path of Earth Service

The Path of Earth Service is the first of the seven paths to higher evolution. If you choose this path, you remain on Earth or in the ashram of one of the seven chohans serving humanity from the inner plane. If you choose this path you must also choose which kingdom (human, animal, plant, or mineral) to focus on based on which would profit most from your abilities.

Terri Sue has chosen this path and Djwhal Khul has told her that she would be spending the next four thousand years serving humanity. You can serve directly, by incarnating, or indirectly, from the spiritual world. The basic goal of this path is to raise the consciousness, frequency, level of love, and initiatory status of humanity and all the other kingdoms. All who choose this path work under Sanat Kumara, the Planetary Logos.

There is also the issue here of choosing the Path of Earth Service on a temporary basis as opposed to a full-time basis. I, for example have chosen the Path to Sirius, but I have been told by Djwhal Khul that even though this is the case, I will be spending a period of time, after leaving this physical body, in Djwhal's ashram working with him much as we are working together now. Djwhal Khul has chosen the Path to Sirius. The interesting thing, however, is that Sanat Kumara has asked Djwhal to remain with the Earth and on the Path of Earth Service during this critical time in Earth's history. In a sense, you might say that Sanat Kumara chose the Path of Earth Service for Djwhal and Djwhal graciously agreed. However, he does a lot of training and work all over the universe in conjunction with this mission. Most people, after ascension and leaving the physical vehicle, will spend some time in Earth service from the inner plane as part of their training.

The Path of Earth Service deals with initiations seven through twelve, which take you up through the galactic level. Djwhal Khul, I believe, is at the ninth initiation in this process. After the ninth initiation you usually leave the cosmic physical universe altogether.

The Path of Earth Service, during this particular phase of Earth's development, is a most spectacular path because of the incredible speeding-up of evolution that is taking place at this time. Earth will make more progress in this forty-year period of history (from 1988 to 2028) than it has in the past 3.2 billion years. This path has been less popular in the past than, for example, the Path to Sirius.

Also, there has been a limit on the number of people who have been allowed to choose this path, and it has become more popular in the past fifty years. The Path of Earth Service is more familiar than any of the other six paths to higher evolution because, of course, it is the plane on which humans are incarnated. In a sense, all are on the Path of Earth Service and have been so for a very long time. The difference between that and what I am referring to in this chapter is that after the sixth initiation and ascension, when a path has been chosen, you serve with full self-realization.

As you remember, there are seven cosmic planes. The seven planes through which humans are evolving are only the seven subplanes of the cosmic physical plane. Djwhal, at the ninth initiation, is just preparing to leave the cosmic physical plane. The Path of Earth Service leads to the cosmic astral plane, as does the Path to Sirius. Some of the later paths lead to the cosmic mental plane and one even leads to the cosmic Buddhic plane.

Buddha, after his ascension, chose the Path of Earth Service. Interestingly enough, he realized later he had made a mistake and Sanat Kumara allowed him to choose the Path to Sirius. Buddha has left the Earth system now and has moved on to his cosmic evolution. Lord Maitreya will soon do the same when his final mission here, during this millennium, is over. The Master Kuthumi will take over the position of the Planetary Christ.

The Path of Earth Service is the only path Sanat Kumara retains the right to, in a sense, draft new ascended masters onto. This, in truth, is a great honor and compliment, for he is saying your great skills and abilities are needed here. In such a case these masters postpone their movement to one of the other paths, although their decisions are recorded. At a later time, in his omniscience, Sanat Kumara will notify them when it is time to leave.

Lord Maitreya will return to Earth at a much later time as the Cosmic Christ, which will be a great event in Earth's evolutionary history. The masters on the Path of Earth Service are working in conscious receptivity to the cosmic astral plane even before graduating to that level because the cosmic astral plane is the true source of the energy of love.

All seven paths lead either to the cosmic astral plane or to the cosmic mental plane. The cosmic astral plane is the Heart of God and the center of pure love. The cosmic mental plane is the plane of the Divine Mind. The cosmic Buddhic plane is the cosmic level of pure reason. All paths eventually lead to the Great Central Sun.

Much training occurs on the inner plane once you have chosen your path. Vywamus told me that there are classes in telepathy, in how to channel (both as a giver and as a receiver), in the science of impression (conveying your will and intent to your manifested body), and in direct Light transmission. There are classes in cyclic evolution that focus on the developmental stages of Earth's history, just as a class on Earth might chart the developmental stages of a baby. The incarnations of the great masters are evidence of key transition points within this developmental model.

Another class involves the study of various planets and their processes of coming into being, looking specifically at Earth's movement from the ideal etheric blueprint into a manifested state. The Earth-school model is, of course, not the only model for planetary evolution in this universe. There are many, many models; in fact, Earth is unique in its usage of emotion for spiritual development.

The Path of Earth Service is one of great teaching, both as a master and as a student, for there is always another level to unfold and another initiation toward which you are moving. The process is not complete until you move through all three hundred fifty-two levels of the Mahatma, so there is a long way to go.

The amount of time spent on the Path of Earth Service varies. In Terri Sue's case it is four thousand years, but it varies with each individual and with what is going on in the divine plan of Sanat Kumara. Many classes are developed on a spontaneous basis as the need arises. For example, this period of Earth's history has brought up many unique issues that past phases of Earth's history have never had to deal with.

Two: The Path of Magnetic Work

The Path of Magnetic Work is the second of the seven paths to higher evolution. If you choose this path, you learn to work with fohat, the essential energy of the solar system, of the Solar Logos, Helios. Fohat energy is differentiated into seven major types. It is specifically with the astral energy of this planet and later of the solar system that you work if you choose this path. You learn to direct the fohat energy into the planetary astral plane to help clear the manmade glamour and delusion. The pure astral energy used on this path is free of delusion, for it is made up of pure unconditional love. On this path, you wield the force of this electrical magnetism under the direction of the Great Ones. Matter of every density and vibration is manipulated in service of the Divine Plan.

On this path, you also learn to work with the great waves of ideas and currents of public opinion on a planetary level. You learn to work with pure solar astral energy, pure galactic astral energy, and later, pure cosmic astral energy. If you choose this path, you must be trained to be an expert in timing and energy manipulation. The pure astral energy, or love energy, that is coming from the higher levels is also expressed as Light and Good Will. It is distributed to the Hierarchy as well as to humanity.

The Path of Magnetic Work takes the master first to the heart of the Sun and work with Helios and then to the cosmic mental plane, pausing only temporarily on the cosmic astral plane. It is through the use of magnetism that the planetary astral body is cleared, hence clearing humanity's consciousness. Djwhal Khul has stated that many initiates who have achieved liberation on the fifth ray, the ray of concrete knowledge, seem to follow this path of magnetic work.

Vywamus has told me that masters who choose this path deal with the concept of polarity balance on a planetary, solar, galactic, universal, and cosmic level and also on a subatomic level. Working with magnetism involves balancing the universal forces. Much work is also focused on the grid lines of the Earth. The Path of Magnetic Work is a cosmic science that applies to creation on many levels. At its highest level it deals with the creation of universes, white holes, black holes, and star polarities. For human purposes, magnetics is focused on a planetary and solar level and is concerned with the evolving consciousness in incarnation.

The first training, Vywamus said, would be an observation class in which you observe how magnetic work is implemented in the cosmic plan. At the second step, you are allowed to experience the magnetic effect on a limited basis. The third step involves the application of magnetics in service to the planet.

An example of the observation phase might be the monitoring of a pulsation coming to Earth from the Galactic Core. The pulsation will cause an electromagnetic change. The master on this path develops great expertise in understanding and working with the effects of these electromagnetic adjustments on personal, planetary, solar, and galactic levels. He also develops an understanding of the relationship between energy and thought and between magnetics and polarity. Magnetics is applied on all levels primarily to maintain unity.

Magnetism is occurring all the time on Earth. There is emotional magnetism that occurs between a man and a woman who are in a romantic relationship. There is magnetism between any two people who are having an intellectual conversation. There is magnetism between any two people who are physically touching each other, for energy is being transferred. You already have some understanding of magnetism and you utilize that understanding in your daily life. The master who chooses the Path of Magnetic Work builds on this understanding in order to deal with humanity as a whole, with the planetary body and solar system, and later with the galaxy and cosmos themselves.

The master choosing this path learns the science of changing mass consciousness and public opinion through the dissemination of electromagnetic pulses and electromagnetic waves of energy. For example, one of the waves or pulses might be connected to the thought form of peace. Rays, colors, and sounds can be used in this way as well. It is on the astral plane, however, that most of this work is being done.

Ascended masters do not operate out of the astral plane because for Earth, it is the plane of delusion. By clearing and purifying the astral plane, they allow humankind to see reality more clearly, for then it is not living in a dark cloud of planetary delusion. It is hard to free yourself from this delusion on a personal level when the entire planet is one massive emotional fog. In this context the importance of such work can be seen. I have often asked the ascended masters to magnetically pull all the etheric mucus out of my field if I am feeling unclear. Masters such as Lenduce or Vywamus can pull clouded energy right out of your field like an instantaneous vacuum cleaner.

The astral-plane delusion around the planet could be likened to emotional smog. The masters on this path, using pure astral energy and the science of magnetics, clear the smog away and then influence consciousness on a planetary level toward the spiritual ideal. Vywamus told me that magnetics is used on all seven of the paths to higher evolution. In truth, it is the foundation for all other paths. Djwhal confirmed this, also, when he said it was one of the first paths to be tread upon after the evolutionary process was set in motion by Sanat Kumara.

Ten percent of humanity chooses this path as opposed to the other seven paths to higher evolution. Vywamus said that the science of magnetics could be described as the "understanding of the way to keep creation together in manifestation." It is to this larger ideal that the masters who have chosen this ideal work on all levels of God's creation.

Three: The Path of Training to Become a Planetary Logos

The Path of Training to become a Planetary Logos is the third of the seven paths to higher evolution. It is the path that Sanat Kumara, Earth's Planetary Logos, has chosen. The masters choosing this path at their sixth initiation are being trained to take up the work of the seven planetary logoi and the forty-nine subplanetary logoi and their assistants for the next system. Each of the seven chohans, or lords, of the seven rays takes on a certain number of students and trains them specifically for this work. The masters choosing this path have a special aptitude for dealing with the psyche and are, hence, considered the divine or cosmic psychologists.

They also have a special aptitude for dealing with color and sound. Every planetary logos has his or her own planet and school for the training of subordinate logoi. There are many schools for the training of planetary logoi. Sanat Kumara attended a school on Venus (see *The Complete Ascension Manual,* chapter 15). Masters choosing this path will study under Sanat Kumara. The initial training is done through a form of higher telepathy from members of the Council Chamber at Shamballa and specifically from two of the Buddhas of Activity who are the core helpers of Sanat Kumara in his work as planetary logos. The next stage will be to travel to Venus as Sanat Kumara did and continue your training there. This will ultimately lead to the cosmic mental plane.

Only 15% of humanity choose this path of the seven paths to higher evolution. The training is long and arduous. The full training to become a planetary logos, which means to embody a planet of your own for which you become totally responsible, can take as long as fifty million years. It must be remembered, however, that time is not experienced in the same way once you leave your physical body. There is really no such thing as time on the inner planes. There are cycles of activity and inactivity. Cycles of inactivity take the form of periods of contemplation and mental activity. Cycles of activity take the form of periods of active energy direction which serve to impress the will of a given planetary logos upon the Council Chamber of the planet with which he is working and possibly upon other planets in the solar system as well.

Vywamus told me that the goal of the planetary logos is to communicate the theme of the cosmic day with which it is involved to all species under its auspices in the shortest time possible. He also told me that three of the main spiritual qualities required for this job are oneness, patience, and love. Sanat Kumara has been incarnated in the Earth, using it as his body of manifestation, for eighteen and one-half million years.

I asked Vywamus about some of the classes available during training. He spoke of a class about time and cosmic planning which deals with how to mesh your specific planetary plan with the plans of other planetary logoi.

He also mentioned a class dealing with multispecies evolutionary development. In the case of this planet, for example, Sanat Kumara is in charge of the development of the mineral, plant, and animal kingdoms as well as of humans, but not all planets have a variety of species. Vywamus talked about another class that is concerned with the eighth dimension and provides training in how to handle incompletion on a planetary level in cases in which a particular theme being impressed on the evolutionary scheme is not working.

One other class that Vywamus mentioned is a class on the subject of communication and oneness. A lot of time is spent on this subject, studying, among other things, how to accommodate change on a large scale. It must be understood that masters on this path are not focused on individual states of consciousness but on the consciousness of the whole and its responsiveness to cosmic issues with which it is involved.

The main focus of the training on the third path is on building the planetary, solar, and cosmic antakarana, or bridge of Light, to God. These masters are building the antakarana of collective humanity, as differentiated from that of a specific individual. The work is done in relationship to the planetary monad, so to speak, and also to other planets. In the case of Earth, one such planet is Venus which is like an elder brother or sister to Earth. From there the planetary antakarana extends to the heart of the Sun, to Helios, the Solar Logos. Helios would then be in charge of building the antakarana to the Galactic Core and Melchior.

In the process of training, masters choosing this path work very closely with the Buddhas of Activity, or Kumaras, who form the core group that helps Sanat Kumara in his work. Eventually the masters in training will become Buddhas of activity themselves, on this planet or, more likely, on some other planet. This will lead to the ultimate goal of eventually embodying an entire planet and becoming a planetary logos.

As a planetary logos, the master's job is to learn to register and express the will of the solar logos who is in charge of the solar system into which he has incarnated, so to speak. Instead of inhabiting a small physical body, as a planetary logos you must embody a whole planet. Instead of working to improve your personal physical, mental, and emotional bodies, you are in charge of expanding the physical, mental, and emotional bodies of all species and of the very planet into which you have incarnated. Quite a job! You can see why a lot of training is needed. The impression of your will upon the planet is achieved through the planetary antakarana. It must be done in a way that respects the free choice of the beings incarnating onto the planet, or karma is created.

As you evolve through God's infinite universe, you keep extending the responsibilities you are given. When the job of being a planetary logos is finished, you might choose to graduate and move on to embodying an entire solar system, as Helios has done. After that, maybe a whole galaxy and then an entire universe, as Melchizedek has done. You must expand gradually, step by step, your mastery and worthiness to take on the next step of responsibility. Most people get overwhelmed just dealing with their own bodies, emotions, and minds. Imagine being responsible for a whole planet, solar system, galaxy, or universe. This is your destiny, regardless of which path you choose. Each initiation you go through, of the three hundred fifty-two leading back to the Godhead, signifies another level of expansion and added responsibility.

In a recent meditation I was talking with Sai Baba, and I requested his help in moving to the next higher octave and initiation and anchoring my fiftieth chakra in my crown chakra. The first thing he asked me was whether I was ready and willing to take on the level of added responsibility that would ensue upon the realization of the prayer request. This is something you should consider as you invoke an acceleration in your own initiatory and ascension process. The higher you go, the more will be expected on all levels, and the more quickly your karma will return to get you off track.

If you choose this path, you will eventually become a directing builder and creator of all forms of planetary life. You will have achieved the perfect synthesis of spiritual will and spiritual love. As the training continues and you move to becoming a Buddha of activity, you add active intelligence of the third ingredient which creates a perfect balance of active love and active will. Before incarnating into your own planet, you will serve as a Buddha of activity on another planet, helping another planetary logos. The supreme goal of a planetary logos is to impress his sevenfold body of manifestation, via its seven states of consciousness and seven chakras, with his will and intention. The training on this path therefore requires an intensive study of the science of impression. As a master in training, you gain experience helping another planetary logos in his work with the sacred planets in the solar system with which he is involved. It must be remembered that everything in God's infinite universe is interconnected and, in truth, one. No planet or planetary logos is an island unto itself.

The work of building the planetary antakarana deals with creating a link to the monad and monadic plane from the three worlds of dense physical expression (physical, astral, and mental). In this process, the antakarana is also built to the planetary spiritual triad (spiritual will, intuition, and higher mind). The final step in this process on a planetary level is building the antakarana from dense physical expression to Shamballa, or the will center of the given planetary logos. Eventually, the antakarana will extend to the seven sacred planets, to Helios, and, in more advanced planetary systems such as Arcturus, to cosmic levels of consciousness and ultimately all the way back to the Godhead.

If you choose this path, it confines you to a particular solar system for an extended period of time. For this reason Sanat Kumara has been esoterically called "The Great Sacrifice." This particular path is not for every-body; however, it holds incredible opportunity for those who resonate with it.

Four: The Path to Sirius

The Path to Sirius is the fourth of the seven paths to higher evolution. It is the path the majority of humanity will follow after ascension. Sirius is considered to be the higher university. Even before ascending, people often travel there during sleeptime to attend classes and receive further training.

It would seem that many of the other paths to higher evolution are more advanced, and the Path to Sirius serves as kind of an intermediate step. For example, I mentioned to Djwhal Khul that I was interested in the number seven path, the Path of Absolute Sonship. He recommended that I take the Path to Sirius first and then later transfer to this more advanced path after I had received the proper initial training.

Sirius is the galactic doorway to this galaxy. It is closely aligned with the Pleiades. The actual star Sirius is a Great Sun. When I speak of Sirius here, I am referring to the inner plane Sirius, in the same sense that Shamballa is the inner plane "capital" of our planet. Djwhal has said that the Great Sun Sirius is to Earth's Solar Logos Helios what the monad is to the spiritual person on Earth. So Sirius is one of the teachers for Helios, who is the president, so to speak, of this solar system.

There is also a close relationship between the Lord of Sirius and Sanat Kumara, Earth's Planetary Logos. Sirius is also connected with the Galactic Core and, hence, with the galactic masters. The relationship between Sanat Kumara and the Lord of Sirius has intensified since Earth has achieved her sacred status in recent times.

There is a close relationship too between Sirius and the Spiritual Hierarchy headed by Lord Maitreya who is now physically incarnated on Planet Earth. The energy evoked is like a triangle with Sirius at the top and the Hierarchy and the Heart of the Sun at the two lower points of the triangle. The energy from Sirius is the principle of cosmic love. Interest-ingly enough, this energy bypasses Shamballa (the home of Sanat Kumara and the will aspect of God) and focuses directly on the Spiritual Hierarchy. Its effect is not felt until after you take your initiation.

The astrological configuration that occurred on April 23, 1994, which happens only once every ninety thousand years, allowed more of this Sirian energy to be anchored. It allowed the Spiritual Hierarchy to anchor a Light package into the brain and heart centers of humanity and served to Light up the grid points of the entire planet. This was an enormous boon; it accelerated your spiritual growth if you were open to it. The ascended masters use this Sirian energy for training disciples for the second, fourth, and sixth initiations.

The entire work of the Great White Lodge is controlled from Sirius. Since the Harmonic Convergence and Earth's move into the beginning of the fourth dimension, humanity has been more closely connected to the Galactic Core and hence to Sirius. The fifth initiation is considered to be the first cosmic initiation of the seven levels of initiation that can be taken on this plane. It is also considered to be the first cosmic initiation from the perspective of Sirius. The second cosmic initiation is the sixth initiation, ascension. The third cosmic initiation is the seventh initiation which is merger with Sanat Kumara and the seventh plane and merger with Shamballa, the will aspect of God. These higher initiations are taken under the influence of the Sirian energy. Metaphorically, it's as though Earth were the master's degree program and Sirius the Ph.D. program for spiritual growth. It also must be understood that Sirius serves this function for a great number of planets in this galaxy, not just for Earth.

The Sirian influence was not recognized or focused upon on this planet until the Lord Maitreya, the Planetary Christ, overshadowed the Master Jesus. Together, they revealed the love of God to humanity. Lord Maitreya was the perfect example and expression of the Sirius initiation.

Djwhal Khul had chosen the Path to Sirius; however, Sanat Kumara asked him to remain with the Earth for a period of time as a personal favor to him, to help in Earth's transition to the New Age. Djwhal Khul graciously agreed and has forgone his cosmic evolution in order to be of service to his brothers and sisters on the Earth. My understanding is that Buddha had originally chosen path number one, the Path of Earth Service. He later changed his mind and chose the Path to Sirius, also. Sanat Kumara did not choose the Path to Sirius but, rather, the Path of Training to become a Planetary Logos. Sirius has often been referred to as the Sirian Lodge or the Blue Lodge. Sirius has enormous influence, not only on this planet but also on this solar system.

Upon leaving Earth and traveling to Sirius after the completion of your mission here, you will automatically become a representative of Earth's evolving conclave. There will be representatives from other planets there, too. One of the things that you will probably do is to teach at the higher university on Sirius. Many of the students in attendance will be from Earth and will arrive in their soul bodies during their sleeptime. Some may come from other planets. Others may be fellow masters from other planets who wish to know more about the Earth's form of evolution.

Besides teaching, you will be attending classes and many meetings. Some of the meetings will be formal and some informal. There will be many opportunities for expanded service work, depending on your unique abilities and aptitudes. Since I have chosen the Path to Sirius, I asked Vywamus how long I would be spending there, in terms of Earth time, and

he said one thousand years. When I asked, "What then?" he said there
were infinite possibilities. I could begin training on another one of the
seven paths to higher evolution; I could become an assistant to a solar
logos; or I could serve on one of the galactic councils, just to name a few
possibilities. Just because you go to Sirius, it does not mean that the
process of initiations stops. There are, in truth, three hundred fifty-two
levels of initiation to pass through before returning to the cocreator level
of complete union with the Godhead.

Sirius receives much guidance from the Universal Core and the
Universal Logos, Melchizedek. Vywamus also told me that Sirius receives
guidance from a star system called Tulobra. Tulobra is a universe that has
achieved complete unification and is from a Source entirely separate from
the Source of this universe.

Vywamus told me that of the seven paths to higher evolution, the Path
to Sirius is chosen by 62% of humanity. I asked Vywamus what I will be
teaching once I reach Sirius. He said it is different for each person,
depending on his unique abilities, consciousness, and skills, but that I
would be teaching a class on the psychology of consciousness development,
with perhaps a specific emphasis on the development of consciousness
through emotions. It must be remembered that many other planetary
systems in this galaxy do not access emotions in the same way as humans
on Earth. The beings from Zeta Reticulum, for example, are not emotional
at all and have more of a mental and group consciousness. Vywamus said
he also saw me teaching teleportation classes in the future. This surprised
me a little since I have not even learned to do it yet.

I then asked Vywamus about the classes I would be attending on
Sirius. He told me that I would be very interested in what he referred to as
universal bridging. This has to do with what I have called the merger of
Source A and Source B — the ascension, in a sense, of the Source of this
universe to a still higher Source. I am actually very interested in this
consciously, so it came as no surprise to me when Vywamus said it.

He also said that I would be interested in something called the null
zone, which is apparently some kind of space-time continuum on the inner
and/or outer planes where all that exists is primordial energy that has not
been activated yet. No seed has been planted into it by the Source, or the
Godforce. Vywamus told me I am currently studying this on Sirius. The
activation of one of these null zones with the cocreator gods could possibly
be one of my later assignments during my stay on Sirius.

Once you ascend, if you have choosen the Path to Sirius, your home
base will be Sirius for a period of time. As Earth is involved with initiations
one through seven, Sirius is involved with initiations seven through twelve.

Shamballa, the home of Sanat Kumara, is a mini-chamber of the expanded chamber that is Sirius. Shamballa is like an outpost of the White Lodge on Sirius. The governing body on Sirius is a Council of Twelve. The focus of their work is not just this galaxy, but the entire universe. Sirius and the Galactic Core are not the same. The Galactic Core feeds Sirius, which is a learning center; Sirius is a part of the Galactic Core. Since Earth went through the Harmonic Convergence and moved into the fourth dimension, it has a direct connection to the Galactic Core and more of a direct connection with Sirius, both through its own contact and through the Spiritual Hierarchy. This connection with Sirius was expanded during the astrological configuration that occurred right before Wesak, on April 23, 1994.

Five: The Ray Path

The Ray Path is the fifth of the seven paths to higher evolution. If you choose this path, you stay on your own ray, the ray your soul or monad is on. (See *The Complete Ascension Manual,* chapter 10.) Choosing this path means you work under the Lord of the World, Sanat Kumara, and the chohan governing your particular ray. If you choose this path, you travel to every part of the solar system in your service work.

It is a very complex path that requires an understanding of intricate mathematics and the ability to use geometry in a manner incomprehensible to the linear human brain. This path is chosen if you find the law of vibration of profound importance. In later stages of this path, you will serve on another planet corresponding to your own soul or monadic ray. This is true unless you are a third-ray soul or monad which means that you will remain in service to the Earth.

In even later stages, you will continue your service work with the Sun and work with Helios. Having thus mastered the Law of Vibration in the solar system, you will then pass on to the galactic levels of consciousness and service. It is at that stage that you pass from your own ray and move on to a corresponding cosmic ray. The subrays the initiates have been on are only subsidiary rays of one of the cosmic rays. For example, this solar system is a second-ray solar system, but other solar systems within this galaxy are likely to be on one of the other of the seven rays.

Each of the seven ray lords, or chohans, has certain qualities to express and certain aspects of life to unfold and manifest. It is with these ray intentions and unfoldments that you are involved if you choose this ray. Many first-ray souls and monads choose this path. Every initiate is on one of the first three rays: rays four through seven are subsidiary rays of the third ray. If you choose the Ray Path you must develop an understanding of the world of cosmic purpose.

The first ray deals with the will aspect of God. This ray path leads you to understand the use of will on a cosmic level. It deals with the will to power, the will to love, the will to knowledge, the will to harmonize, the will to act, the will to Cause and the will to express. These seven aspects of will form the basis of training for this path. If you choose one of the other seven paths to higher evolution, you ultimately reach the same goal; however, this is the line of least resistance for first-ray initiates. For this reason it is initiates of the first and second ray who choose this ray path most often.

Djwhal Khul, in the Alice Bailey book, *The Rays and the Initiations*, has said that the first-ray initiates who choose the Ray Path must learn to negate their "isolated unity" and must study the beauty and value of differentiation. The first-ray initiate tends to be more independent in his wholeness. The movement toward differentiation leads to a mysterious esoteric training in the development of multiple identification. This, I believe, has to do with the development of your multidimensional nature and the ability to focus and comprehend many, many places simultaneously.

If you are a second-ray initiate who chooses the Ray Path, you must learn to negate your "attractive and magnetic tendencies" and learn the meaning of "isolated intention with a multiplicity of goals." The attractive and magnetic quality is the key attribute of the second-ray initiate. You must learn to develop the abilities of all the rays as you move into your cosmic evolution. If you are a second-ray initiate, the exclusiveness has to become an inclusiveness in a much larger and greater world of God-realization. (In such exclusiveness, there is no aspect of separation, as the word commonly implies amongst humanity.)

The training given on this path will lead you to a sacred planet or to some other solar system that will correspond with Shamballa on this planet, where the Will of God is anchored. The goal you eventually reach is a sphere of activity where "sublime purposes and divine intentions" are worked on under the guidance of cosmic intelligence.

Six: The Path on Which the Solar Logos Himself Is Found

The Path on which the Solar Logos himself is found deals with the training process to become a solar logos. This path is different from the third path, which trains you to become a planetary logos. Whereas the previous five paths included a period of intermediate work on the Earth or on Sirius, the sixth path leads directly to cosmic planes of consciousness.

The Solar Logos for this solar system is Helios. Sanat Kumara, the Planetary Logos of Earth, might be considered a disciple of Helios, just as you, as an initiate, are a disciple of Sanat Kumara. In this regard, Sanat Kumara has begun to take on certain cosmic responsibilities, just as humans have begun to take on certain planetary responsibilities.

Certain masters of a very high initiation from the previous solar system form an esoteric group around Helios and help him in his work.

The real home of these great beings is on the cosmic Buddhic plane. Again, there are seven cosmic planes, but Earthlings deal only with the first one, the cosmic physical plane. Humans are evolving through only the seven sublevels of this first cosmic plane. The next six, moving in order up toward the Godhead, are the cosmic astral, cosmic mental, cosmic Buddhic, cosmic atmic, cosmic monadic, and cosmic logoic.

One of the main jobs, or focuses, of Helios is the development of cosmic vision, or the development of the cosmic third eye. The small group of high-level initiates who work with Helios form, esoterically, the "pupil of his cosmic third eye."

There are only a few initiates who chose this path and who are qualified to take this path. Gradually, over eons of time, certain masters have qualified and have taken the place of the original members of the group, allowing those great beings to move on to even higher levels of cosmic evolution. The great beings move on to a cosmic center around which Earth's system and even the great system of Sirius revolve. Only an occasional initiate has the necessary qualifications, for it involves a certain type of response to cosmic vibration. It requires a specialization in inner sight and the development of a certain degree of cosmic vision.

Interestingly enough, more devas and angels pass on to the Path of the Solar Logos than do humans. Human beings in the past have passed on to it via the devic evolution which can be entered by transference to the Ray Path. Djwhal Khul, in the Alice Bailey book *The Rays and the Initiations*, said that it is on the Ray Path that the two evolutions can merge, and from the Ray Path the sixth path can be entered. In more recent times, however, special dispensations have been received which allow an initiate to pass directly on to the Path of the Solar Logos without entering the devic or angelic evolution.

If you are an initiate choosing this path, you are in training to become a solar logos eventually. Sanat Kumara is one example of this, but it is not necessarily true of all planetary logoi. Some planetary logoi of other planets do not automatically desire to become solar logoi. Vywamus told me a very interesting thing: Sanat Kumara has been considering the possibility of leaving the position of Planetary Logos of Earth and letting another planetary logos take his place. He has been with the Earth now for over 18.5 million years; although from the perspective of humanity, this is an incredibly long period of time, from a cosmic perspective he is a very young planetary logos.

This sixth path is one on which, as an initiate, you work a great deal with angels. Eventually you are allowed to enter the Council Chambers of the Sacred Planets before progressing into the group that works directly with the Solar Logos. To reach this level of work can take incredibly vast amounts of time, from humanity's perspective. When a master finally achieves this level, he is given the cosmic responsibility of becoming the custodian and distributing agent for certain energetic principles. For example, Venus was originally the custodian of the principle of Mind, which was brought to Earth from Venus by Helios, Sanat Kumara, and his fellow Kumara brothers as a pure gift to embryonic humanity.

In a similar way, if you are an initiate treading this path, you will eventually distribute other such energetic principles throughout the solar system and cosmos under the guidance of the Solar Logos, until your training is complete and you are ready to take on the cosmic responsibilities of embodying an embryonic solar system.

Seven: The Path of Absolute Sonship

The Path of Absolute Sonship is the seventh of the seven paths to higher evolution. It is the path leading to the sonship of a cosmic being higher even than Earth's Solar Logos, Helios. This path forms a triangle between the Planetary Logos, Sanat Kumara, the Solar Logos, Helios, and a cosmic being who has been referred to as "the one about whom naught may be said." This path also relates our Solar System to the constellation of the Great Bear.

Djwhal Khul, in the Alice Bailey book *The Rays and the Initiations*, has said that there is another triangular formation composed of "one stream of energy emanating from the Great Bear, another stream of energy issuing from the Heart of the Sun or from our Solar Logos, and the base line constituted of the seven streams of energy which come from our Seven Sacred Planets." This triangle produces the relationship between Earth and her solar system, galaxy, and universe. Its purpose is to help this solar system bring the nonsacred planets to the point of spiritual liberation. Sacred status for a planet might be considered to be when it takes its third initiation. It is through this triangular formation that all the great avatars enter this system. Sai Baba is one example.

In a personal conversation I had with Djwhal Khul, I told him that of all the seven paths to higher evolution, I was most attracted to this seventh path. His guidance for me was that I should first take the Path to Sirius in order to get the proper preliminary training. Then later, it would be possible to transfer over to this path if it is still my desire to do so at that time. I pass this information on to you, for I believe it applies to many of the advanced paths to higher evolution.

Summation of the Seven Paths to Higher Evolution

The material I have presented in this chapter is a little esoteric in nature and needs to be grasped with your right brain as much as with your left brain. The seven paths to higher evolution deal with cosmic levels of reality that are nonlinear and, in truth, extremely difficult to explain, no matter what your level of spiritual development.

I have attempted to give you some basic information so that you have enough understanding to begin to think about your choice. The most important thing to remember is what Djwhal Khul has said in *The Rays and the Initiations*: "I should, however, remind you that every effort to live rightly, beautifully, and usefully, to control the mind and to achieve loving understanding, lays the foundation for the right decision at the sixth initiation." Your monad already knows the right path for you. It is just a matter of tuning into your inner guidance.

The rapid development of humanity, even since the early parts of this century when the Alice Bailey books were written, has changed the Hierarchy's views of the seven paths of evolution for humanity. Humankind is no longer entering cosmic evolution blindly; the decision is being made much more consciously, with open eyes and based upon true revelation. The mental and intuitive development of humanity is so much greater than it was in the past. Love and intelligence distinguished the masters until three hundred years ago; love, intelligence, and will now distinguish humanity. It is only in this century that the information on the seven paths to higher evolution has even been revealed to human consciousness in written form.

One other important factor in understanding the paths to higher evolution is to understand that the seven paths become four paths, owing to the fact that the solar system in which Earth resides is of the fourth order. Djwhal Khul, in *The Rays and the Initiations*, says the seven paths to higher evolution merge in the following manner: the initiates upon path one "fight their way" onto path six; the initiates upon path two "alchemise themselves" onto path seven; the initiates upon path four have a free range of options.

Those initiates who have not achieved full mental development but are more emotionally based must pass to the sun Sirius, there to undergo tremendous mental stimulation, for Sirius is the emanating source of Mind. In hierarchical terms that position is referred to as being a lord of compassion rather than a master of wisdom. One is not better than the other, for the ideal is always balance. The masses of humanity are still astrally based, however, and are still Atlantean in nature. Again, over 60% of humanity has chosen the Path to Sirius, the training ground and prep school for some of the other, more advanced paths.

The following chart might be helpful in consolidating some of the esoteric information presented in this chapter. It is my heartfelt hope and prayer that this chapter has shed some "Light" for you on this most mind-expanding subject.

The Seven Paths to Higher Evolution

This chart is from the Alice Bailey book *The Rays and the Initiations*, pages 426–427. I am very grateful to Alice Bailey for her groundbreaking work in this area.

One: The Path of Earth Service

Attributes . . . . Wise compassion

Source . . . . Constellation of the Dragon, via Libra

Method . . . . Twelve cosmic identifications

Hierarchy . . . . The sixth

Symbol . . . . A green dragon issuing from the center of a blazing sun; behind the sun and overtopping it can be seen two pillars on either side of a closed door

Quality gained . . . . Luminosity

Two: The Path of Magnetic Work

Attributes . . . . Responsiveness to heat and knowledge of rhythm

Source . . . . An unknown constellation, via Gemini

Method . . . . The entering of the burning-ground

Hierarchy . . . . The third and fourth

Symbol . . . . A funeral pyre, four torches, and a fivefold star mounting toward the sun

Quality gained . . . . Electrical velocity

Three: The Path of Training to become a Planetary Logos

Attributes . . . . Cosmic vision, devic hearing, and psychic correlation

Source . . . . Betelgeuse, via Sagittarius

Method . . . . Prismatic identification

Hierarchy . . . . The fifth

Symbol . . . . A colored cross with a star at the center and backed by a blazing sun surmounted by a Sensa Word

Quality gained . . . . Cosmic etheric vision or septenary clairvoyance

Path Four: The Path to Sirius

Attributes . . . . Cosmic rapture and rhythmic bliss

Source . . . . Sirius via the sun, which veils a zodiacal sign

Method . . . . Duplex rotary motion and rhythmic dancing upon the square

Hierarchy . . . . Veiled by the numbers 14 and 17

Symbol .... Two wheels of electric fire, revolving around
an orange cross, with an emerald at
the center

Quality gained .... Unrevealed

Path Five: The Ray Path

Attributes .... A sense of cosmic direction

Source.......... The Pole Star via Aquarius

Method .... A process of electrical insulation and
the imprisonment of polar magnetism

Hierarchy .... The first and the second

Symbol .... Five balls of fire enclosed within a sphere;
sphere is formed of a serpent inscribed with
the mantra of insulation

Quality gained .... Cosmic stability and magnetic equilibrium

Path Six: The Path on Which the Solar Logos Himself Is Found

Not given......... Not given

Path Seven: The Path of Absolute Sonship

Not given......... Not given

I would like to take this opportunity to acknowledge Alice Bailey and her extensive work. Hers is the first material about the seven paths to higher evolution ever made available to humanity in written form. The foregoing chart is from *The Rays and the Initiations*, which I used, along with *Initiation, Human and Solar*, in the preparation of this chapter. The material from the books provided a basic understanding that was then supplemented by channelings from Djwhal Khul and Vywamus. For more information on the seven paths to higher evolution, I highly recommend these two books.

13

Ascension Meditations, Techniques, and Insights

*Gaia (Earth Mother) officially took her
ascension initiation on December 12, 1994.*
Djwhal Khul

Kabbalistic Tree of Life Meditation

The following ascension technique is one of the most profound I have ever experienced. It is meant to be done in four separate meditations – first on a planetary level, then on a solar level, then on a galactic level, and then on a universal and cosmic level. The planetary meditation should be done in the ascension seat in Shamballa under the guidance of Sanat Kumara. The solar meditation should be done in the Golden Chamber of Helios in the Solar Core. The galactic meditation should be done in the ascension seat in the Galactic Core of Melchior. The universal and cosmic level of this meditation should be done in the Golden Chamber of Melchizedek under the guidance of Melchizedek.

To begin this meditation, ask to be taken to the ascension seat and the ascension temple on the level you are choosing to work with. Greet the guide of that level and then request that the Tree of Life of that level – planetary, solar, galactic, or universal and cosmic – be fully anchored and activated into your four-body system.

Request that the first of the ten Sephiroth, the one in the crown called Kether, be fully opened and activated. Wait one minute for this to take place.

Request that the Sephiroth of Chokmah, or wisdom, be fully opened and activated. Wait one minute.

Request that the Sephiroth of Binah, or understanding, be fully opened and activated. Wait one minute.

Request that the Sephiroth of Chesed be fully opened and activated. Wait one minute.

Request that the Sephiroth of Geburah, or serenity, be fully opened and activated. Wait one minute.

Request that the Sephiroth of Tiphareth be fully opened and activated. Wait one minute.

Request that the Sephiroth of Netzach be fully opened and activated. Wait one minute.

Request that the Sephiroth of Hod be fully opened and activated. Wait one minute.

Request that the Sephiroth of Yesod be fully opened and activated. Wait one minute.

Request that the hidden Sephiroth of Daath, or knowledge, be fully opened and activated. Wait one minute.

Request then that the openings and activations be made permanent and stable.

Then ask for the anchoring and activation of your Zohar body of Light at the planetary, solar, galactic, or universal level. Sit, then, in silence and enjoy the sensations.

Then call forth a downpouring of the Ain Soph Or (Boundless Universal Light).

A variation would be to call on the archangels associated with each of the ten Sephiroth to help in the activation:

Kether.	Metatron
Chokmah	Ratziel
Binah	Tzaphkiel
Chesed	Zadkiel
Geburah	Chamuel
Tiphareth	Michael
Netzach	Uriel
Hod	Raphael
Yesod	Gabriel
Malkuth	Sandalphon

Ask Melchizedek to open the hidden Sephiroth of Daath, or knowledge.

End the meditation by saying, "Kodoish, Kodoish, Kodoish, Adonai Tsabayoth" ("Holy, holy, holy is the Lord God of Hosts").

One more addition to this meditation would be to chant the names of God associated with each Sephiroth. I would recommend saying them three times for each Sephiroth:

Kether.	Ehyeh
Chokmah	Jehovah
Binah	Jehovah Elohim

Chesed . . . . . El
Geburah . . . . . Elohim Gabor
Tiphareth . . . . YHWH
Netzach . . . . . Jehovah Tsabayoth
Hod . . . . Elohim Tsabayoth
Yesod . . . . . . Shaddel El Chai
Malkuth . . . . . Adonai Malekh

The final addition to this profound meditation would be to invoke the cosmic Tree of Life. Do this by calling forth the Beloved Presence of God, the Council of Twelve at the three hundred fifty-second level of creation.

Call forth the twenty-four elders that surround the Throne of Grace.

Call forth the twelve mighty elohim and the twelve archangels that surround the Throne of Grace.

Call forth the Mahatma, the Avatar of Synthesis.

Then request that the cosmic Tree of Life be anchored for yourself, your group, all of humanity, and the Earth, herself. Request that each of the ten cosmic Sephiroth on the cosmic Tree of Life be opened and activated on a permanent basis. Request the healing of all separation between Heaven and Earth. Request the opening of the cosmic hidden Sephiroth of Daath.

This Tree of Life meditation in combination with the ultimate ascension meditation (see chapter 9) is guaranteed to activate you spiritually in the most awe-inspiring ways you can possibly imagine. I have recorded these two meditations on audio tapes which can be ordered from Light Technology Publishing.

Ascension Seats on the Ashtar Command Ships

In the meditations Caryn and I do together, we often travel to the ascension seats on the Ashtar Command starships. Caryn has a very strong connection to the Ashtar Command so I asked her to share her experience of working with their ascension seats:

I recently attended a meeting on the inner planes with the Ashtar Command and the Hierarchy of Planet Earth. We discussed a more expansive ascension program. There are ascension seats on many of the Ashtar Command ships and many people go to these seats unaware during sleep. The commanders and crews of these Ashtar Command ships warmly welcome you aboard.

The ascension seats on the various ships look very similar. The ascension processing is conducted in a circular room with the ascension seats in a circle in the center of the room. Coming down from the heavens and encompassing all of the seats is the ascension column of divine Light from the Source. There are instrument panels in the background. The ships are usually orbiting around the Earth. Some of the ships have a clear dome above and below the seats, so while you are integrating the divine Light you can observe the beautiful Earth, Gaia, below, and the heavens above.

While the ascension seat is activated you might experience a warmth or a flash or heat. You might feel a tingling sensation throughout your body as the old karma, or dross, is leaving your body's cells. Send love and forgiveness as you release this old karma; claim that it is no longer a part of your life. Claim personal grace in your life so that the process will accelerate. Transmute the karma with a violet flame or the violet ray.

There are various ships you can go to (and I might add that it is your etheric body that actually goes). You might enjoy visiting the ship of Ascended Master Ashtar, the commander of the Ashtar Command. Another terrific ascension facility is located on Commander Esola's ship. He is a tall blond Pleiadian ascended master. You might also enjoy Ascended Master Korton's ship.

Lord Pleiades has his own gigantic mothership with ascension seats aboard. The ascension facility is located in a lovely garden area where there are beautiful plants and where it is very peaceful. The ascension seats are in a circular formation. The ascension column of divine Light comes down from the heavens and through the ship, encompassing all the seats. There are clear domes above and below so that you can enjoy the beauty of the heavens, the Earth, and the garden while you are integrating Light. It is quite a wonderful experience!

Before you go to sleep at night, or during meditation, ask to be taken aboard one of Ashtar Command ships. Ask for Light integration and ascension processing. Place yourself in an orange-gold bubble of Light to seal your nerve endings and auric field. Call upon the twelve archangels to guide, guard, and protect you, in love and life and Light. Call upon your Mighty I Am Presence by saying, "I Am That I Am." Place yourself in a living Light merkabah vehicle. The basic merkabah vehicle looks like this: ◆

Call upon your favorite ascended master to assist your process, along with the ship's commander and crew. Call upon Archangel Michael to watch over and protect you. Once aboard the ship you will find great safety and protection.

It is your etheric body that actually goes to the various ascension seats; there is actually a transference of Light from the etheric body to the physical body. Conversely, when you sit in an established ascension column of Light here on Earth, the Light goes directly into your physical body. This process is called the spiritualization of the dense, physical-body matter. There is an activation of the Lightbody and an integration of your personal divinity from the Source.

The Twelve Bodies

Melchizedek has said that you actually have twelve bodies, which extend all the way up through the universal level. In meditation, you can call forth all twelve bodies, extending to and from the universal level, to anchor and activate in your four-body system on Earth.

Vywamus' Electrical Work

Vywamus is an expert at electrical rewiring and recircuiting. Call on him for help in rewiring your spiritual bodies so they can hold a higher Light quotient and so you can handle the higher levels of initiations and the fifty chakras.

Vywamus' Future Initiation

Djwhal Khul has said that a time to remember is November 1997; at that time, Vywamus, who is the oversoul for Planet Earth, will be taking a major initiation. That will end the magnetic frequency that will have been in place for three years and that is connected to the photon belt which is now affecting Earth and humanity. Mark that date on your calendar, for when Vywamus takes an initiation, the entire planet and all of humanity will be affected by being upraised.

Zeal Point Chakra

Call forth the complete opening and activation of the zeal point chakra in the back of the head. This helps to create the Lightbody. It is magenta in color.

Djwhal Khul's System of Pattern Removal

Djwhal Khul has a special technique that he teaches his students for the removal of patterns. He recommends that you imagine a blue triangle above your head. As faulty, negative patterns arise, put them in the blue triangle and let them be burned up by the spiritual energies. In a session he will identify a particular topic he is focusing upon and list the patterns he says are operating concerning that particular subject. After reading them off, you put them in the blue triangle and get rid of them. Try this technique. It can be quite helpful.

The Sacred Garden Ascension Seat of Buddha and Quan Yin

Caryn and I, during our meditations, often go to the sacred garden ascension seat of Buddha and Quan Yin for ascension activation. This is a new ascension seat that we have recently discovered, and it is a most enjoyable one!

El Morya's Sacred Glen Ascension Seat

Another new ascension seat in which Caryn and I have also found great pleasure and enjoyment is in the sacred glen of El Morya, who is a wonderful ascended master. He invites you there for spiritual rejuvenation and ascension activation.

Merging Ascension Seats

An ascension technique you might try is the blending and merging of ascension seats. For example, if you are in El Morya's Sacred Glen ascension seat you can request that it be blended with the ascension seat in the Great White Lodge on Sirius or with Melchizedek's Golden Chamber on the universal level. This can be done with any of the ascension seats. An overlapping occurs of planetary, solar, galactic, and universal ascension seats. I, personally, am very drawn to the Golden Chamber of Melchizedek, so I like to blend his ascension seat with those of the other guides with whom I work.

Channeled Dancing

One other very important ascension technique is what I call channeled dancing. After you have invoked all the energies, then allow your body to move in a free-flowing fashion. Let the higher-frequency energies move your body. This will facilitate the anchoring of the energies into the physical vehicle. It will also allow you to meditate for a much longer time and can be helpful if you start to get tired during a particular meditation. The final key to the ascension process is to anchor into the physical vehicle all that has already been anchored into the etheric vehicle. Movement can be a very helpful tool in this regard.

Channeling Sound

After calling on the higher-frequency energies, then allow them to make sounds through your vocal cords. Vywamus is especially good at this. This might also be called channeled toning. It will help you to raise your vibrations, clear your field, and create certain profound spiritual activations.

Repairing the Etheric Vehicle

Many Lightworkers do not realize that the etheric vehicle can be damaged just as the physical vehicle can be damaged. The etheric is the blueprint for the physical body. If the etheric vehicle is damaged, the physical body is going to find it almost impossible to heal. Call to the White Brotherhood Medical Assistance Program healing team to repair your etheric body and to tighten and balance all your grids.

Confusions

There is much discussion among Lightworkers about the twelve strands of DNA, the twelve chakras, the twelve rays, the twelve initiations, the twelve dimensions, and the twelve bodies. They are all very profound states of consciousness within which you can integrate the energies.

However, there is the belief among some Lightworkers that the integration of all of these energies will take you to the three hundred fifty-second level of the Mahatma, the level of the Godhead. This is untrue. The integration of these energies does not take you even to the galactic level. As Vywamus has said, total mastery of this planet takes you not more than three-quarters of an inch up a ten-inch ruler. For example, the twelfth chakra is only a fourth-dimensional chakra.

Chakras one through seven are of the third dimension.

Chakras eight through fourteen are of the fourth dimension.

Chakras fifteen through twenty-two are of the fifth dimension.

Chakras twenty-three through twenty-nine are of the sixth dimension.

Chakras thirty through thirty-six are of the seventh dimension.

Chakras thirty-seven through forty-three are of the eighth dimension.

Chakras forty-four through fifty are of the ninth dimension.

Even when you anchor chakra fifty, you are no more than one inch up the ten-inch ruler. To think you are at the top of creation once you have anchored the twelfth chakra is illusion.

Another confusion among Lightworkers is the belief that you can go beyond the seventh initiation (or the twelfth initiation, depending on which system you are using). Many Lightworkers think they are taking their seventeenth initiation, or something of the sort. That is also illusion, the glamour and delusion of the negative ego. If you go beyond the seventh sublevel of the seventh (twelfth) initiation, you will lose your physical body. The only exception to this occurs in the descent of an avatar such as Sai Baba, the Lord Maitreya, or Kuthumi. They have materialized bodies at galactic or universal levels of initiation.

This also applies to the twelve dimensions. There is a belief that the twelfth dimension takes you to the three hundred fifty-second level of the Godhead, the highest cosmic logoic plane in Djwhal Khul's system. This is not true. The twelfth dimension takes you only one inch up that ten-inch ruler. Think about it. If you can anchor the ninth-dimensional chakras by anchoring the fiftieth chakra in the crown and you are still operating on a planetary level, how could the twelfth dimension be the level of the Godhead? There is a tendency of the negative ego to think that you are more evolved than you really are.

Before you evolve to the three hundred fifty-second level of the Godhead, you must evolve through the solar level, the galactic level, the universal level, the many source levels, and the cosmic level before you reach the Godhead. Even Sai Baba, who is the highest spiritual being on this planet and who is a universal avatar, is operating somewhere around the twentieth to twenty-fourth level.

Watch out for the negative ego. In my opinion, that is the number one lesson for Lightworkers around the planet. The negative ego always wants to be the best and likes to compete and compare. This is why it is wise not even to talk about your level of initiation unless it is clearly appropriate to do so.

The twelve rays are really just subrays that have been toned down over and over again through the hierarchical levels. The Lightworkers on this plane, no matter what level of initiation, do not, in truth, go beyond the level of Melchizedek, the Universal Logos. It is possible to tune in to higher levels, but this is the true ceiling that all Lightworkers work with, according to Melchizedek himself. That is a big enough stretch.

The Mahatma is the highest energy that can be accessed from this plane. However, at the level of schooling Planet Earth has reached, you do not have a lot of access beyond the Universal Logos. It is a sort of ring-pass-not for this planet. On occasion, as a special divine dispensation, you might be able to go beyond that just to observe, but beings on those levels are not actively involved with this level of schooling; the Earth is still very young in the cosmic scheme of things.

Another confusion concerns the twelve strands of DNA. They are integrated into the etheric body, not the physical body. It is only when you complete the seven levels of initiation (the twelfth initiation) that the process of transferring the twelve strands into the physical vehicle really begins.

The twelve bodies exist at the universal level or below. There are many more bodies beyond that. No matter what level you are on, you cannot integrate the twelve bodies because you have not yet reached the galactic or universal level in terms of realization. You can channel those energies in a toned-down fashion, but you will not realize them until you have evolved to the level of Sai Baba, for example.

Djwhal Khul has said that the two most highly evolved beings on this planet now are Sai Baba in India and the Lord Maitreya in England. Humanity is blessed to have a universal avatar and a galactic avatar incarnated simultaneously. An aspect of Kuthumi is incarnated too, and we have recently been told that Jesus (Sananda) has also incarnated during this period of the externalization of the Hierarchy.

The Lord Sai Baba has said that the true definition of God is "man minus ego." Let this thought be present when you think about defining your level of evolution.

The Meaning of Ascension

Ascension really means that you are carrying a certain amount of Light in your four-body system. I have come to understand that many people who ascend and many who have taken all seven levels of initiation are still very unclear. Ascension does not mean perfection on all levels. I know some seventh degree initiates who are still very much run by their negative egos, others who are still victims of their emotional bodies, still others who have prosperity issues or issues concerning lack of self-worth and self-love, and others who are dealing with health lessons. They are all wonderful, sincere, God-seeking people whom I am proud to call my friends and colleagues. However, everyone has blind spots and there is not one on this planet who does not have to watch out for the glamour, illusion, and maya of the negative ego.

You will be exactly the same as you are now when you complete your initiations except that you will be able to hold more Light. You might have developed the first-ray qualities but not the second-ray qualities, or you might have developed the third-ray traits but not the others. I realize that this might be a shock to you, but I tell you for an absolute fact, it is true.

The positive side is that God has not made the requirements so difficult that they are impossible to achieve. What I have come to understand is that ascending is much easier than I had thought it was. This information is important because there are many teachers walking around who have ascended but still present teachings that are unclear or unintegrated in some respects. Just because you have completed all initiations or have raised your Light quotient to 99%, it does not mean that you are beyond your ego or are psychologically clear and completely integrated in your understanding.

So do not give your power to anyone, and always be discerning. Trust God within yourself, no matter where a person claims to be in terms of his level of initiation. This is not to say that what a person has to offer is not of value, for indeed it may be. You just have to be discerning as to when the ego is getting in the way, and where the teachings might be illusionary.

Even Sanat Kumara and Vywamus have said that they still have small remnants of negative ego they are working on clearing. If they are still clearing, do you think anyone on this plane is free? You must become a master not only on the spiritual level, but also on the psychological level and on the physical level. You must also become a master of all the rays, even if your monad and soul are on a specific ray.

Sanat Kumara has told me that this is one of the dangers of these times. He said that people are advancing spiritually with incredible speed, but their mental, emotional, and physical bodies are not evolving as quickly. This problem is rampant around the planet, so it is important to be aware of it in yourself and to avoid being gullible in terms of the spiritual teachers you work with.

I have come to understand clearly now that ascension has more to do with spiritual development than it has to do with mental, emotional, and physical development. That is why, if you want to ascend, you should focus on the building of your Light quotient. If you truly want to realize God, then also master your mental, emotional, and physical vehicles in service of spirit and, above all else, transcend negative ego consciousness!

One last confusion has to do with the Light quotient and what it really means. The initiations are basically an index of the amount of Light you are carrying. Even when you achieve the 99% Light quotient, you are still operating at a planetary and solar level. You have not even entered into galactic realization, let alone universal realization. The ability to achieve these very high levels of Light quotient so quickly is a new dispensation. In the past, it was done much more slowly which allowed time for the mental, emotional, and physical bodies to catch up and which allowed for the development of some of the more advanced ascension abilities.

Mass Ascension for Planet Earth and the 12:12

The 12:12 on December 12, 1994, was a great success on a planetary level, according to Ascended Master Djwhal Khul. The 12:12 was much more significant than most people realized. It marked two major spiritual events. The first was the movement of Planet Earth herself (not humanity) from the fourth dimension into the fifth dimension. In essence, the Earth took her ascension. It was during the Harmonic Convergence in 1987 that Planet Earth moved from the third dimension into the fourth dimension. The Earth is in a state of spiritual evolution just as humanity is and is in the process of completing her seven levels of initiation also.

The second major spiritual event marked by the 12:12 was the opening of the spiritual window for the mass ascension of humanity. The Wesak Festival (the Festival of the Buddha) on May 14th, 1995, is when humanity, on a mass scale, began to walk through that window. The success of the 12:12 was that the window was opened extremely wide, much wider even than Sanat Kumara and the Spiritual Hierarchy had expected. That allowed greater numbers of people to walk through the window. May 14th began a five-year window of mass ascension for Planet Earth. Never before in the 3.1 billion years of the existence of Planet Earth have so many members of humanity taken their ascension. The event is unprecedented. A relatively small number of advanced initiates had already walked through the window; Wesak began the large-scale movement for humanity.

Spiritual Job Opportunities

One of the experiences many of you will begin having after you have completed your ascension process and initiations is that of being offered spiritual job opportunities. You are all part of the next wave, so to speak. A great many of the previous wave are slowly, but surely, preparing to move on to their cosmic evolution. For example, Djwhal Khul told us that he is preparing, around the year 2012, to move on to his cosmic evolution on his path to the Great White Lodge on Sirius. He told us that a great may of his senior disciples will be going with him. Lightworkers on Earth will be filling a great many of these posts in the seven ashrams and approximately forty nine subsidiary ashrams of the Christ, Lord Maitreya. Even Lord Maitreya will soon be moving on, as Kuthumi will be taking over his post in approximately two thousand years. This is the natural evolution of all planetary, solar, galactic, universal, and cosmic hierarchies throughout creation.

Certain job positions in the spiritual government have already been offered, and many of you will be offered similar positions. This is something to be aware of. If you are accelerating your ascension process, you can be forewarned that "much is given, but much is also expected." This is a direct quote from Djwhal Khul and Melchizedek. The higher the initiation level, the greater the responsibility and the more service work is required.

Much of the work for these positions occurs at night on the inner planes during sleep. Djwhal Khul told us that certain senior members of the current Spiritual Hierarchy will still be around to help us in our conscious training when we make our transfer to the inner plane. He said that we would be in that position for approximately one hundred and twenty-five years. Then we would transfer the work to someone who is a part of the wave just behind us and we would move on to the Great White Lodge on Sirius as the hierarchical chain of command continues.

Earth Life after Ascension

How long do you stay on Earth after you complete your seven levels of initiation? This seems to be variable, depending on a number of factors: first, the contract you made with the Lords of Karma before you came in; second, free choice. Even when your contract is up, you can choose to stay longer if you wish to. There seem to be certain windows of exit. Djwhal told me that I had a window around the year 2012. I have not decided yet whether I will remain on Earth or leave at that time. I am not yet ready to make that decision.

This brings up the issue of physical immortality which is not an automatic occurrence. The amount of spiritual current running through your bodies when you hold a 99% Light quotient will definitely make you younger, stronger, and healthier; that is certain. But it does not guarantee physical immortality. You must decide if that is the way you want to use your energy. For example, when Djwhal Khul learned to maintain physical immortality, he was an older man and did not want to use his energies in that manner. If your energies are used for youthing, then they are taken away from other focuses.

Loving Earth Life

Djwhal Khul has told us that an absolute requirement for graduating from Earth life is loving Earth life. The attitude of wanting to escape from life on Earth and looking at it as a prison is faulty thinking, and it guarantees that you will have to remain here. Earth and the material universe are, in truth, one of the many heavens of God. If you knew how many beings would give their eye teeth, so to speak, from the inner plane to trade places with you, you would be amazed! This Earth school, especially now at this extraordinary time in its history, is one of the most sought-after schools in the entire universe. It is a tough school, but Djwhal Khul has told us that having it on your "spiritual resume" will be a real boon to your cosmic evolution. Earth, in truth, is a planet of love and joy, and it is your job as a Lightworker to set an example and be a Lightbearer for the coming age.

Thymus Chakra Activation

The thymus chakra is a chakra between the heart and the throat. It is turquoise in color. Call forth to Quan Yin on the inner plane and request the opening and full activation of your thymus chakra to accelerate your spiritual evolution, no to metion boosting your immune system.

The Ascension and Resurrection Flame

Call forth the ascension and resurrection flame from the ascension temples on the inner plane and from your own Mighty I Am Presence. Request that it pour forth through your crown chakra into your four-body system. Request that it first flow through and purify your physical vehicle, then your etheric vehicle, then your astral vehicle, then your mental vehicle, then all your spiritual vehicles. Ask that it pour through and purify your seven major chakras and all your minor chakras. Call forth a raising of your vibration to that of the Christ.

The Council of Twelve for This Cosmic Day

Call forth, when you are having one of your deeper meditations, an ascension blessing by the Council of Twelve for this cosmic day. I would recommend doing this while sitting in the ascension seat in the Golden Chamber of Melchizedek.

Ascension Activation with the Seven Mighty Archangels

In meditation, call forth Archangel Michael and call forth a downpouring of his energies of protection with help from his legions of angels.

Secondly, call forth Archangel Jophiel and request the ascension energies of illumination and wisdom.

Then call forth Archangel Chamuel and request the ascension energies of love, tolerance, and gratitude.

Call forth Archangel Gabriel and request the ascension energies of resurrection and purity.

Call forth Archangel Raphael and request the ascension energies of concentration and truth.

Call forth Archangel Uriel and request the ascension energies of peace and devotion.

Call forth Archangel Zadkiel and call forth the ascension energies of culture, refinement, diplomacy, ordered service, and ascension itself.

Call forth Archangel Metatron and the combined forces of the seven above-mentioned archangels and request an ascension acceleration the likes of which you have never received before. Request that they remain with you and work with you on a full-time basis until you complete your ascension and seven levels of initiation. Request Light quotient building and the anchoring of your higher chakras and your twelve strands of DNA.

Call forth a balancing of the feminine and masculine energies within yourself from the feminine counterparts of these archangels, Faith, Christine, Charity, Hope, Mother Mary, Aurora, and Amethyst. Request a balancing of your four-body system and request that a pink rose appear in your heart.

Call forth, specifically, your ascension angels to help you in these activations and openings.

Call forth, finally, a rain of blessings from the seraphim, cherubim, thrones, dominions, virtues, powers, principalities, archangels, and angels for yourself, your group, all of humanity, and the Earth herself.

Ascension Activation with the Seven Mighty Elohim

Go, again, to the Golden Chamber of Melchizedek and sit in the ascension seats to get plugged into the universal current. After achieving a deep state of relaxation and attunement, call forth the seven mighty elohim and the Council of Elohim.

Call forth first an ascension blessing from the first-ray elohim masters, Hercules and Amazonia.

Call forth a second-ray elohim ascension blessing from Apollo and Lumina.

Call forth a third-ray ascension blessing and activation from Heros and Amora.

Call forth a fourth-ray ascension blessing and activation from Purity and Astrea.

Call forth a fifth-ray ascension blessing and activation from Cyclopia and Virginia.

Call forth a sixth-ray ascension blessing and activation from Peace and Aloha.

Call forth a seventh-ray ascension blessing and activation from Arcturus and Victoria.

Call forth an alignment with the elohim computers in the Earth.

Chant the name "Elohim" for several minutes to begin this meditation in order to magnetize their energies to you and immerse yourself in their vibration. Elohim is one of the most holy of all the names of God. Request that this blessing be transferred to the Earth Mother herself and to all Lightworkers consciously seeking their ascension.

Call forth a downpouring of the sacred scriptures.

Cosmic Grounding

After doing your spiritual meditations, it is a good idea to call forth, on a regular basis, cosmic and spiritual grounding for yourself and your group. It is important to do this for the purpose of getting the high-frequency energies into your physical vehicle and not just into your metaphysical bodies. This is also a great service to the Earth Mother who is greatly in need of blessings and energies.

Call forth Archangel Sandalphon to help in this regard, for this is his specialty. Request his help in creating a grounding cord down to the center of Earth. Request his help in creating roots from your feet deep into the Earth. Request his help in fully opening your foot chakras. Also request the help of Gaia herself in this grounding process. Request that all the energies you have received in your heavenly meditation now be transferred into your physical body and then into Gaia to help accelerate her evolution. See yourself as a channel, a conduit for bringing the higher energies into the Earth. See and feel Gaia's gratitude.

Upon completion of this process, call forth the energies of Gaia to come upward through your feet and to mix with the downpouring energies from the Heavenly Father and spiritual forces. Ask Archangel Sandalphon to help in the proper balancing and mixing of these energies. Ask the Earth Mother for help in accelerating your ascension process from a grounded perspective.

Golden Pyramid of Light

Call to Archangel Metatron and call forth an anchoring and activation of a golden pyramid of Light to anchor around yourself or around the group with which you are working. Call then to Thoth and ask that the energies from the Great Pyramid in Egypt transfer and align with your golden pyramid and that it become a permanent structure in your home.

Request that it also serve as a protective spiritual structure to allow in only energies of the Christ. Request that it be aligned with the Great Central Sun. Request that it become a temple of Light and initiation for all who enter.

The Forty-three Christed Universes

Call forth to Melchizedek while sitting in his Golden Chamber and request the anchoring of the energies of the forty-three Christed universes from the Source of this cosmic day. This is a very special blessing and is not a regular invocation. It should be asked for only once.

The Physical Body becomes Etheric

As you complete the seven levels of initiation and build your Light quotient to the 98% level, you find it becomes important to transfer into the physical body all that is contained in the Lightbody. Such transference has been going on all along, but the Lightbody has not been completed until this point. Once it has been completed the focus is to make the physical body more of an etheric body.

When humanity first came to Earth, beings were all more etheric in nature and did not have dense physical bodies. In essence, humanity is moving back to that state of consciousness. The Earth's having taken her ascension at the 12:12 makes this movement a little easier for all physical bodies on the Earth. The dense physical body will still be visible to third-dimensional eyes when it becomes more etheric, but when seen by spiritual eyes, a major difference will be obvious, and abilities such as teleportation will come more easily.

Meditations for the Matrix-Removal Program

The matrix removal program is used to clear the negative ego's faulty programs from your four-body system. For this particular meditation, call Vywamus and Djwhal Khul and any other master you are intuitively inspired to request. Ask first for a general clearing of all fear-based programs that are hindering your spiritual growth. You will feel them moving out of the top of your head. Then request that they focus on your physical body and ask them to remove any and all fear-based programs lodged there. Then request that they move into your etheric body and remove any fear- based programs that are blocking your ascension. Move on to the astral body and request that they remove all fear-based programs and spiritual weeds from your astral, or and emotional body. Then request that they move to your mental body and remove all thought forms of an imbalanced and negative nature. Then move to your spiritual bodies and request that they be cleared.

After each one of these mini-meditations, request that the programs be completely removed from your soul and from the Akashic Records. You must give your permission for them to do this. You could spend a long time meditating for this particular ascension technique – I am sure this meditation could be done many, many times.

During another meditation, go through each of your seven major chakras. Begin with the first chakra and request the matrix removal program to remove all imbalanced energies and fear-based programs preventing you from achieving your ascension in the first chakra. Then do the same for each of the other six chakras.

Call forth the spiritual vortex from your own Mighty I Am Presence to clear your field. Then call forth the cosmic fire to cleanse your four-body system and chakra column and request that all astral residue be burned up. Then call forth the Medical Assistance Program healing team to perfectly balance your chakras and four-body system. Do this for an hour a day for twenty-one days and you will be absolutely amazed by how much negative energy has been removed from your field. Request that they do it at night while you sleep until 90% to 95% of your fear-based programming has been removed. If you want to raise your vibration and build your Light quotient, this is one of the fastest ways.

Once you have made some headway with your personal material, then you can begin doing world service work and clearing fear-based programs for humanity as a whole. You can actually do both at the same time. When doing it for humanity, also call in some of the galactic and universal masters such as Vywamus, Lenduce, Metatron, Sanat Kumara, Lord Maitreya, Sai Baba, the Lord of Arcturus, and the Lord of Sirius to make sure the work gets done quickly and efficiently. At the end, always request a clearing of your field and the removal of all etheric mucus from it by means of the magnetic healing abilities of Vywamus or Lenduce. They can just vacuum up the etheric mucus instantly. Clearing fear-based programs from humanity and from the Earth Mother's body is a tremendously important service you can perform.

Chakra Toning Meditation

Begin with the first chakra and for one minute chant the sound "o." Move to the second chakra and chant the sound "shu," pronounced "shuck," for one minute. Then move to the third chakra and chant the sound "ya." Move to the fourth chakra and chant the sound "wa," pronounced "yawn." Move to the fifth chakra and chant for one minute the sound "he." Move to the sixth chakra and chant the sound "hu," pronounced "hue." Move to the seventh chakra and chant the sound "eye" for one minute. This will completely tune up and open all seven chakras. It might be good to do this meditation after you do the matrix removal program on your chakras.

The Twelve Rays Meditation

This meditation is designed to balance your energies and to get you used to calling on energies of the twelve rays. Begin the meditation by invoking your own Mighty I Am Presence and call forth the first ray, the red ray. Feel the will and dynamic power flowing through you. Any time you need more will power and alignment with the Will of God, call on this energy. Call on it when you are feeling lazy and are procrastinating.

Then call forth the second ray, or blue ray, of love and wisdom. Feel how it is different from the first ray. When you feel deficient in love and wisdom, call on this ray.

Then call forth the third ray, the yellow ray of active intelligence. Note how it feels and how it is different from the second ray. You can do this as you are reading this book; experience it as you are reading about it. When you need more active intelligence, call on this ray. You invoke it by just saying the number of the ray or the color or the quality it embodies. Any one of these three methods will work equally well.

Then call forth the fourth ray of emerald green, which is the ray of harmony. When you want more harmony, call on this ray. When you want to invoke more artistic energy and beauty and healing, call on this ray. See how it feels now. Feel how it is different from the previous ray.

Call forth the fifth ray of orange, which is concrete science. Be aware of how this feels. This is a good ray to call on when you are doing mental research of some kind or studying for a test.

Now call forth the sixth ray of indigo, which embodies the quality of devotion and idealism. When you want to cultivate this quality – for example, when you go to church – call upon this ray. When you are losing your feelings of enthusiasm for your spiritual path, call this ray. Experience how it feels right now as you are reading. It takes just a few seconds and comes in instantly when you call on it. Feel the mastery at your disposal with the ability to call in any ray or quality you need at any time.

Now call in the seventh ray, the violet ray of ceremonial order and magic. Sense how it feels to be in this ray. This ray is good for the transmutation of negative energies or negative situations. It is good for grounding and the cultivation of spiritual order.

Call in the eighth ray of seafoam green which is the higher ray of cleansing. When you feel a need to clean your aura and four-body system, call on this ray. Feel how it feels right now. If you are fasting or are in need of purification, call on this ray.

Now call in the ninth ray of blue-green. This is the ray that attracts the body of Light and creates joy. When you want more joy in your life or if you are getting too serious, call on this ray. You will immediately feel happier. If you wish, the Arcturians can even send it to you from their starships, and I will bet you any amount of money you will not be able to stop yourself from smiling, once they turn on the juice. Try it! Do you see the mastery you have over your mind and emotions through affirmations, prayer, and the invocation of these rays? Most people stay stuck instead of just calling for the energies they need.

Now call forth the tenth ray of pearlescence. This ray fully anchors the Lightbodies. There are two bodies of Light, the soul body of Light and the monadic body of Light. Constantly call on this ray until you take your ascension to insure soul and monadic infusion and merger, which is what ascension is.

Call forth the eleventh ray of pink-orange. This is the energy that is the bridge to the New Age. Call it forth now and experience how it feels so you will remember it for your spiritual tool kit.

Call forth, now, the twelfth ray of gold. This is the energy of the New Age and is the energy of the Christ consciousness. It is one of my favorite rays and I call on it often. The actual ascension energy is a combination of this gold ray with white. Call in the twelfth ray now and experience how it feels. Call in the ascension energy now and feel the slight variation.

The Importance of Meditating

Meditation is the key to your ascension. As you spend more and more time meditating, you will experience the subtle variations of the rays, the different ascension seats, and the various spiritual masters with whom you work. It is good to vary your meditations to avoid boredom and to keep up your divine enthusiasm. This book has provided you with a potpourri of meditations and ascension techniques that will just about guarantee your ascension if you use them with any regularity.

Meditate all day long and when you sleep at night. Even while your mind is focused on a normal job, these energies can be working for you. Do these meditations in groups and with friends and spread them around the planet. I was never a good meditator myself until I got into this kind of meditation; it is fun and is a continual downpouring of divine nectar and healing balm for all my bodies. There is no better feeling in the world than the experience of the constant immersion in the spiritual current in its various forms. Every person on Planet Earth can experience it with the invocation of any of the spiritual techniques in this book.

The main goals are to have fun, to experiment, and to meditate as much as possible. Make your life one constant, ever-changing meditation that ranges from one ray, master, ascension seat, or ascension technique to another. That will give you the direct experience of having God with you all the time. It will prevent you from seeking your wholeness outside of yourself. The experience of the energy is the key. If you happen to be able to perceive the energy clairvoyantly or clairaudiently, so much the better, but it is not necessary in the slightest in order to achieve your ascension. I know this for an absolute fact. Call forth the higher-frequency energies and experience the subtle and sometimes not-so-subtle God intoxication that they can produce. The spiritual path on Earth can be very difficult; however, the healing balm that will come to you as aresult of the constant invocation of spiritual energies will make you strong and give you faith, for you will unmistakably experience them, no matter what your level of initiation. The more you practice, the more quickly you will ascend, for every day, your Light quotient is increasing.

Service is important. However, you do not have to be a world teacher or a famous person to ascend. The vast majority won't be. The key is to integrate Light through, work, sleep, exercise, relaxation, socializing, and meditation, constantly invoking the Godforce by means of the techniques I have shared. Bathe in God's divine current and do not let go until God blesses you.

Djwhal told us the two key ingredients in achieving ascension are building your Light quotient and service. Never compete or compare! As Jesus said in *A Course in Miracles*, "To have all, give all to all." What you hold back from your brother and sister, in truth, you are holding back from yourself. We all share one identity as the Eternal Self; all else is illusion. "Nothing real can be threatened. Nothing unreal exists. Herein lies the peace of God."

Melchizedek's Cosmic Computer

When my ascension group reached the 98% Light quotient level and went through the seventh sublevel of the seventh initiation, we were, by the grace of God, granted a new dispensation which is available to all. Many will take advantage of it during sleeptime, but it is my job to bring many of these usually unconscious processes to the conscious level. This special dispensation available at the 98% Light quotient level is a cosmic computer which Melchizedek is in charge of and which the Arcturians use on the motherships. It is specifically designed to take the fire letters, key codes, and sacred geometries that have been programmed into the etheric body and the Lightbody and to actualize and transfer them into the physical body.

Remember that there are three stages involved in anchoring the fire letters, key codes, and sacred geometries, as there are in the anchoring of the higher chakras: there is the anchoring and activation, the actualization, and the utilization. Once you reach the completion of the seventh initiation and the 98% Light quotient and have practiced the meditations in this book and in *The Complete Ascension Manual*, pretty much everything necessary will be anchored.

The next step is the physicalization, the transfer from etheric to physical. This applies to the DNA also. The mini-tornadoes are one technique for doing this but Melchizedek's computer is incredible. It systematically, in a very precise, orderly manner, lights up certain keys and sets of keys in your four-body system. Certain organs, glands, and brain centers light up. Each one is like a key that unlocks the next sequence. The computer can also be programmed to anchor and activate the five sacred languages.

You will all reach the 98% Light quotient level and complete the seven levels of initiation in a much shorter time than you now realize is possible. If you really apply the techniques and stay totally focused on your spiritual path, it is possible to build your Lightbody at the rate of twelve to fifteen Light quotient points a year. I am not saying everyone will do this. However, it is possible, and the committed might be able to do it even faster. That is equivalent to taking an initiation every one or two years. Most of you reading this book are already at the third, fourth, or fifth initiation, and a few are even farther along.

Figure it out: there are only seven levels of initiation, so at that pace, everyone could quite easily achieve the 98% level between the years 1995 and 2012. Ascension is much easier to achieve than you realize – if you have the information. What has been lacking has been the knowledge of what to do. Many people are spinning their wheels because they are focusing on spiritual practices that are not as effective as they could be for the achievement of the goal they are trying to reach. Every day, just live like God, do your service work, and build a little more Light quotient. Much more is occurring on the inner plane than you realize. Once you begin working with these tools, you are made a part of an ascension wave, a group on the inner plane, and the masters automatically help you move along because of your commitment to practicing these ascension techniques.

Once you reach the 98% level, which all of you will (and I really mean this!), call on the cosmic computer of Melchizedek. Request that it be programmed to anchor all fifty of your chakras. Build your Light quotient to the 98% level, transfer your DNA into the physical, fully complete and stabilize your seven levels of initiation, and help your physical body become an etheric body so you can learn to teleport.

When looked at clairvoyantly, there appears to be a sort of lightning storm that surrounds this process. As the sets of key codes fire, these spiritual lightning bolts seem to work metaphysically with the firing process to fully activate and actualize the process. It feels really "enlightening."

Cosmic Journey Meditation

The following meditation seems a fitting way to end this chapter.

Begin by becoming very relaxed and comfortable in a place where you will not be disturbed. The idea of this meditation is to go on a cosmic journey from the bottom to the top of creation.

Begin by establishing your grounding cord to the very center of the Earth while simultaneously reaffirming and consciously establishing your antakarana, or bridge of Light, up through the soul and the monad all the way through the three hundred fifty-two levels of the Godhead and back to Source. Call forth Metatron and Archangel Michael, requesting divine protection and also requesting that they be your guides on this cosmic journey. Call forth your personal merkabah for the journey.

First, travel into the center of Earth where you can blend and merge with the Earth Mother, Gaia. Send your spiritual body there. Meld with her lovely energy as she greets you, and share her love.

Now travel to Shamballa in the center of the Earth. Here you can experience a thriving world that most of humanity is unaware of. Ask permission now to be taken by Metatron and Michael to one of the spiritual temples in the Hollow Earth. Experience the energy there.

Now travel up through your grounding cord, up through your chakra column, and out though your crown chakra in your merkabah, with Metatron and Archangel Michael at your side. Travel to the ashram of Djwhal Khul. He greets you and invites you to look around and to stay a while and meditate in one of the garden courtyards or meditation rooms in his facility. Experience the vibration and sanctity of this sacred space. Stay a while if you like and meditate with Djwhal.

Now travel upward to the inner-plane ashram of His Holiness, the Lord Maitreya. Lord Maitreya is the Master of Masters, the Teacher of Teachers, and the Planetary Christ. He welcomes you with open arms and asks you to sit and meditate with him for a little while. Sit with him and blend with his energies. Ask for his ascension blessing.

When you feel complete, travel upward again to the ascension seat in the courts of Shamballa. Sanat Kumara greets you and welcomes you. Sit with him for a while and meditate. Tune in to the vibrations of the Planetary Logos. Note how Shamballa feels different from the places you have traveled to previously. Feel the spiritual current running through your body from the ascension seat. Ask for Sanat Kumara's ascension blessing, which he happily gives.

Travel now to the central core of the solar system, to the ascension seat in Helios' Golden Chamber. Helios comes to greet you. Sit in the ascension seat and blend with the energies of Helios. Feel how the solar energies differ from the energies of Shamballa. Feel the solar current running through your four-body system. Stay and enjoy the solar current while your four-body system is beginning to get revved up with Light. Remain as long as you like.

When you are ready, travel to the Great White Lodge on Sirius. Visit His Holiness, the Lord of Sirius, and sit in the ascension seat. You have now moved up to the galactic level in your cosmic journey. Be aware of how refined the energy is at this level. It has a new quality. You are becoming much more expansive. Feel the galactic current from the Great White Lodge and the Lord of Sirius running through your physical, etheric, astral, mental, and spiritual bodies. Request an ascension blessing from the Lord of Sirius and call for the Light packets of information to be infused. Stay for a while and enjoy the great blessing you are receiving.

Now travel to the ascension seat in the Galactic Core and visit Melchior. He welcomes you with open arms and bids you meditate with him. Tune in and experience the subtle difference between the Galactic Core and the Great White Lodge on Sirius. Feel the spiritual currents pouring through you from the Galactic Core and Melchior. Ask Melchior for his ascension blessing and activation, and meld and blend with his energy.

Now travel to the ashram of Lenduce, the higher aspect of Vywamus. This is an even more refined level of consciousness. Request to be placed on his ascension seat and feel the divine current pouring through you. Call for his help and his blessing on your spiritual path.

Now move to His Holiness Sai Baba's inner-plane ashram at the universal level, which is blended with his physical ashram in Putaparti, India. Ask to sit in the love seat of Sai Baba to experience the love, the sweetness, the succor of Sai Baba, the Cosmic Christ and Universal Avatar. Ask for Sai Baba's blessing and help on your path of ascension. Feel or see him sprinkle his vibuti ash on your head as a blessing. Call for his help in building your spiritual wattage and Light quotient. Completely bathe in his energy, for there is nothing quite like it in God's infinite universe. Once touched by Sai Baba, you will never again be the same. A being of this magnitude has never before incarnated on Earth. Request that he be an advocate on your behalf, regardless of your spiritual path or religious orientation.

When you feel complete, travel to visit the Grand Master himself, His Holiness, the Universal Logos, Melchizedek. Request to be seated in the ascension seat in his Golden Chamber. Experience the universal spiritual current pouring through your veins. You have now reached one of the pinnacles of creation for this Earthly school, a most holy and refined space. Ask for Melchizedek's blessing on your path of ascension. Feel, see, or hear this blessing take place. Tune in now, and feel the cosmic pulse of the universe as you sit here. You have truly entered the Holy of Holies now that you have been granted access to this Golden Chamber. Come here often in the future to experience directly the universal aspect of your divinity.

Now request to be taken even higher still, through the seven cosmic planes and up through the three hundred fifty-two levels of the Mahatma to stand before the Throne of Grace and the Godhead, the Source. The Light is so brilliant and refined at this level that you withstand it only with the help and grace of Melchizedek, Metatron, and Archangel Michael. The love emanating from the center of this Light is unfathomable.

Standing before the Creator is the Cosmic Council of Twelve that runs the entire cosmos. It is from here that the twelve rays emanate. In the background can be vaguely seen the twenty-four elders who also surround the Throne of Grace. The energies of the Mahatma, the Avatar of Synthesis, can be seen extending from the Creator all the way downward to the material universe. As you look down from this pinnacle, you can see the seven heavens, or seven cosmic planes. If you tune in and focus, you can see the seven mighty archangels and the seven mighty elohim in the background. If you tune in to your inner ear, you can hear the incredible sound of celestial music.

Ask to be placed now in the Cosmic Pillar of Light and the cosmic ascension seat. Stand or sit now, and feel the God current pouring directly through you. Feel, also, the energies of the Mahatma pouring through you, charging up your spiritual battery and refining and raising the frequency of your electrical system. Take time to sit in the silence of the Holy of Holies at this highest cosmic level that can be reached, and blend and merge with the Presence of God. Return home in this holy instant and experience your true identity, unity, and oneness with God. Let all illusion drop away. "Be still and know that I am God . . . I and the Father are One."

Now speak directly to God, the Creator of the infinite universe, and pour forth your deepest and most heartfelt prayers. Pray now as you have never prayed before. Pray for ascension, healing, prosperity — whatever it is you need and want. Then share with God how you plan to serve Him and give back to creation. Ask that you be consciously linked with Him/ Her forevermore. Know that, in truth, you have always been linked and that there is an aspect of you that already lives at this level; it is just waiting for you to catch up, so to speak, and realize that which you already are. In truth, you are already God, but the process of creation is such that you must consciously demonstrate your Godhood through planetary, solar, galactic, universal, and cosmic dimensions in order to return to the home whence you originated.

Now feel yourself grounded back into your physical body on Earth, directly and consciously linked with the Godhead and with all the cosmic masters and ascension seats throughout the three hundred fifty-two levels of the Godhead. You are now forever transformed and cosmically expanded. You will forevermore live like a God, like a cosmic citizen which, in truth, is what you are. Make a spiritual vow now to hold the state of consciousness you have tuned in to in this meditation and to never allow yourself to forget and fall back under the spell of matter and negative hypnosis.

This time, you return home consciously; that is the process of initiation through which you are moving, the three hundred fifty-two levels of the Mahatma, each initiation being a greater expansion of Light and a greater expansion of your identity and service.

The first step while on Earth is to become a planetary teacher and to set a good example. Then you become a solar teacher, then a galactic teacher, then a universal teacher, then a cosmic teacher. You cannot take shortcuts, and you must prove yourself worthy at each stage before you are allowed to move to the next one; that is how the hierarchical chain of spiritual life you are in functions. Eventually, you will return home because, in truth, there is only one being in the infinite universe, and that is God. All share in this one identity, as the Eternal Self. The fall never really happened; you just think it did.

In truth, God's creation has always remained in oneness, but all creation is in the process of demonstrating at higher and more expansive levels of consciousness and responsibility. As you evolve, you will each, in the future, be in charge of solar systems, galaxies, universes, multidimensional or parallel universes, and, eventually, the entire cosmos. Such is the destiny of all, and the purpose of life is to shorten the necessary time, for time and space are temporary conditions, needed only while there are still students who have not graduated from the material universe. Eventually, all will graduate and ascend, including Earth herself and including the material universe herself, the Cosmic Mother.

God has breathed out the infinite universe and is now in the process of breathing it back into His/Her Eternal Womb. Your destiny is so much more grand than you have previously realized. It is good to remember this as you return to Earth each time so you don't become immersed in overidentification with matter and the pettiness of the lower self and negative ego. Remember this in the way you deal with your spouse, children, family, work associates, friends, and strangers, who, in truth, are your brothers and sisters. Arguments, grudges, lack of self-worth or self-love, competition, jealousy, violence in any form, attack thoughts, selfishness, fear, judgments, gossip, self-centeredness, and so on are way beneath such a noble being as yourself.

Eternally remember this in the way you live your life from this moment forward, and live like the God you in truth are. As *A Course in Miracles* says, it is time to own your grandeur, but not your grandiosity. All are equal, for all are God. People are just on different levels of realizing what is already so. Never forget that the infinite universe is really just a mirror: what you experience is your own state of consciousness, projected.

How you treat your brothers and sisters is literally — and I mean literally — what you are giving to yourself. Hold back love from any brother or sister, and you have short changed yourself because of the illusion of the negative ego. You receive in life exactly that which you give. It is not up to God, it is up to you. God has already given you everything; the question is, what will you give to yourself? If you want God, it is quite simple: give God to everyone and everything. This means give love, Christ consciousness, joy, total cooperation, and complete egolessness to everyone and everything. If you give your all and hold back nothing from your brothers and sisters and all God's creation, then God will hold nothing back in return. In essence, when you give all, you get all. Salvation is already yours. The question is whether you will hold it back from yourself due to the faulty, separative thinking of the negative ego.

As Master Jesus said, "Be ye faithful unto death, and I will give thee a crown of life." Hold on to this state of consciousness, to this ideal and never let go of it, even for an instant. Your spiritual victory, your ascension, your inner peace, your joy, your prosperity, your enlightenment are secure and inevitable!

Namasté.

Meditation for Ascension and Chakra-Clearing

Caryn created the following meditation and we both used it quite a bit early in our ascension processing. We also used it when emotional issues were on the surface in a major way. We feel that this particular ascension meditation could be very helpful to Lightworkers, so to end this chapter, I have included it for your enjoyment and edification.

Before beginning this ascension meditation, please find a comfortable place to sit. Then invoke the Pillar of Light down from the heavens, through your body, and into Gaia, the Earth. Continue bringing Light into your body, and extend the Light out through your chakra system, creating a shield over the front and the back of each chakra. Leave the shields in place and continue to expand the Light from your being, creating an oval shape around yourself. You are now sealed in your oval and protected by your shields within the sacred Pillar of Light.

Now please ground yourself into the center of the Earth by extending a copper cord from the bottom of your spine, down into the center of the Earth.

Then call forth guides to facilitate and assist you, for example, Sananda, Mary, Merlin, Ashtar, Helios, Buddha, Paramahansa Yogananda, Quan Yin, Isis, Serapis Bey, Sanat Kumara, Babaji, the Pleiadians, Melchizedek, Quetzalcoatl, Moses, Maitreya, and Sai Baba. Also always call forth Archangel Michael to watch over and protect you. Then, please call forth Archangel Uriel, Archangel Gabriel, Archangel Raphael, Archangel Zadkiel, Saint Germain, Mahatma, who is the Avatar of Synthesis, Metatron, and any other personal guides.

Please invoke your I Am Presence, your Christed Overself Being, your higher self by saying I Am That I Am. Allow your I Am Presence to surround you. Your I Am Presence actually does most of the work in the ascension process.

Proclaim, "I wish to begin the ascension processing now. I Am That I Am. I activate the thymus chakra. I Am That I Am. I activate the unified chakra. I Am That I Am. I am allowing Archangel Michael to cut all unwanted aka cords, and I send love to these beings. I Am That I Am."

Now, please place yourself in the Ascension Flame of the Dove. The Ascension Flame of the Dove is white, representing peace and grace, and pink, representing unconditional love.

Now, please place yourself in the living Light merkabah vehicle. The merkabah vehicle will accelerate the quickening, or will accelerate your personal vibrational rate. You will now meet Serapis Bey, your personal guides, and Mahatma, the Avatar of Synthesis, in the Temple Luxor. They will assist your ascension processing.

Please place a ball of golden-white Light in each of your chakras. Start with the root chakra; then the second chakra, then the third chakra, then the fourth chakra, then the fifth chakra, then the sixth chakra, then the seventh chakra, and then into as many chakras as you are comfortable with beyond your body.

Please call forth Mahatma, the Avatar of Synthesis. Visualize a tube of aquamarine blue coming down from the heavens, filling all of your bodies. Then through the aquamarine energy, bring in or invoke the Mahatma energy. See this energy as brilliant Light. Allow this energy to permeate your essences, all of your bodies.

Now please call in Saint Germain and ask him to send the Violet Flame up through your entire chakra system. The Violet Flame will transmute any negativity to a higher vibration.

Please focus on your root chakra. See your root chakra as a ball of red Light. Become a very tiny person and go into the root chakra. Check to see if you get an impression of any issues that might be held there. The issues might be surrounding survival or creativity. If something comes into your mind that needs to be looked at and healed, please use powerful clearing affirmations regarding unconditional love, forgiveness, and divine grace. [Affirmations can be found at the end of this meditation.]

Please focus on the second chakra, which is orange. See yourself as that tiny person again, and go into the second chakra. Reach out and tune in to any issues that might be stored in the second chakra. The issues might involve pleasure or pain. The issues might center around your personal sexuality. The issues might concern your wounded inner child. Whatever the issues are, it is time to look at them and heal them. This is that wonderful, magical, healing moment in your life. Please use the divine healing affirmations at the end of this meditation.

Now please move to the third chakra, which is yellow. Once again, become that very tiny divine being. Go into the third chakra and take a good look around. What do you see or sense? What issues come to mind? This is the center that is concerned with your personal power and your personal fears. This is where the logical mental thought processes are centered. You might encounter something you fear. It is time to face that fear and heal it. Heal the fearful situation with the divine healing affirmations. Fear is not real; it is something that has been created. Create a new mental house, free of fear.

Focus now on your heart chakra. This chakra is a ball of lovely emerald green Light. Become that tiny divine person again, and go into your heart chakra. Put out your feelers for the issues being held there. The heart deals with the issues surrounding love and love relationships, with that wonderful person who broke your heart into a million pieces. Take a good look. Use the powerful healing affirmations to heal and balance your heart. Now, please look at the threefold flame in your heart. See if the pink, the blue, and the gold flames are balanced. If they are not, add whatever is needed. This is the area where you balance the energies from above with the energies from the Earth below. Make sure these energies are balanced. You might see a beam of golden-white Light coming down to you from the heavens and a beam of radiant silver Light coming up to you from Gaia, the Earth. The two beams of Light meet evenly and smoothly in your heart chakra.

Move on to your throat chakra, the fifth chakra. See it as a ball of blue Light. Transform yourself into a tiny person and go into the chakra. See if there are any unresoved issues there. The issues might be about communication. Is there something you cannot talk about, or is there someone you cannot talk to? Heal the situation with the divine affirmations. If you are working with a person in this sacred space, tell him or her what is wrong and how you are feeling. Once again, heal the situation with the divine affirmations.

Now focus your energy on the third eye chakra, the sixth chakra. See a sphere of indigo Light. This is your visionary center. Become a tiny person and see if there are any issues there. If there is any work to be done, use the affirmations to create a divine healing.

Please move to the seventh chakra, the crown chakra, or Godhead. This is your connecting link to all that is and ever will be. It can be seen as a ball of white Light, with some violet or lavender and some gold. This is where the thousand-petaled lotus is located. Send that tiny divine aspect of yourself into the crown chakra and check for any problems. If you find some problems, heal them with the affirmations.

While remaining in the crown chakra, pull up the ball of orange Light from the second chakra. Leave the red Light of the root chakra in its place, for the Earth associated with the root chakra will protect you during the entire ascension process. Now please focus on the third chakra, and pull the ball of yellow Light into the crown chakra. Now focus on the heart chakra, and pull the lovely emerald green ball of Light into the crown chakra. Move on to the throat chakra, pulling the blue Light up into the crown. Focus on the third eye chakra, and pull the ball of indigo Light into the crown chakra.

Now focus on the crown chakra. There you see a lovely ball of golden-white Light with some violet or lavender in it. Now you see, situated in the crown, all the colors of all the chakras, with the exception of the root. You see that each ball of colored Light represents one of your bodies. When you pull up the balls of Light associated with the bodies, the bodies ascend.

Now please activate your first seven chakras and blend them to make a column of white Light. Activate the five upper chakras to make a column of golden-white Light. Now blend the columns of gold and white Light together and receive your golden-white Light halo. Experience your Christed self.

[If you do not want to do the full meditation now and are just saying affirmations, please start here.]

Place yourself in the Pillar of Light. Place yourself in your merkabah vehicle and allow it to spin clockwise. Call in Mahatma, the Avatar of Synthesis. Call in Sananda. Call in Metatron, Archangel Uriel, Archangel Raphael, Archangel Gabriel, Archangel Zadkiel, and Saint Germain. Call in Archangel Michael for protection, and to cut all aka cords. Send love to those who are being uncorded. Now please meet Serapis Bey, the guide in the temple at Luxor. They will watch over and monitor your ascension processing.

Have Saint Germain send the Violet Flame of transmutation up from the bottom of your feet and through your entire system. You can ground yourself into the center of the Earth with the copper cord at the bottom of your spine. You also have the option of grounding yourself into your I Am Presence; that can be accomplished by simply handing over the copper cord at the bottom of your spine to your I Am Presence.

Affirmations

Please declare these affirmations out loud:

I allow the lifting process to begin now. I Am That I Am.

I activate the thymus chakra. I Am That I Am.

I activate the unified chakra. I Am That I Am.

I am rebundling my twelve-stranded DNA now. I Am That I Am.

I am filling my entire brain and ductless glands with Light. I Am That I Am.

The Amrita, fire letters, sacred geometries, and key codes are now fully activated, reestablishing divine memory within my Lightbody. I Am That I Am.

I allow my original blueprint grids to be reinstated through axiatonal alignment. I Am That I Am.

I am a divine manifester, a divine alchemist. I Am That I Am.

I stop the aging process now. I Am That I Am.

I reprogram my pituitary gland to give forth the lifegiving hormones. I Am That I Am.

I breathe in sustenance for my body from sunlight. I Am That I Am.

I am on good terms with and am peacefully cocreating with all my brothers and sisters. I Am That I Am.

I allow the quickening of my vibratory frequencies. I Am That I Am.

I am resonating at fifth-dimensional frequencies. I Am That I Am.

I am allowing the standing waves of my third-dimensional and fourth-dimensional body envelopes to resonate with the blueprint and the harmonic frequencies of the fifth dimension. I Am That I Am.

(Optional: I am placing under myself a small speck, the size of a match flame, of the Cosmic Fire. I Am That I Am.)

I am becoming transparent. I Am That I Am.

I step-up and step-down my energies with divine nonchalance, with divine grace and ease. I Am That I Am.

I am ascending now in divine love, divine peace, and divine grace. I Am That I Am.

I am the Light, I am the resurrection. I Am That I Am.

I experience completion. I Am That I Am.

You should eat lightly when you are doing this kind of clearing work and meditation. Heavier foods such as red meats bring down your vibratory level. It should also be noted that the full moon and the actual spinning of your physical body clockwise will accelerate the quickening process.

14

Kabbalistic Ascension Techniques

*Treasury of Light — a realm of habitation
where the Elect of the World work with all
tablets and documents.*

The Book of Knowledge:
The Keys of Enoch

One of the most profound books ever written on this plane of existence is *The Book of Knowledge: The Keys of Enoch* by J.J. Hurtak is. It is truly a revelation of God. It is also, in truth, more of a science book than a spiritual self-help book, and for that reason is a little more difficult to read than most spiritual books. I value this book and the time I have spent studying it as one of my greatest treasures.

The Keys of Enoch embodies the true teachings of the Kabbalah as Melchizedek, Metatron, and Archangel Michael would teach them. Years of studying the material have allowed me to create ascension techniques and activations based on some of the abstract information in this book. The ascension techniques garnered from this material are among the most profound ever created. I suggest buying *The Keys of Enoch* in order to refer to the glossary where you will find the terms I have used, such as the Kabbalah, the Tree of Life, the Zohar, the Body of Knowledge, the Torah, or the Divine Scriptures of YHWH (not to be confused with the Earthly Torah of traditional Judaism, which is beautiful but is not the ultimate revelation of YHWH), the elohim, and Metatron. This information will fire keys within you as nothing you have ever come across before.

I suggest reading the introduction to *The Keys of Enoch* first, then the entire glossary, and then each of the sixty-four Keys before actually reading the text of the book. Even if that is all you do, the book would be worth its weight in gold. It is the spiritual revelation of YHWH and Metatron.

The Sixty-four Keys

Call to Metatron in meditation to anchor and activate, through your third eye and crown chakra, all sixty-four Keys of Enoch on planetary, solar, galactic, universal, multi-universal, and cosmic levels in your consciousness and multi-body system in all five sacred languages (Hebrew, Tibetan, Egyptian, Chinese, and Sanskrit).

Anchoring the Bodies

Call forth from Metatron a permanent anchoring and activation of your Electromagnetic body, Epi-kinetic body, Eka bodies, Gematrian body, Overself body, anointed Christ Overself body, Zohar body, and higher Kadmon body.

Melchizedek Crystals and Diamonds

I asked Melchizedek if there is any special tool that could help to anchor the twelve bodies. He said that he could anchor a certain type of Melchizedek crystals and diamonds that would help to accelerate the process. Ask for them in meditation when you are focusing on anchoring the solar, galactic, and universal bodies.

A Melchizedek Tidbit

I asked Melchizedek what level he was operating out of in terms of the seven cosmic planes of which Djwhal Khul speaks in the Alice Bailey material. Again, we are working only on the seven planes of the cosmic physical plane. Melchizedek said he was operating out of the fifth to the seventh cosmic plane; that would be the cosmic atmic to the cosmic logoic. After hearing this I became aware of how blessed humanity is to have a being of such spiritual magnitude in charge of the entire universe and available to the Lightworkers of Earth.

Clarification of Twelve Bodies

Melchizedek has clarified the twelve bodies. The first seven bodies correlate with the seven subplanes of the cosmic physical plane through which all of humanity is evolving. However, the eighth and ninth bodies, to which I referred as the soul and monadic bodies, are a little different from what I first thought they were. The eighth body does not refer to the individualized soul body because that anchors at the third level, or third initiation, correlating with the higher mental plane; the eighth body is the higher correspondence, the soul body that contains all the lives of the soul extensions and the parallel lives that must be integrated.

The ninth body is the integration of all the soul extensions and parallel lives from your entire monad which equal one hundred forty-four — that is, the twelve higher selves that make up the monad, each higher self incarnating twelve soul extensions or personalities into physical existence. All one hundred forty-four of these must be incorporated as part of anchoring the ninth body.

You might say the eighth and ninth bodies are the group soul and the group monad, rather than the individualized soul and monad. The individualized monad is anchored at the fifth, sixth, and seventh initiations: at the fifth initiation it anchors in consciousness; at the sixth, or ascension, it anchors completely; at the seventh, the completion of the process takes place.

If you are working with *The Keys of Enoch* and the seven bodies that are referred to there (the Zohar body of Light, the Overself body, the Anointed Christ Overself body, the Electromagnetic body, the Epi-kinetic body, the Eka bodies, the Gematrian body), Melchizedek says they refer to the same twelve bodies I have outlined.

It must be understood that there are bodies beyond these twelve that will be anchored upon graduation from physical existence. They might be called cosmic bodies. Melchizedek has told me that there are also cosmic chakras beyond the fifty with which humanity is able to work. However, at some point, chakras as most people understand them no longer exist because of the multidimensional, nonlinear qualities of those realities.

I asked Melchizedek the purpose of the higher bodies. The anchoring of the cosmic bodies such as the solar, the galactic, and the universal allows you to travel spiritually through those planes. Their anchoring also allows the clearing of karma on a much more expansive level.

Deca Delta Light Emanations

Call forth from Metatron the anchoring and activation of all Deca Delta Light Emanations from the ten Light Superscripts of the Divine Mind.

The Seventy-two Areas of the Mind

Call to Metatron and Melchizedek to spiritually illuminate the seventy-two areas of the mind.

Anchoring the Yod Spectrum

In meditation, call forth Metatron and ask for the permanent anchoring of the Yod Spectrum which includes the complete spectrum of divine fire letters which raise the consciousness of all individuals and codes them for spiritualized biological transmutation, cell by cell. Request that this be done on planetary, solar, galactic, universal, multi-universal, and cosmic levels. The solar body of Light, as it is now starting to come in, is forming a second layer of fire letters underneath the planetary body.

The Zohar Body of Light

Call in meditation to Metatron and Master Enoch and request a permanent anchoring and activation of the Zohar body of Light, the overself body, and the Anointed Christ Overself body, as described in *The Keys of Enoch*. (There might be some overlapping of theoretical systems here; however, I believe in being as comprehensive as possible to be sure nothing is missed. The Kabbalistic teachings trigger certain keys that other systems might not. Metatron and Master Enoch will know what to do. Request that they continue this work until it is complete.)

Anchoring the Teleshift Light Field

Call in meditation to Archangel Michael for a divine anchoring and activation of the Teleshift Light Field on a permanent basis. The Teleshift Light Field protects your mind so it can adapt to new and higher frequencies of Light integration.

The Divine Template of the Elohim

Call to Metatron, the Council of Elohim, and the twelve mighty elohim to fully anchor and activate the divine template of the elohim and/or the divine Light-grid of divine wisdom on a permanent basis so you may receive the highest wisdom of God, or YHWH.

The Holy Spirit, Shekinah

Call forth the Holy Spirit, Shekinah, for a true baptism by the living Light to prevent anything from coming between you and the Father who art in Heaven.

The Father's Eye of Divine Creation

Call to Metatron to anchor and activate the Father's Eternal Eye of Divine Creation into your third eye and multibody system.

The Nogan Shells

Call to Metatron to anchor the Nogan Shells of YHWH so you can experience and contemplate the ecstasy of God. Ask to be momentarily united completely with the living Light.

Temple Sanctuary of Light

Call to Metatron to anchor in your meditation room the Temple Sanctuary of Light of YHWH.

Zohar, Shekinah, and Christed Light

Call to Metatron and ask to be placed in an envelope of Zohar, Shekinah, and Christed Light and request that he now help you to build your eternal garment of Light on a permanent basis.

The Scriptures of Light

Call to Metatron to anchor the Scriptures of Light and the direct revealed Word of God and YHWH.

The Lay-oo-esh

Call forth to Metatron to anchor the Lay-oo-esh (Pillar of Light) around yourself on a permanent basis and in your home on a permanent basis.

Anchoring the Alhim

Call forth to Metatron for a downpouring of the Alhim (infinitesimal particles of spiritual Light).

Energy Tablets of God's Law

Call to Metatron to fully anchor and activate on a permanent basis the ark and the energy tablets of God's Law.

The Hyos Ha Koidesh

Call forth in meditation to the Hyos Ha Koidesh, the highest servants of YHWH, for an ascension blessing and activation.

The Ten Commandments

Call to Metatron for an anchoring of the Light packets of information from the true Ten Commandments. Call forth the ten Light superscripts within the unique pyramid grids of Light that are the foundation of life and cosmic law in the Father's universe.

Tablets of Creation

Call to Metatron and Enoch to anchor the Light packets of information from the tablets of creation that are connected with the scientific keys of living Light to the mansion worlds of YHWH.

Garment of Shaddai

Call to Metatron for a permanent anchoring of the Garment of Shaddai into your four-body system which, in truth, is Metatron himself!

The Super Electron

Call to Metatron to anchor and fully activate within your multibody system a divine infusion of the Super Electron for unification of the subparts of the local universe as described in *The Keys of Enoch*. Request that all existing electrons be replaced on a permanent basis with these Super Electrons of Metatron.

The Biostratus

Call to Metatron for the full anchoring and activation of the biostratus, a spiritual-genetic superhelix which was lost after the fall and which can now be fully reinstituted.

The Celestial Family of God

Call to the Hsakamim (the thirty-six watchmen of YHWH's program) to help reconnect you and the family of man to the celestial family of God.

Spiritualized Blood Chemistry

Call to Metatron to anchor the universal and cosmic energies necessary to transform your blood chemistry. Ask for this so your blood chemistry can be freed from Earth-bound dimensions and so that it can operate on the next orbital level of the Universal Mind.

Ain, Ain Soph, Ain Soph Or

Call forth a downpouring from Metatron and YHWH of the Ain, Ain Soph, and Ain Soph Or. This is the Limitless Light, the Eternal Light of YHWH.

The Language of Light

Call to Metatron for an anchoring of the communication system of the language of Light on a conscious basis so spirit can communicate directly from all levels of YHWH's creation.

The Divine Word

Call forth from Metatron an anchoring and activation of the divine work, the divine letters, the divine Lights, the divine powers, and the divine intelligence so you can experience the Godliness, Glory and Virtue of God in full manifestation and expression on Earth.

Revelation of YHWH

Call forth to the YHWH, the Cosmic Council of Twelve, the twenty-four elders who surround the Throne of Grace, the twelve mighty elohim, the Metastronane, the twelve mighty archangels, the Hyos Ha Koidesh, and Melchizedek for direct, ongoing, permanent revelation on Earth of YHWH and the Throne worlds of YHWH.

The Coat of Many Colors

Call forth to Metatron for an anchoring of the coat of many colors, which corresponds to the brilliant and splendid structure of the heavenly Jerusalem through the Zohar body of Light and the seventy-two sacred areas of the mind.

Gifts of the Holy Spirit

Call to Metatron, Melchizedek, Archangel Michael, and the Shekinah for the anchoring of the gifts of the Holy Spirit. Call forth the divine love, the creative power, the divine wisdom, and the gifts thereof in the name of the Father, YHWH.

Call forth the traditional gifts of the Holy Spirit, as well as the ability to speak in spiritual and scientific tongues and angelic languages, the ability to see and work with the angelic teachers of the Light, the understanding of the mysteries of the Shekinah's, the Son's, and the Father's kingdoms, the power of resurrecting the dead. Also call forth the full anchoring of the Lord's Mystical Body as the trinity power of the

Godhead on Earth so you can spiritually transform the substance of the Earth for the Glory of God.

The City of God

Call forth from Metatron, Melchizedek, and Michael an anchoring of the City of God, the City of YHWH, into yourself, your home, and your externalized ashram, so the material universe can also manifest the glory of God.

The Covenant of YHWH

Call forth an anchoring, activation, and reaffirmation of the Covenant of Fire and Light of YHWH. Call this forth from Metatron for an anchoring, activation, and reaffirmation of the Covenant of Israel and of the Covenant of Light. Call for an anchoring and activation of these covenants so that you can act as a blueprint for the implanting of greater knowledge and greater responsibility on Earth.

The Nag Hammadi Codices and Scriptures

Call forth from Metatron and Melchizedek an anchoring of Light packets of information from the Nag Hammadi codices and the scriptures of the Three Veils of Light. Request this so you can develop a greater understanding of the Melchizedekian knowledge of the Lightbody.

Resurrection

Call to Metatron, Melchizedek, and the Holy Spirit for a complete and total resurrection and transfiguration of your four-body system so you may be restored into the Father's image through Christ and into the heavenly Adam Kadmon body in the fullness of the Holy Spirit. Request to be made into a temple of the Holy Spirit.

The Torah Or

Call forth from Metatron and Melchizedek a permanent anchoring and activation of the Torah, or the divine tablets, scriptures, and documents of YHWH and his many Trees of Life. Request that this book of Light commissioned by the Ancient of Days (YHWH) now be transferred, over a period of forty days and forty nights, into your Earthly brain consciousness and four-body system as a special divine dispensation from the presence of the throne of YHWH himself. Request that this be made manifest through the power and glory of Metatron, Melchizedek, Archangel Michael, and the Council of the Elohim. Ask for this as you have never asked for anything before, so you can more perfectly reflect the glory and spiritual grandeur of God.

The Treasury of Light

Request of Metatron, Melchizedek, and Archangel Michael that you be directly connected to the Treasury of Light where the elect of the God's infinite universe work with the tablets and documents of YHWH. In receiving this sublime blessing, give your solemn oath to practice benevolence, love, and peace among your brothers and sisters and to practice the laws of God as they are practiced in the higher worlds. Call forth an anchoring, on a permanent basis, of the primordial Torah of YHWH himself.

Jesus, Moses, and Elijah

Call forth from Metatron, Melchizedek, and Archangel Michael an anchoring and activation of the wisdom exemplified by Moses, the word exemplified by Jesus, and the vehicle of Light exemplified by Elijah.

Overself Bodies

Call to Metatron, Melchizedek, and Archangel Michael for a full anchoring and activation of all your overself bodies which include the elohistic lords, the paradise sons, the Orders of the Sonship, the Christ overself-body, the overself-body leading to self-realization, and the synthesis of all vehicles.

Operation Victory

We call to Metatron, Melchizedek, and Archangel Michael to now institute Operation Victory through the high command for yourself, your family, your ashram, for the Earth herself, and for all of humanity.

Ordination by the Spirit of YHWH

Call to Metatron, Melchizedek, Archangel Michael, and the Holy Spirit, Shekinah, to be officially ordained by the spirit of YHWH as a messenger of Light with the authority to teach and demonstrate as a basic pillar and witness to the Kingdom of God.

The Celestial Marriage

Call to Metatron, Melchizedek, and Archangel Michael for the celestial marriage of personality, soul, spirit, God, and all celestial bodies lying therein! End this ceremony by chanting the words "Ehyeh Asher Ehyeh" and "Kodoish, Kodoish, Kodoish, Adonai Tsabayoth, Holy, Holy, Holy is the Lord God of Hosts!"

The Higher Kabbalah

Call to Metatron and Melchizedek for a permanent anchoring and activation of all Light packets of information from the anointing wisdom of the higher Kabbalah revealed by the living messengers of YHWH.

Scrolls of Weights and Measures

The scrolls of weights and measures, as described in *The Keys of Enoch*, are the sacred alphabet and the seventy-six names of God that hold together the structure of creation and the higher evolution.

In meditation, call forth the Sacred Scrolls of Weights and Measures and request the help of Metatron to completely anchor and activate these scrolls on a permanent basis within your multibody system.

The Seventy-six Sacred Names of Metatron

The higher Adam Kadmon body, as described in *The Keys of Enoch*, is the perfect divine blueprint body. It is actually composed on the seventy-six sacred names of Metatron. In meditation, call for the complete anchoring and activation of this higher Adam Kadmon body and of the seventy-six sacred names of Metatron so that they infuse your consciousness and four-body system (physical, astral, mental, spiritual) on a permanent basis.

The Three Seals of Creation

This Kabbalistic meditation is a little esoteric. It can be found in *The Keys of Enoch*, pages 273 to 274. That Key talks about the need break three seals to merge with the Creator. This particular technique might not be for everyone; however, I feel the insight is quite profound, even though I don't claim to understand it completely.

Invoke Metatron, requesting that the seal of the breath by the vibration of the sacred name merge with the seal of the body of creation of the higher Adam Kadmon body of Light.

Call to Metatron to break the seal of the body of consciousness so you are finally prepared to add your name to the names of the sacred who ascend to the Presence of the Throne of God. Call to Metatron and the archangels to come and receive you.

In *The Keys of Enoch* Metatron is considered the third and final seal for he is the final seal for all the bodies of Light that have descended into the lower worlds. Request now that that seal be opened and that Metatron be the bridge for you between the higher and lower worlds.

You might want to read or chant the seventy-six sacred names of Metatron while doing this meditation, even though some of them are a little hard to pronounce. I would also recommend doing the Tree of Life meditation and then doing all of the *Keys of Enoch* invocations in the same meditation for a really awesome Kabbalistic activation. Adonai!

The Ascension Angels

There are specific angels in God's infinite universe that have been given the specific focus by God of being in charge of the process of ascension. With the help of Metatron, the King of all the Angels, call forth a team of Ascension Angels to work with you on a full-time basis to help you to ascend and to help Earth and your friends and humanity as a whole to ascend. These angels, being specifically trained in this process, can be an invaluable help.

The Color Yods

Within the Yod spectrum of Light are the various color Yods, or color sequence of Yods, that will be uniquely beneficial to each person's ascension process. In this ascension technique, call forth Metatron to anchor the unique sequence of color Yods that will completely open the fifth circulatory system, which allows all chakras to share the same pulse of transfigured Light.

The Pillar of Light and the Shekinah

In meditation call forth from Metatron the anchoring of the Pillar of Light and the anchoring of the Shekinah (Holy Spirit) so that they radiate through all your bodies, building the imperishable Garment of Light so you can go through the time zones of this world into the presence of the Father's throne. Also request the anchoring and activation of the full Alpha and Omega Spectrum of Light for personal and cosmic ascension.

Star Codes of Melchizedek

Call to Metatron and Melchizedek for the anchoring and activation of the Star Codes in Melchizedek's universe that specifically relate to full God-realization on Planet Earth.

The Keys of the Melchizedek Priesthood

Call forth to Grandmaster Melchizedek, the Universal Logos, to transfer the keys of the Melchizedek priesthood that you are worthy of holding and embodying them in divine service to humanity.

Light Thresholds

Call to Metatron, Melchizedek, Michael, Jesus, Moses, and Elijah to now fully activate your Light Thresholds in the Father's program of salvation so you may completely ascend on Earth according to the blueprint of YHWH's living word and so you may be the embodiment of the collective Messiah and also become the Anointed One of the prophets, of the priests, and of heavenly Israel.

The Light Geometries

Call to Metatron and Melchizedek to fully anchor the Light geometries which can mathematically arrange each of the energy meridians to make them energize the etheric and physical vehicles.

Shekinah's Life Force

Call to Metatron and the Holy Spirit, Shekinah, to infuse your multibody system on a permanent basis with the Shekinah's Life Force so you may be prepared for the full anchoring and activation of your twelve bodies and the full completion of your seven levels of initiation.

Activation of Epi-kinetic Body

Call forth from Metatron and Melchizedek a full activation of your Epi-kinetic body and biological plasma for the ability to project and teleport between dimensions. Also ask that corresponding chakras be activated.

Eka Body Activation

Call forth Metatron and Melchizedek to fully activate your Eka body so you can develop the ability to time-travel in service of the Divine Plan.

The Rock of Salvation

Call to Metatron and Melchizedek for an anchoring of the Rock of Salvation which represents the foundation of God's wisdom in the world of form. Call forth the twelve energy foundations of the heavenly Jerusalem. Ask to become, within your own being, the altar of Jehovah which contains the wisdom codes of the Divine Plan for salvation.

Electromagnetic Coding

Call to Metatron and Melchizedek to fully anchor and activate your electromagnetic coding. Ask that your electromagnetic body be filled with Light. Ask that your physical body be coded into other regions of consciousness in this local universe. Call forth the ability to occupy all twelve bodies of Light so you may be of greater service.

The Sephirothic Knowledge

Call to Metatron and Melchizedek to be anointed with the highest triad of Sephirothic knowledge with a permanent Light grid over your head if you are deemed righteous enough to receive such a blessing.

The Divine Seed of the Elohim

Call to Metatron, Melchizedek, Archangel Michael, the Council of Elohim, and the twelve mighty elohim as a special divine dispensation to fully activate the divine seed of the elohim. Call forth this elohim seed which is the "image and similitude of divine creation." Call forth this divine thought form enclosed in a protective envelope of Light from the Treasury of Light of YHWH himself.

The Dead Sea Scrolls

Call to Melchizedek and Metatron to anchor the Light packets of information from the Dead Sea Scrolls which were the sacred teachings of YHWH and a spiritual community of Melchizedek followers. Call forth into your consciousness and multibody system those Light packets of information that are pertinent to your evolutionary progression.

The Divine Recorder Cell

Call to Melchizedek and Metatron to fully anchor and activate your divine recorder cell to work in conjunction with the Deca Delta Light emanations and the unique pyramidal energy network to facilitate the anchoring of the ten Light Superscripts of the Divine Mind.

Opening the Mind Locks

Call to Metatron and Melchizedek to bring forth the living flame geometries of color and sound with the keys of YHWH to open all mind locks in your consciousness so the divine mind of Metatron and Melchizedek can directly seed your innermost mind.

Opening the Seven Seals

Call to Metatron and Melchizedek to fully open the seven seals as described in The Keys of Enoch so you may be directly linked with the cosmic Tree of Life. Ask now to be made one with the eternal mind of the I Am at the highest cosmic level.

The Gates of Light

Call to Metatron, Melchizedek, Archangel Michael, the Sons of Light and the Sons of God, the B'nai Or and the B'nai Elohim, to fully open the Gates of Light.

The Ancient of Days

Call to be taken to the Throne of Grace to visit the Ancient of Days, the Recent of Days, and the Future of Days, YHWH himself, and call forth a special divine dispensation ascension blessing and activation. Ask to merge as fully as you are able with the Light of all Lights.

The Keys to the Universes

Call to Metatron, Melchizedek, and Michael to fully anchor and activate the keys to the Father universes, the keys to the Son universes, and the keys to the Shekinah universes.

Biological Codes for the Christ Race

Call to Metatron to anchor and activate all biological codes of the Christ race for yourself and for humanity.

Cosmic Pyramids of Light

Call to Metatron, Melchizedek, and Michael for the anchoring of the cosmic pyramids of Light for planetary and cosmic ascension activation and so you may become a whole Lightbeings.

The Structural Pattern of Living Light

Call forth Metatron and Melchizedek to fully anchor the structural pattern of living Light within your entire being and multibody system so you may become the embodiment on Earth of the Kingdom of Light.

Activation of the Messiahship Within

Call to Metatron, Melchizedek, and Archangel Michael to fully activate your Messiahship within so you can be of greater service to humanity.

Revelation of the Holy Scrolls of Burning Light

Call to Metatron, Melchizedek, and the Council of the Elohim for a revelation of the Holy Scrolls of Burning Light to be programmed into your third eye and crown chakras, a direct gift of revelation for humankind.

The Divine Plan of YHWH

Call to Metatron, Melchizedek, and Archangel Michael to now fully anchor and activate the divine plan of YHWH into our consciousness and multibody system.

The Cosmic Book of Knowledge

Call to Metatron, Melchizedek, and the Council of the Elohim for an anchoring of the Light packets of information of YHWH's Book of Knowledge at the highest cosmic level so that you may embody and demonstrate this knowledge and information on Earth as a new divine dispensation to the Shekinah universe. Call this forth directly from YHWH himself.

Removal of All Veils of Light

Request that Metatron, Melchizedek, and Archangel Michael now remove all veils of Light so you can fully know and experience the glory of God and hence can share it with your brothers and sisters in God.

Removal of the Veil of Time

Call to Metatron, Melchizedek, and Archangel Michael to remove the veil of time so you can live in both the nonlinear and linear worlds simultaneously and with no obstructions.

The Divine Attributes

Call now to Metatron, Melchizedek, and the Council of Elohim for a full-spectrum anchoring of all divine and cosmic attributes and archetypes on a permanent basis so you can more fully reflect the glory of YHWH.

The Tetragrammaton

Call forth now from Metatron and Melchizedek a special divine dispensation for the anchoring of the most blessed Hayavah, or Tetragrammaton, that it may be inscribed upon your inner mind and be the inspiration for your every thought, word, and deed.

The Throne Light Pyramid of the Next Universe

Call forth Metatron to now anchor and activate into your being the throne Light pyramid of the next universe if this prayer be in harmony with God's will. Call forth the help of Melchizedek, too, for this most sublime and sanctified blessing.

The Living Energy Codes
Call to Metatron, Melchizedek, and Archangel Michael to fully anchor and activate the living energy codes so their coded nucleic membranes can attach to the larger membrane of the universes of YHWH.

The Ophanim
Call to Metatron and the Ophanim to reveal the Glories of the Throne as the servants of living man. Call them forth as a divine dispensation for this entire physical incarnation so YHWH may be known more directly on Earth.

Scriptures of the Luminaries to Come
Call to Metatron and Melchizedek to fully anchor and activate the Light packets of information from the scriptures of the luminaries to come.

The Dove and the Serpent
Call to Archangel Michael and Metatron to fully anchor and activate the Dove of Ascension and to banish the serpent of glamour, illusion, and maya.

Codes of the Luminaries
Call forth from Metatron and Melchizedek a divine anchoring and activation of the codes of the luminaries.

The Hidden Divine Word
Call forth Metatron, Melchizedek, and the Council of the Elohim to fully anchor, as a special divine dispensation, the hidden divine word at the end of consciousness.

The Image of the Elohim
Call to Metatron and Melchizedek for the full and complete anchoring of the Image of the Elohim. Call forth the last Adam Kadmon blueprint that occurs at the end time.

The Flame of YHWH
Call forth from Metatron, Melchizedek the flame of YHWH to be fully anchored now and activated on a permanent basis forevermore. Call forth this divine dispensation from the Creator so that you may carry the flame of YHWH forevermore within your being and live in a field of glory and Light. Request this so that all you touch and serve will directly experience the "energies of great rushing" and hence upraise themselves into sons and daughters of Light and into the Great White Brotherhood. (See Key 2-1-0 in *The Keys of Enoch.*)

Light Vibrations of the Sacred Names

Call forth from Metatron and Melchizedek the Light vibrations of the sacred names of YHWH to fully anchor and activate now.

Cosmic Light Packets

Call to Melchizedek and Metatron and request the anchoring of the Light packets of information from the sacred scriptures of Metatron, the sacred scriptures of Melchizedek, the sacred scriptures of the Cosmic Council of Twelve, the archangelic sacred scriptures of Light, and the sacred scriptures of the Hyos Ha Koidesh.

Knowledge of the Next Universe

Call forth from Metatron and Melchizedek the sacred knowledge of the next universe through the wavelengths of the sacred names of Metatron. Ask that these sacred names and wavelengths be fully anchored and activated now, on a permanent basis.

Chromosome Transformation

Call forth Melchizedek and Metatron to fully anchor the geometries and color codes that will allow the structure of your chromosomes to reflect the energies of Metatron and Melchizedek across all Light time zones.

Image of the Luminaries

Call forth from Metatron and Melchizedek a permanent anchoring and activation of the image of the luminaries.

The Arc of Light and the Twelve Faces of Consciousness

Call forth from Metatron and Melchizedek the arc of Light to fully anchor and activate the twelve faces of this consciousness time zone in order to fully reveal life within life. Ask that all crystalline systems be activated within this arc of Light. Call forth the message of deliverance from the seraphim. (See Key 3-0-9 in *The Keys of Enoch.*) Also call forth the living Light grid mechanisms to transform all enzymes into the divine image of the elohim and to align properly with the third eye under the guidance of Metatron.

Quanta Mechanical Corpuscles of Light

Call forth from Metatron and Melchizedek a full anchoring and activation on a permanent basis of the Quanta Mechanical corpuscles of Light to help you fully evolve into a whole Light being. (See Key 3-1-6 in *The Keys of Enoch.*)

The First and Last I Am of YHWH

Call forth from beloved Metatron and Melchizedek the first I Am of YHWH and the last I Am of YHWH and request that this revelation be fully anchored and activated within your divine matrix now.

The Ten Pictures of Light

Lastly, call to YHWH, to the Cosmic Council of Twelve, to the twenty-four elders that surround the Throne of Grace, to the twelve mighty elohim and the Council of Elohim, to Metatron and the twelve mighty archangels, to the Hyos Ha Koidesh, to the Mahatma, to the Paradise Sons, to the creator gods, to Archangel Michael, and to Grandmaster Melchizedek, the universal teacher. Call forth a profound divine dispensation from the throne of YHWH. Call forth a permanent and full anchoring and activation of the ten pictures of Light to connect yourself and the evolving universe of your I Am to the living universe of Ehyeh Asher Ehyeh, the YHWH of the living, everlasting Light. Amen.

Kodoish, Kodoish, Kodoish Adonai Tsabayoth!
Holy, Holy, Holy is the Lord God of Hosts!

Summation

I would like to acknowledge once again J.J. Hurtak and his extraordinary *The Book of Knowledge: The Keys of Enoch*. This book served as the catalyst and inspiration for the forgoing ascension techniques. It is a book you should have in your library if you are a sincere Lightworker. The ascension techniques based upon this material will allow you to integrate vast amounts of information without having to worry about logical comprehension of much of what is being said in the text. It is a book that is meant to be read more with your right brain than with your left brain. This chapter should help to facilitate that process.

Ehyeh Asher Ehyeh!

The Ultimate Kabbalistic Huna Prayer and Meditation

Create a Huna prayer and address it to the cosmic and planetary masters you like to work with. Request a two-year anchoring and activation plan. The following list contains seventy-six cosmic activations. I recommend reading through the prayer and meditation one time to set the anchoring process in motion. The following is an example you might use.

Beloved Presence of God, YHWH, Mahatma, Council of Elohim, Metatron, twelve mighty archangels, Cosmic Council of Twelve, twenty-four elders that surround the Throne of Grace, Melchizedek, Lord of Sirius, Lord of Arcturus, Sai Baba, Vywamus, Lord Maitreya, Sanat Kumara, Djwhal Khul, Babaji, El Morya, Kuthumi, Serapis Bey, Paul the Venetian, Hilarion, Master Jesus (or Sananda), Saint Germain, Ashtar Command, Melchior, and Helios:

With all my heart and soul and mind and might I now call forth from the Throne of God, the Golden Chamber of Melchizedek, and Sanat Kumara, our Planetary Logos, a two- to five-year ascension activation program for my personal and cosmic ascension. I also request ascension activation for my core ascension group and for all sincere ascension seekers on the entire planet. I also request ascension activation for the Earth Mother if she would like to receive this blessing.

As I go through this prayer, I ask that these activations be given as I request them and that they also be programmed into the ascension seats and Light quotient building program with which I am involved and which I am officially invoking now.

I request that this program, once invoked, continue twenty-four hours a day, seven days a week, three hundred sixty-five days a year, until I achieve a 99% Light quotient, the anchoring of my fifty chakras, completion of my seven levels of initiation, the anchoring of my twelve strands of DNA, the anchoring and activation of my twelve bodies, and full God-realization on all levels. I request that this take place at night while I sleep, also. It is now time for all of humanity and the Earth to fully complete their ascension. I invoke this now!

Metatron and Melchizedek, please completely anchor and activate, this day and over the next two years until fully complete, the following seventy-six keys, as stated in *The Keys of Enoch* and in the inner-plane Book of Knowledge.

Anchor and fully activate the sixty-four Keys of Enoch on solar, galactic, universal, multi-universal, and cosmic levels in all five sacred languages.

Anchor the Deca Delta Light emanations from the ten Light Superscripts of YHWH.

Anchor the fifty chakras, the twelve bodies, and the Melchizedek diamonds and crystals.

Anchor the Nogan shells of YHWH on a permanent basis.

Anchor the divine template and the Light grid of the elohim permanently.

Anchor YHWH's Tablets of Creation.

Anchor the the cosmic Torah Or of YHWH.

Anchor the scriptures of Melchizedek.

Anchor the scriptures of Metatron.

Anchor the elohim scriptures.

Anchor the Light packets of the higher Kabbalah of YHWH and Melchizedek.

Anchor the cosmic Tree of Life permanently; open all Sephiroth.

Anchor the seventy-six sacred names of Metatron and YHWH.

Anchor YHWH's living energy codes.

Anchor YHWH's Book of Knowledge.

Anchor the gifts of the Holy Spirit as described in *The Keys of Enoch*.

Anchor the scrolls of weights and measures.

Anchor the the keys of the Melchizedek priesthood.

Anchor the highest triad of Sephirothic knowledge.

Anchor the divine seed of the elohim.

Anchor the keys to the Father, Son, and Shekinah universes.

Anchor the biological codes for the Christ race.

Anchor the scriptures of the luminaries

Anchor the codes of the luminaries.

Anchor the hidden divine word of YHWH.

Anchor the image of the elohim permanently.

Anchor the flame of YHWH on a permanent basis.

Anchor the knowledge of the next universe as described in *The Keys of Enoch*.

Anchor the ten pictures of the Light of YHWH as described in Key 64.

Anchor the entire treasury of the Light of YHWH on an ongoing, nonstop basis for the next two years until the twelve dimensions and bodies and the fifty chakras have been completed.

Illuminate permanently the seventy-two areas of the mind.

Anchor the complete Yod spectrum.

Anchor the permanent Teleshift Light Field for divine protection.

Anchor permanently the Father's Eye of Creation.

Anchor permanently the Garment of Shaddai, the Lightbody of Metatron.

Anchor the superelectrons and microtrons so they can replace all existing electrons.

Anchor the biostratus, the genetic superhelix, and the twelve strands of DNA.

Anchor Light frequencies to spiritualize our blood chemistry.

Permanently anchor Ain, Ain Soph, and Ain Soph Or.

Bestow an ordination by the spirit of YHWH.

Anchor the celestial marriage of our twelve bodies.

Please anchor the star codes of the Melchizedek universe.

Anchor Light geometries to permanently energize our etheric and physical vehicles.

Anchor divine recorder cells as described in *The Keys of Enoch*.

Give us a permanent infusion of Shekinah life force.

Let there be a baptism by the Holy Spirit.

Please open all mind locks.

Open all seven seals so we may be directly linked to the cosmic Tree of Life.

Complete the opening of the Gates of Light all the way up to YHWH and his Treasury of Light.

Anchor the cosmic pyramids of Light on a permanent basis.

Activate our Messiahship within.

Anchor the Robe of Power of Djwhal Khul.

Anchor the Robe of Power of Melchizedek.

Allow the permanent anchoring of the sword of Lord Michael.

Remove at this time all veils of Light.

Remove all veils of time.

Allow a permanent anchoring of the tetragrammaton upon our inner minds.

Allow a permanent anchoring of the Divine Plan of YHWH.

Anchor the Light pyramid of the next universe of YHWH.

Anchor and activate all living energy codes so that our nucleic membrane can attach itself to the larger membrane of the universe of YHWH.

Anchor the scriptures of luminaries to come.

Anchor the sacred geometries and color codes to transform our chromosomes into the blueprint of YHWH.

Anchor the Light packets of information from the Nag Hammadi codices and scriptures so we can develop a greater understanding of the twelve Light bodies.

Anchor on a permanent basis the electromagnetic body, Epi-kinetic body, Eka body, Gematrian body, overself body, Anointed Christ Overself body, Zohar body of Light, higher Adam Kadmon body, and the Lord's mystical body.

Permanently anchor our overself bodies (the elohistic lords, the Paradise Sons, the Orders of the Sonship, and the Christ overself body, and the overself body as described in *The Keys of Enoch*).

Permanently anchor the twelve foundations of the heavenly Jerusalem.

Anchor and activate all pertinent Light packets of information from the Melchizedek Dead Sea Scrolls.

Fully anchor and activate the structural pattern of Living Light.

Anchor the quanta mechanical corpuscles of Light.

Lastly, by the grace of God, anchor the entire Treasury of Light of YHWH.

We request that our crown chakras be directly connected by a cylinder of Light with this treasury, under the guidance of Metatron and Melchizedek. We also request that the ascension columns in our ashrams be connected with this treasury if that be in harmony with God's will.

We now pray with all our hearts and souls and minds and might that these seventy-six activations we have invoked continue now on a nonstop basis for the next two years or until the twelve levels are fully realized. We are 100% serious about what we have invoked and ask, by the grace of God and if we are deemed worthy, to be given the cosmic blessings we have asked for.

Kodoish, Kodoish, Kodoish Adonai Tsabayoth!

Holy, Holy, Holy is the Lord God of Hosts!

Our beloved subconscious minds, we hereby ask and command that you take this thought form prayer, with all the mana and vital force needed and necessary to manifest and demonstrate this prayer, to YHWH and the Cosmic Council of Twelve, the Elohim Council, and the archangelic councils through Melchizedek and Metatron.

Amen.

Beloved Presence of God, Melchizedek, Metatron, and Archangel Michael, let the Rain of Blessings fall!

Amen.

15

Cosmic Ascension

*It is through the anchoring and
activation of the fifty chakras and the twelve
bodies that true God-realization on
this plane is actualized.*

Melchizedek

This chapter contains some of the most awesome material I have ever compiled in my entire lifetime. I have attempted, with the help of Melchizedek, the Universal Logos, to put together a cosmic map that depicts the course a person travels to achieve what I am now calling cosmic ascension. It must be remembered that the ascension you are now mastering is just planetary ascension; you have not yet achieved solar, galactic, universal, multi-universal, or complete cosmic ascension at the three hundred fifty-second level of the Godhead. The cosmic map on the next page outlines the process of planetary ascension and also charts the course for full cosmic ascension through the seven cosmic planes and forty-eight dimensions of reality back to the Godhead and undifferentiated Source.

A Deeper Explanation

As you can see, this cosmic map is packed with information. I will attempt to provide a deeper explanation of what it all means.

As I have said, it is possible to anchor all fifty chakras, to build a 98.99% Light quotient, and to complete the seven levels of initiation (or twelve initiations, depending on what system you use). These are the spiritual limits for this planetary system while still incarnated in a physical body. The anchoring of the fifty chakras, the eighth- and ninth-dimensional chakra grids, takes you to the ninth dimension of reality. Ascension,

COSMIC MAP

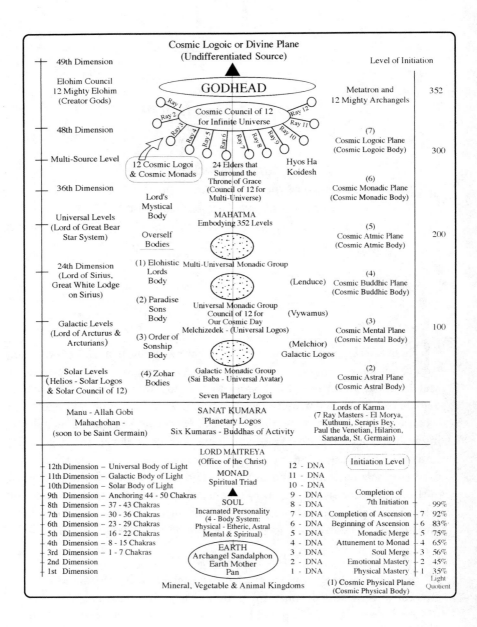

49th Dimension	**Cosmic Logoic or Divine Plane** **(Undifferentiated Source)**	Level of Initiation
Elohim Council 12 Mighty Elohim (Creator Gods)	**GODHEAD**	Metatron and 12 Mighty Archangels	352
	Cosmic Council of 12 for Infinite Universe Ray 1 – Ray 12	
48th Dimension		(7) Cosmic Logoic Plane (Cosmic Logoic Body)	300
Multi-Source Level	12 Cosmic Logoi & Cosmic Monads	Hyos Ha Koidesh	
36th Dimension	24 Elders that Surround the Throne of Grace (Council of 12 for Multi-Universe)	(6) Cosmic Monadic Plane (Cosmic Monadic Body)
	Lord's Mystical Body	
Universal Levels (Lord of Great Bear Star System)	MAHATMA Embodying 352 Levels Overself Bodies	(5) Cosmic Atmic Plane (Cosmic Atmic Body)	200
24th Dimension (Lord of Sirius, Great White Lodge on Sirius)	(1) Elohistic Multi-Universal Monadic Group Lords Body	(Lenduce) (4) Cosmic Buddhic Plane (Cosmic Buddhic Body)
Galactic Levels (Lord of Arcturus & Arcturians)	(2) Paradise Sons Body (3) Order of Sonship Body	Universal Monadic Group Council of 12 for Our Cosmic Day Melchizedek - (Universal Logos)	(Vywamus) (Melchior) Galactic Logos	(3) Cosmic Mental Plane (Cosmic Mental Body)	100
Solar Levels (Helios - Solar Logos & Solar Council of 12)	(4) Zohar Bodies	Galactic Monadic Group (Sai Baba - Universal Avatar) Seven Planetary Logoi	(2) Cosmic Astral Plane (Cosmic Astral Body)
Manu - Allah Gobi Mahachohan - (soon to be Saint Germain)	SANAT KUMARA Planetary Logos Six Kumaras - Buddhas of Activity	Lords of Karma (7 Ray Masters - El Morya, Kuthumi, Serapis Bey, Paul the Venetian, Hilarion, Sananda, St. Germain)

	LORD MAITREYA (Office of the Christ)		Initiation Level
12th Dimension – Universal Body of Light		12 - DNA	
11th Dimension – Galactic Body of Light	MONAD	11 - DNA	
10th Dimension – Solar Body of Light	Spiritual Triad	10 - DNA	Completion of
9th Dimension – Anchoring 44 - 50 Chakras		9 - DNA	7th Initiation	99%
8th Dimension – 37 - 43 Chakras	SOUL	8 - DNA	Completion of Ascension	7	92%
7th Dimension – 30 - 36 Chakras	Incarnated Personality	7 - DNA	Beginning of Ascension	6	83%
6th Dimension – 23 - 29 Chakras	(4 - Body System: Physical - Etheric, Astral	6 - DNA	Monadic Merge	5	75%
5th Dimension – 16 - 22 Chakras	Mental & Spiritual)	5 - DNA	Attunement to Monad	4	65%
4th Dimension – 8 - 15 Chakras	EARTH	4 - DNA	Soul Merge	3	56%
3rd Dimension – 1 - 7 Chakras	Archangel Sandalphon	3 - DNA	Emotional Mastery	2	45%
2nd Dimension	Earth Mother	2 - DNA	Physical Mastery	1	35%
1st Dimension	Pan	1 - DNA		Light
	Mineral, Vegetable & Animal Kingdoms		(1) Cosmic Physical Plane (Cosmic Physical Body)	Quotient

remember, is the fifth dimension of reality; the seventh initiation is the sixth dimension of reality. It is the anchoring of these higher chakra grids that allows you to incorporate the higher dimensions even though your initiations stop until you complete your mission on Earth. Melchizedek has recently said that it is actually possible to anchor through the twelfth dimension on this plane.

There is a very important distinction that must be made having to do with the difference among actualizing, activating, and anchoring. The limits of planetary ascension are such that it is possible to actualize the seven levels of initiation, to activate the fifty chakras, and to anchor the twelve dimensions. So in a sense, you are allowed to go higher than the seven levels of initiation, even though you will not be able to fully actualize those levels while still in a physical body. You can, however, activate and anchor the higher levels. You are laying the foundation for future evolutionary progress, which will make it much easier to pass through the higher initiations, beyond the seventh, when you continue your cosmic evolution.

The Twelve Bodies

You can integrate dimensions ten through twelve, which go beyond even the fifty chakras, by anchoring and integrating your twelve bodies into your current nine-body system. The four-body system includes the physical, astral, mental, and spiritual bodies; I refer to nine bodies because after you complete your seven levels of initiation and anchor and activate your fifty chakras, that is what will have been incorporated. The nine bodies are as follows:

Physical/Etheric body
Astral body
Mental body
Spiritual body

Expanded understanding has now made it clear that the spiritual body is itself made up of nine bodies:

1. Buddhic body
2. Atmic body
3. Monadic body
4. Logoic body

These first seven are connected to the seven subplanes of the cosmic physical plane. The next two bodies are the

5. Group soul body of Light
6. Group monadic body of Light

Remember, when you integrate the tenth ray, you anchor the body of Light. There are, in actuality, two bodies of Light:

the soul and the monadic bodies of Light. The soul body of Light is integrated at the third initiation; the monadic body of Light is integrated at the fifth, sixth, and seventh initiations. The final three bodies to anchor and integrate are the

7. Solar body of Light
8. Galactic body of Light
9. Universal body of Light.

These three bodies, as they are integrated, allow you to incorporate what might be called the twelve levels, or the twelve dimensions.

As you see, at this point you are going beyond planetary mastery and planetary ascension for the first time and are moving now toward solar, galactic, and universal attunement. It must be understood here that the anchoring and integration of these three bodies make up only the first baby steps toward attuning to the highest levels; in actuality, according to Melchizedek, there are forty-eight dimensions of reality on the way back to Source.

The Forty-eight Dimensions of Reality

The forty-eight dimensions between here and the Godhead are the same as the three hundred fifty-two levels of the Mahatma and the same as the seven cosmic planes. Remember that the level you are working on here is the cosmic *physical* plane; there are seven cosmic planes. The ninth initiation (in Djwhal Khul's system, the eight and ninth initiations cannot be taken while in a physical body) signifies the time when you graduate from the cosmic physical plane and go on to the cosmic astral plane, or cosmic mental universe.

The seven cosmic planes are:

Cosmic physical plane
Cosmic astral plane
Cosmic mental plane
Cosmic buddhic plane
Cosmic atmic plane
Cosmic monadic plane
Cosmic logoic plane

While on Earth, you are evolving only through the first plane, not having even entered the next six. That is why Vywamus has said that completing the seven levels of initiation means having moved scarcely three-quarters of one inch up a ten-inch ruler.

In summary: the forty-eight dimensions, the three hundred fifty-two levels of the Mahatma, and the seven cosmic planes are all the same thing.

Melchizedek has said that after you evolve through the forty-eight dimensions, there is a final transfer that takes place to what he calls the forty-ninth dimension, and it is there that you merge with the Godhead.

There is some overlapping that takes place, however: the solar levels are at approximately levels nine through eighteen; the galactic levels are at approximately levels twelve through twenty-four; the universal levels are at approximately levels twenty-four through thirty-six; and the multi-universal levels back to Source are approximately levels thirty-six through forty-eight.

The Twelve Strands of DNA

The twelve strands of DNA are related to the twelve dimensions of reality. The first step is to move them into the etheric body. The next step is to anchor them into the physical body. This cannot be fully accomplished until you have anchored the twelve bodies. The twelve bodies allow the first attunement to the more cosmic levels of evolution.

Misunderstanding about the Light Quotient

As I have already stated, the highest Light quotient that can be achieved while still in a physical body is 98.99%. How can this be if you are still only one inch up a ten-inch ruler? It is because that percentage applies only to this planetary school. When the same scale is applied to the full cosmic school of God's infinite universe, then reaching the 98.99% Light quotient level means you are really at only the 8% to 10% level on the cosmic scale. The above scale applies to every single person on Planet Earth – with two exceptions: the Lord Maitreya and Sai Baba. These two beings are the two highest beings, in a spiritual sense, on this planet, according to Djwhal Khul. Lord Maitreya holds 10% Light quotient on the cosmic scale. This is enormous. No being has ever held this much Light while retaining a physical body, except one. That is Sai Baba, whose Light quotient is 31% on the cosmic scale. This was told us by the Lord Maitreya himself.

After you graduate from this Earthly school and go on to cosmic evolution, you will switch over to the cosmic scale. On the planetary-level scale, 98.99% does not even reach the solar level, let alone the galactic or universal level. Melchizedek is somewhere around the thirty-sixth dimension or thereabouts, being a universal avatar. Lord Maitreya is working in the twelfth through the twenty-fourth dimensions. It is only an avatar (one who is God-realized at birth) who can come in at a level higher than that of the system with which all other beings on a planet are working.

It also must be understood that no one from the three hundred fifty-second level has ever incarnated on this plane of existence. First, there is no reason for that to happen; and second, Earth is not sufficiently evolved for it even to be considered. With Sai Baba on the planet now, it is the first time a universal avatar has ever physically incarnated. Sai Baba has said that he is a seventeen-point avatar in the Hindu system and that such an incarnation has never before occurred in the history of this planet. That is a direct quote from Sai Baba himself.

Many spiritual schools and religions on this planet think they are attuning to or have reached the ultimate level; in truth, that is illusion. As Sai Baba has said so eloquently, "God is blocked by the mountain range of ego." The Lightworkers on the planet must be discerning in regard to such matters.

Even Sai Baba is less than one-third of the way through his cosmic evolution. The signs of his achievement are his totally unconditional love, his egolessness, his complete selflessness, and his ability to materialize physical objects at will, right out of the ethers, which is a God-given ability, not any form of magic or reliance on devas or spirit guides. He can teleport and can even create two physical bodies simultaneously. He has absolute omnipotence, omniscience, and omnipresence. These are the characteristics of a true avatar. The same could be said of the Lord Maitreya.

The Cosmic Monadic Level

You merge with your monad when you achieve your ascension; that is what ascension is. It is the fusion of personality, soul, and monad in the physical body. There is also, however, a cosmic monadic level on the higher planes. As you evolve into the cosmic levels of evolution, monads group together, forming in a sense, larger monads.

It would probably be helpful to start at the top of creation.

At the very pinnacle of creation, there is the Godhead, or undifferentiated Source. Right below the Godhead is the cosmic Council of Twelve for the infinite omniverse. The Council of Twelve for this universe is at a much lower level on the ladder of creation than is the cosmic Council of Twelve, and that is another confusion among many Lightworkers.

There are many councils of twelve, each at a different dimensional level. Above the Council of Twelve for this Cosmic Day is another Council of Twelve for the multi-universes. Extending from the Council of Twelve at the cosmic level are twelve rays. The twelve rays worked with on Earth are so stepped-down that they have little or no resemblance to the twelve cosmic rays. They are stepped-down in voltage from the multi-universal level through the universal level, through the galactic level, through the solar level, and down to Planet Earth. The voltage here is only one-tenth of what it is on the cosmic level.

Extending from the cosmic Council of Twelve are what might be called the cosmic monads. Melchizedek has said there are twelve of them, and there are twelve cosmic logoi who are in charge of these monads. All monads, or I Am Presences, come from one of the twelve cosmic monads. The microcosm is like the macrocosm: on a planetary level each monad creates twelve souls who then create twelve personalities who incarnate; on the cosmic level it is the same.

Moving down the hierarchical ladder of creation, you can see the breakdown of the twelve original cosmic monads. At each level there is a god or logos who is in charge of the expansion from Source. Melchizedek has said that it is possible to call for the anchoring of and to merge with your galactic and universal monadic groups. I have recently begun doing this myself and I recommend it.

After the Council of Twelve, Melchizedek said that there are the twenty-four elders that surround the Throne of Grace. There are also the Council of the Elohim, the seven mighty elohim, Metatron, who is the head of the archangels, and the seven mighty archangels. The Arcturians operate out of the very high galactic levels as does the Great White Lodge on Sirius, but both have easy access to the higher universal levels. Vywamus operates out of the higher galactic and universal levels and Lenduce out of levels higher still.

Sanat Kumara, Vywamus, and Lenduce form the ultimate trinity for this planetary system. Lord Maitreya, who is on Earth and living in London, just precipitated a physical body out of the ethers. Sai Baba, having incarnated into a baby's body, will remain here until around 2025 A.D. Then he will go to the spirit world for two years and then will return in a triple avatar incarnation. His name in his future incarnation will be Prema Sai Baba.

Forty-three universes make up the Source of this Cosmic Day. The Cosmic Day for this universe is 4.3 billion years long; 3.1 billion years have passed, so in 1.2 billion years, this Cosmic Day will be closed down and will return to a Cosmic Night which may or may not last as long. The Cosmic Night will be a time of incubation and inner activity before the next Cosmic Day begins.

A Warning to Lightworkers

Some schools of spiritual thought that are in touch with cosmic levels teach that it is all right to see as unimportant and to ignore the Spiritual Hierarchy and the planetary leaders — Sanat Kumara, Lord Maitreya, El Morya, Kuthumi, Djwhal Khul, Paul the Venetian, Serapis Bey, Hilarion, Jesus (Sananda), and Saint Germain. Those schools believe that because they have gone beyond that level, it is not important. This can also be true of the Solar Hierarchy and even of the Galactic Hierarchy, in some cases.

This is an improper attitude and it will backfire. It is like being at the junior high school level and saying you are not going to listen to or respect your high school or college teachers, but will pay attention only to professors with Ph.D.s. That is not the way the universe works, and it is a manifestation of the negative ego. As Djwhal Khul has said, there are many glamours on the spiritual path that you must watch out for.

There is absolutely nothing wrong with working with the cosmic teachers, and I highly recommend it. You must, however, know your place in the hierarchical scheme of things. You must not try to skip a level of schooling.

Every person on Earth, whether you like it or not, is connected to one of the seven ashrams of the seven chohans of the seven rays. Which one you are connected with usually has to do with the ray configuration of your monad and soul. There is a lot of overlap in the work of the different ashrams and where you are is determined by individual preference and by your attunement at any given time in your life. The key is to work on all three levels simultaneously, not try to skip the lower ones. For example, I work out of Djwhal Khul's ashram on the first level, and then I work with Lord Maitreya on the next level up, whilst simultaneously working a lot with the Arcturians and the Great White Lodge on the galactic level and also with Melchizedek, the archangels, and others at the cosmic level. I love the cosmic levels the most, and I would not be telling the truth if I did not admit it. However, I do not try to skip the Spiritual Hierarchy or any other level. If you do, it will actually slow down your progress, not speed it up. The key word here is integration.

Just because you have ascended, it does not mean that your mental body has perfect understanding. It does not mean that you are clear of the distortions and glamours of the negative ego. It does not mean that your emotional body or even your physical body is totally clear, either. It is time to let go of the myths and fantasies about what ascension really is.

Some ascended masters you meet who come into the forefront of public attention will have great abilities to bring in Light. Others will have a clear mental and psychological understanding of things. Others will have a clear emotional understanding. Still others will bring through healing abilities. Some will have great channeling abilities, others accurate clairvoyance, and others high teachings. Those in the true vanguard will have combinations of these. None will have everything, no matter what they say. Be discerning. Use your own intuition. Take the best from each teacher with whom you work and throw out the rest.

Just because a particular ascended teacher you work with has a big ego or has some distortion in his or her mental or emotional understanding or has some health lessons in no way discounts the possibility that he or she might have some information of great value to offer you. Do not get caught up in perfectionism or there will be no teachers for you, including yourself.

Ascension and the completion of the seven levels of initiation and incorporation of the twelve dimensions does not mean perfection or perfect integration or mastery on all levels. Ascended masters will have strengths and weaknesses in different areas, depending on their ray types and other factors too numerous to account for. The ideal is to be balanced and integrated and to master and perfect all levels. This is easier said than done, I am sure you will agree. Watch out for the negative ego which will tell you that you have done it when, in truth, you have not. The ones who have done it are at the forty-ninth dimension of reality and at the three hundred fifty-second level of the Godhead; they have achieved cosmic ascension, not merely planetary ascension!

The Lightbody

There is a lot of discussion about the Lightbody among Lightworkers around the planet, and that is good. Basically, the Lightbody grows as you build your Light quotient and is completed when you reach the 98.99% Light quotient level and also fully anchor and merge with your soul Lightbody, your monadic Lightbody, your solar Lightbody, your galactic Lightbody, and your universal Lightbody.

When the universal Lightbody is anchored and merged with, the physical body becomes more etheric in substance, even though it can still be seen. That is when you become able to teleport to the inner-plane ashrams and attend meetings in your physical body. At that point you can also teleport the physical body anywhere on the physical planet and you can materialize objects. Having the ability to do these things tells you that you have merged with your universal Lightbody. Make the building of your Lightbody one of your prime focuses on the path to ascension.

The Great Central Sun

There is frequent use of the term "the Great Central Sun" among Lightworkers, but there is also a lot of confusion about what it means. The reason for this confusion is that there are a great number of great central suns, not just one: there is the solar Great Central Sun, the galactic Great Central Sun, the universal Great Central Sun, the multi-universal Great Central Sun, and the ultimate cosmic Great Central Sun which, in essence, is the Godhead. This is a wonderful term; however, it is important to be clear about which one you are referring to.

The Atomic Body

The atomic body is the body that contains the atoms. You want your atomic body to be filled not only with the monadic energies, but also with the solar, galactic, and universal energies. Request, in meditation, that the atomic body be filled with the microtrons, which are a refined level of spiritual energy and spiritual current. Ask for this specifically from Metatron.

The Cosmic Stations

A universal-level invocation I recommend is the invocation of the anchoring of the twelve heavenly astrological houses and the twelve Cosmic Stations. This is guaranteed to accelerate your spiritual progression.

The Mantle of the Christ

Call forth in meditation from Melchizedek, Melchior, Helios, and Sanat Kumara the universal, galactic, solar, and planetary anchoring of the Mantle of the Christ.

The Cosmic Threefold Flame

Call forth Archangel Michael for the anchoring of the cosmic Blue Sword of power and manifestation. It is blue in color with lightning bolts coming out of it. Call for it to empower you to manifest your service work into the world. Anchor this sword into your right hand.

Secondly, call forth the Divine Mother energies to anchor into your left hand the pink and magenta rose of cosmic love which serves to balance the cosmic power you now hold in your right hand.

Thirdly, call forth the cosmic golden scroll and golden robe of Melchizedek which embody the cosmic wisdom. See the golden scroll come in through your crown chakra. This golden scroll, hence, forms a triangle at the top of your head with the blue sword and the pink-magenta rose of the Divine Mother. You have now anchored the cosmic and planetary threefold flame of divinity.

Archangel Michael's Robe of Protection

Call to Archangel Michael. Request that his divine robe of protection be placed around you at all times throughout this incarnation, allowing in only the energies of the Christ.

The Twelve Bodies and Your Spiritual Name

Each of your three higher bodies on the solar, galactic, and universal levels is connected to an aspect of yourself that is already functioning on those levels, just as your own higher self and monad are living beings and spiritual intelligences. In meditation, go first to the monadic level, the level of your Mighty I Am Presence, and ask for your spiritual name. Then call forth and travel up to your solar, galactic, and universal Lightbodies and see if you can get your universal name.

You might consider changing your name legally to that name or just using that name inwardly or with your friends. My name, Joshua David, is not the original name given me at birth. Approximately fifteen years ago I changed my name to Joshua which is my monadic and universal name on the inner planes. Doing this had a very profound effect on me and people I had known my whole life told me immediately that I looked like a Joshua. The name I was given at birth was a good name for the earlier part of my life. However, as I started to evolve I needed a name I could grow into, one that contained my full spiritual potential. Even if you do not change your name officially, I would recommend connecting with your universal name, for it is a touchstone for connecting with this aspect of self.

Anchoring the Divine Mother and Father Energies

In the process of my final review of this book before I sent it to the publisher, I was inwardly guided that the book was quite complete but that the one area that needed to be represented a little bit more strongly was that of the Goddess and Divine Mother energies. In considering this point, I decided to call my dear friend Caryn to share the guidance I had received. We brainstormed a bit over the phone, and she volunteered to write a meditation that would truly honor the Goddess and the Divine Mother in perfect balance with the Divine Father energies.

It seems appropriate that Caryn and I, as female and male, would collaborate to write a meditation that would honor both energies in their perfect, divine balance. This meditation is a little bit longer than most of the other meditations in this book, but because the Goddess and Divine Mother energies are so neglected in this world, I am giving her a prime spot in this book as a way of honoring her on both Earthly and spiritual levels.

Divine Mother and Father Energies Meditation

Please place yourself in a bubble of golden-white Light. Now call upon your twelve personal archangels to guide, guard, and protect you in love, Light, and life.

Call upon any of the Divine Mother/Father energies to assist you in this integration and balancing process: call upon Mary and Jesus, Nada and Sananda, Quan Yin and Buddha, Isis and Osiris, Athena and Ashtar, Lakshmi and Vishnu, Radha and Krishna, Sita and Rama, Parvati and Shiva, Chandra (the Moon) and Surya (the Sun), or the Divine Mother/Father energies from the Source.

See before you the pink flame. the pink rose, and the pink lotus. The pink flame, rose, and lotus represent the divine Mother, Goddess, yin, receptive, sensitive, gentle, caring, loving energies.

Starting at your feet, allow the pink flame, rose, and lotus to rise gently up your left side, stopping at the left side of your heart chakra. Here, at the left side of your heart chakra, allow the pink lotus energies to overlay the pink rose energies. Send the pink flame through the center of these divine, loving, Goddess-flower energies. As the pink flame burns through the center of these beautiful flowers, the petals open slowly, anchoring these divine, pink, loving Mother energies more fully in your heart chakra. Take the pink flame now and spread it through your many-body system. Please pause for a moment and allow these divine pink Mother energies to fully integrate.

See before you now the blue flame, the blue rose, the blue lotus. The blue flame, rose, and lotus represent the divine Father, God, yang, outgoing, externalizing, energetic, powerful energies.

Starting at your feet allow the blue flame, rose, and lotus to rise gently up your right side, stopping at the right side of your heart chakra. Here, at the right side of your heart chakra allow the blue lotus energies to overlay the blue rose energies. Send the blue flame through the center of these divine Father-flower energies. As the blue flame burns through the center of these flowers, the petals open gently, anchoring more fully the divine Father energies within your heart. Now take this divine blue flame and spread it through your entire many-body system. Please pause for a moment to allow this divine integration and balancing to take place.

See before you the golden flame, the golden rose, and the golden lotus. The golden flame, rose, and lotus represent the divine Christed energies, the Christ Consciousness, the Mantle of the Christ, and the Christed wisdom.

Starting at your feet, allow the golden Christed energies, the golden flame, rose, and lotus, to rise up the center of your body, stopping at the upper center area of the heart chakra. The pink flame, rose, and lotus are on the left. The blue flame, rose, and lotus are on the right. The golden flame, rose, and lotus are at the upper center, forming a triangle. This important trinity is referred to as the threefold flame of power (blue), love (pink), and wisdom (gold).

Allow the golden lotus energies to overlay the golden rose energies. Now bring the golden flame through the center of this divine flower. The golden flame allows the petals of the golden flowers to open, gently anchoring the divine Christed energies more fully in your heart.

Now please send the golden Christed flame energies through your many-body system, anchoring the Mantle of the Christ in your expansive body realities. Please pause, allowing the divine Christed energies to fully integrate and balance.

Now focus once again upon your heart chakra. See the triangular trinity of the threefold flames: pink (the love flame) on the left, blue (the power flame) on the right, and golden (the Christ flame) at the upper center. At the same time, see the correlating rose and lotus flowers. The three flames should be evenly burning, extending one and one-half to two inches out. If they are not burning evenly, enhance or fan the flames so that they are. Pause for a moment to feeling the divine inner balance and integration.

The focus of this Golden Age is the heart. When you speak from this divinely balanced heart platform your world is filled with greater joy, harmony, and peace. you are truly operating from a positon in which there can be expansive, loving cocreation.

Now visualize a heart before you. Place the three flames within the heart, and send the heart to the center of the Earth. Spin the heart with the threefold flame within it. This will help the Earth, Gaia, receive a divine balancing. Now expand the heart, letting it surround the Earth so that the Earth and all of her inhabitants receive this divine balance as well.

Now simultaneously send St. Germain's Violet Flame to the center of the Earth and through your twelve-body system. Transmute any negative or discordant energies. Continue expanding the Violet Flame so that all of the Earth and her inhabitants are transmuted, as the balanced threefold flame burns evenly in your body and throughout the entire Earth.

Now visualize a pink heart. Send it to the center of the Earth. That pink heart represents your infinite, limitless love, the Divine Mother energy. Expand the heart so that your love encompasses the entire Earth. Now release the pink heart and let it flow into a liquid pink. Please surround, embrace, and hold the Earth and all of her inhabitants with your expansive, limitless, liquid pink love.

The Attainment of the Fifth Dimension

It must be understood that a million people in the history of the Earth have ascended. They have attained the fifth dimension and even moved beyond it to the sixth dimension. It is not a new phenomenon, Djwhal Khul has told us; the only thing that is new is the number of people who are ascending in a mass wave. This began to occur at the Wesak Festival of 1995, May 14th.

The Earth Mother

I have a special request of all Lightworkers on the planet who read this book: every time you meditate and go to the ascension seats, call in your higher chakras, build your Light quotient, and ask for acceleration, ask that it all be done also for the Earth Mother, Gaia. She is in exactly the same kind of evolutionary process humans are in but on a planetary level. Make her part of your core group; make her your ascension buddy. As your fifty chakras are anchored, hers will be anchored, too. It is such an easy thing to do . . . and the effects on her, if everyone bands together to do this, will be extraordinary.

Earth has taken such abuse from humanity; this is a divine gift humanity can offer to Earth as recompense. One of my new projects is to get all the Lightworkers around the planet to do this. I talked to Melchizedek about this and he said it would be a wonderful idea. I know the Earth Mother will be very grateful. Join me in this cause so she can complete her seven levels of initiation and so she can merge with her twelve dimensional bodies and her twelve planetary strands of DNA and all the rest. I feel her joy and gratefulness as I speak of this. Share the idea with all your friends and spread it around the planet: the Earth Mother, Gaia, is now your new ascension buddy in all your spiritual work!

Cosmic Axiatonal Alignment

In meditation, call not only for a planetary axiatonal alignment, but also call for a cosmic axiatonal alignment. While you are at it, call forth the anchoring and activation of the Zohar body of Light, the Kabbalistic term for the higher Lightbodies. Sometimes certain words act as triggers to activate certain energies, and the Zohar body of Light is certainly one of these. Also call forth the energies of full completion of your seven levels of initiation.

Council of Twelve Ascension Activation

Call directly to the Beloved Presence of God, the cosmic Council of Twelve, the twenty-four elders, the twelve cosmic logoi, Mahatma, the twelve mighty elohim, Metatron, and the twelve mighty archangels for an ultimate cosmic and planetary ascension activation for yourself, for your core ascension group, for the Earth Mother, and for all sincere ascension seekers and candidates on the planet in all ashrams of the Christ.

The Cosmic Great Pyramid Meditation

This meditation is specifically designed to help you anchor your twelve bodies, most specifically your monadic, solar, galactic, and universal bodies of Light.

Begin the meditation by calling on Thoth, Melchizedek, the Lord of Sirius, the Lord of Arcturus, Isis, and Osiris. Call forth your core ascension group to join you and also request that the Earth Mother join you so she can receive her twelve planetary bodies. Before continuing this meditation, refer to the ultimate ascension meditation in chapter nine and slowly call in all the energies listed there. This will get you warmed up and plugged in.

Then specifically request the anchoring of your twelve bodies. The key to this meditation is to anchor the bodies one at a time. Many of you have probably already anchored seven or eight of them, if not more. If you have not ascended yet, begin with the atomic body; then anchor the monadic body, the logoic body, the solar body of Light, the galactic body of Light, and the universal body of Light. If you have already ascended, then start with the solar body of Light, and anchor the last three cosmic bodies.

Another key to this meditation is to do it slowly. Take at least ten minutes for each body. These bodies look like actual beings who are already living and operating on the higher levels. Melchizedek told me that the specific occurrence that allowed us to tap into this level was my creation of the Tree of Life meditation. That was the trigger that told these higher bodies that we were ready to anchor them permanently. If you have not done that meditation, do it first, before doing this one.

Go to the ascension seats in the King's Chamber of the Great Pyramid. Call in the solar body of Light, for example, and ask that it permanently anchor and activate. It will slowly descend and merge. You might experience a kind of spiritual lightning that helps to facilitate the alchemical transformation. Also call forth the fire letters, key codes, and sacred geometries that go with each body. Each of the bodies will serve to bridge worlds and to create your personal connection to more expansive states of consciousness.

When the solar body of Light fully anchors along with the fire letters, visualize the pyramid, which is actually a double pyramid (in other words, there is an upsidedown pyramid going into the Earth; the pyramid, hence, looks like a diamond merkabah). Request that the Great Pyramid and/or diamond merkabah pyramid begin spinning in a clockwise motion to help you integrate this body. Then see a second merkabah spinning in the opposite direction simultaneously. (I talked about that previously as a tool for teleporting.) Let them spin for at least seven minutes, or longer if necessary.

Call on the Arcturians to use their advanced technology to help you. The body of Light that is coming in is like a grid, and this new grid must be united with your existing grids. The Arcturians have technologies that can help in this process. You can also call on Vywamus for help, as well as calling on Thoth and Melchizedek.

When the solar body is anchored, request that the merkabah pyramid stop spinning. Then go through the exact same process for the galactic body of Light. It looked to me like a white-robed being when it came in. Caryn's and my bodies of Light were attending a meeting in the Great

White Lodge on Sirius, so it took a few minutes for them to come in. Go through the same process: ask for the corresponding fire letters, key codes, and sacred geometries; then spin the merkabah and wait about seven minutes, or more if you like. Then stop the spinning.

Call forth the universal body of Light from Melchizedek, along with the corresponding key codes, fire letters, and sacred geometries. Request that the merkabah spin again, and again wait seven minutes. When that is complete, you are ready for the next step.

Once again, call in the energies listed in the ultimate ascension meditation. This time you should incorporate them all at a much higher level. Then spin the merkabah one more time to integrate that which you have invoked.

When that is complete, request that the Great Pyramid, or the diamond merkabah, move upward as though it were on an elevator and connected by a line of Light from Earth to the Godhead. This line of Light connects you with the forty-eight dimensions of reality. At the level of schooling present on Earth, this meditation should focus on the twelve dimensions of reality and twelve bodies that take you to the level of Melchizedek, the Universal Logos. Going beyond that would be unrealistic; you would not be able to actualize it, so there is really no purpose in trying. It is better to focus on that which realistically can be actualized and integrated. So Melchizedek has told us.

After you invoke it, you will experience the Great Pyramid, or diamond merkabah, moving very slowly upward from the fourth dimension to the twelfth dimension. You are still inside the pyramid in the King's Chamber. The energies will build and diffuse as you incorporate each level. Request that the process continue until it is complete.

Currently, the incorporation of the cosmic bodies seems to be a seven-day process. Realize that you can do it in a bilocated state of consciousness — in other words, after your regular meditation, ask that the process continue in your spiritual body while your physical self relaxes, does chores, eats dinner, watches television, and so on.

At the end of this meditation you will have the experience of being merged with all twelve dimensions of reality through the merger with your twelve bodies. An aspect of each of these higher bodies will remain permanently with you, although it will take a little time to fully integrate all the energies and consciousnesses of the bodies.

Sai Baba is the only being on the entire Earth who has not only merged with all twelve dimensions, but has also taken the initiations that fully actualize that level. That is why he is referred to as the Cosmic Christ.

Continue to invoke these bodies in every meditation you do, and see yourself within your mental and emotional bodies as a planetary, solar, galactic, universal, and even cosmic citizen through not only the physical universes but also through all universes and all dimensions of reality. See all extraterrestrial species, no matter what they look like, as brothers and sisters in Christ.

I am now referring to the ultimate cosmic Christ at the highest cosmic level; Sai Baba and the Lord Maitreya are stepped-down reflections of that level. It is time to expand your limited thinking about who and what you think you are. In truth, there is a body and fully realized aspect of yourself already functioning at the three hundred fifty-second level of the Godhead just waiting for you to expand yourself through the initiation process and realize all the different levels so it, too, can merge with you. The integration of your twelve bodies is a major step in this direction.

Many of the integrations in this book will allow you to move through your future initiations more quickly once you leave this physical body. After you achieve all the limits of planetary mastery (99% Light quotient, fifty chakras, completion of seventh initiation, twelve bodies, twelve dimensions, twelve strands of DNA) you will then be ready to apply the same principles to the macrocosm. You will start over, in a sense, and begin working on your cosmic Light quotient, cosmic chakras, cosmic initiations, cosmic dimensions, and the integration of your higher cosmic bodies in a more actualized manner. The process will be very similar, for the microcosm is like the macrocosm, as Thoth-Hermes said.

The one major difference will be that you won't have a dense physical body and you will no longer be operating within linear time. The focus of your service work will be more expansive. Each level, as you move up in your evolution, has a kind of ring-pass-not. You must demonstrate your ability to master each level before you are allowed to expand to the next level of service. Each initiation you take is just an expansion of your spiritual size, of the focus of your spiritual service work, and of the amount of Light you are able to hold. Can you imagine – on a cosmic scale, you are holding only between 6% and 8% Light. You will eventually evolve back to the Godhead and hold 100% Light; that is the cosmic Divine Plan.

If you are familiar with Sai Baba, you know what a being holding 31% cosmic Light can do. (See the chapter about him in *The Complete Ascension Manual*). It is far beyond what even Jesus and Lord Maitreya did together two thousand years ago. You will all do these things and more, for that is your cosmic destiny.

The Seventy-two Areas of the Mind

The Keys of Enoch refers to the seventy-two areas of the mind. In meditation, call forth Melchizedek and Archangel Jophiel to illuminate, on a permanent basis, the seventy-two areas of the mind.

Anchoring the Higher Bodies

Soon after learning about the potential of anchoring and integrating solar, galactic, and universal Lightbodies, I dreamed that I found a ring that had one very beautiful diamond in it and space for three others that were missing and, in a sense, waiting to be filled in. The meaning was quite clear: the diamond that was present in the ring was symbolic of the fact that I had just realized the planetary Lightbody by completing the seven levels of initiation, stabilizing the 98% Light quotient, and actualizing the thirty-six chakras, having installed the eighth- and ninth-dimensional chakra grids (the fifty chakras) and having anchored the nine bodies (physical, astral, mental, Buddhic, atmic, monadic, logoic, soul body of Light, and monadic body of Light), and the twelve strands of DNA. The three empty settings represented the solar body of Light, the galactic body of Light, and the universal body of Light. (We had been invoking the solar body of Light for some time, but I came to realize that these last three bodies do not anchor until the planetary body is complete.)

In my meditations, the complete planetary body looked like an actual skin, or layer, of fire letters surrounding the entire body. I came to realize that the key to anchoring and building the next three bodies is to work specifically with the logos in charge of each level. Since we were working on the solar body, it made sense to work with Helios. When that body was complete I would then work with Melchior and the Lord of Sirius on the next level up, and after that, with Melchizedek and also Sai Baba for the universal body.

Caryn, Marcia, and I were all very excited about this process, because it was the first time we had transcended this planetary system in terms of true realization. We had invoked the cosmic levels thousands of times, but we had not previously attained a sufficient level of initiation and Light quotient to be ready to anchor and fully integrate the next step. As with the higher chakras, the first step is to call to the masters on the inner plane and have them anchor, or install, the grids for the three cosmic bodies. The next step is to fill them in, so to speak. Have the logos at that level work with you on a permanent, twenty-four-hour-a-day basis until it is complete.

I do not yet have a sense of how long this will take, but I have a feeling that the entire process is going to move along at a much faster pace than I had originally expected. The key to all spiritual work is to be efficient and ask directly for what you want. Have the masters work twenty-four hours a day, seven days a week until that has been completed, and then begin working on the next level.

The process of spiritual growth is not really complicated. It is just that most people have not known what to ask for. That is why I have written this book. It cannot be put more simply: just make the requests outlined herein, and let the masters do the rest. But they are not allowed to do this work unless you ask for it, for they are not allowed to interfere with free choice. After making the invocations, your job is to focus on your service work and on demonstrating God in your daily life.

Dematerialization Practice

Do the ultimate ascension meditation and at the end of it, while in the Golden Chamber of Melchizedek (or in the ashram of Djwhal Khul or that of one of the chohans of the seven rays) ask for the master's help in learning to dematerialize. That is the first step in the practice of teleporting. It feels really good and the amount of energy that comes in is incredible!

The Logos of the Great Bear Star System

The Logos of the Great Bear Star System is the higher aspect — the cosmic level — of the Lord of Sirius and the Great White Lodge, who is the higher aspect of the Solar Logos, Helios. They could be likened to the personality, soul, and monad. Ask, in meditation, to tune into this great and majestic being, the Lord of the Great Bear Star System; request anchoring and merger with his great energy and request an ascension blessing and acceleration. Call forth a direct experience of his energy. Request to be permanently aligned with his energy. Request that the energies of the Great Bear Star System, the Lord of Sirius and the Great White Lodge, and the Solar Logos, Helios, form a trinity of guidance for you and be incorporated into your being. Also request that your consciousness be aligned and merged with the seven great beings who ensoul the seven stars of the Great Bear Star System.

Cosmic Anchoring of the Divine Masculine and Feminine

Call forth the anchoring of and merger with the perfected divine archetypes of feminine and masculine at a point of perfect balance on cosmic, universal, galactic, solar, and planetary levels. Call this forth directly from the Great Central Sun on a cosmic level; from Melchizedek, the Universal Logos; from Melchior, the Galactic Logos; from Helios and Vesta, the Solar Logoi, and from Sanat Kumara, the Planetary Logos. Call forth perfect and divine feminine and masculine anchoring and coding on all levels.

Cosmic Chakra Alignment

You can align your chakras with the logoi on the planetary, solar, galactic, universal, and cosmic levels. Begin this ascension invocation with

Sanat Kumara. Call to Sanat Kumara and request that your chakras be perfectly aligned and merged with Sanat Kumara's chakras on a permanent basis.

Next, call to Helios, the Solar Logos. Request that your chakras be perfectly aligned and merged with Helios' chakras and the seven planetary logoi who, in truth, make up his chakras.

Next, call to Melchior, the Galactic Logos. Request of Melchior that your personal chakras now be perfectly aligned and merged with his galactic chakras on a permanent basis.

Now call to Melchizedek, the Universal Logos, and request that your personal chakras be perfectly aligned and merged with his universal chakras on a permanent basis.

Then call forth the Multi-universal Logos, whose name is too sacred to be known, and request that your personal chakras be aligned and merged with his multi-universal chakras on a permanent basis.

Next, call forth directly to God and request that your personal chakras now be perfectly aligned and merged with his cosmic chakras on a permanent basis.

Merger with the Cosmic Monad

Call to God, the cosmic Council of Twelve, the Mahatma, and Melchizedek, and request that your personal, individualized monad now be completely aligned and merged with your cosmic monad on the cosmic monadic plane of creation, on a permanent basis.

Secondly, request that all monadic groupings on multi-universal, universal, galactic, and solar levels also be perfectly aligned with your cosmic monad and personal monad with which you are now merging on Earth.

For the first time, call forth the process of cosmic ascension, that it now be set in motion in conjunction with planetary ascension. The clarion call is going out to all aspects of self on the three hundred fifty-two levels of the Mahatma to come together now and to be put on notice to work for this one unified cosmic goal.

Direct God Current

After one of your deeper and more cosmic meditations, call forth from the Godhead, the undifferentiated Source, a direct downpouring of God-current. Let it come directly from the infinite Creator, as a divine dispensation to yourself, your core group, and the Earth Mother, to heal the separation between Heaven and Earth. Then call forth a direct merger with God, the undifferentiated Source on Earth.

Archangel Metatron

Call forth Archangel Metatron to work with you on a full-time basis to help you anchor your fifty chakras and twelve bodies, and to help in the building of your Light quotient to the 99% level.

Archangel Sandalphon

Call forth Archangel Sandalphon to help you on an ongoing basis to build your physical body into an etheric body. Also ask Archangel Sandalphon to help you transfer your twelve strands of DNA into your physical vehicle. Metatron and Sandalphon are the archangels on the top and the bottom of the Tree of Life. Metatron is the ultimate spiritual aspect, and Archangel Sandalphon is the ultimate for Earthly grounding of spiritual energies.

The Triple Overshadowing Merger Request

Call to Ascended Master Djwhal Khul (or to the planetary master of your choice), Lord Maitreya, and Melchizedek for a permanent overlighting and deeper merger and penetration by their energies on a permanent basis. On a planetary level, it is a good idea to choose one of the chohans of the seven rays: El Morya, Djwhal Khul (taking over for Kuthumi), Serapis Bey, Paul the Venetian, Hilarion, Jesus (Sananda), or Saint Germain.

You are connected with one of the seven rays and the master thereof, and you work in that ashram at night while you sleep. It is a good idea to work with the masters of all the rays at one time or another and also to study in each ashram. However, each of you will gravitate, at higher initiations, to one particular ashram which will be your home base, so to speak. You can also change your overlighting prayer request at a future date; the ascended masters will not take it personally.

If you want to accelerate your evolution, you want to work as closely as you can with the ascended masters. Evolution is speeded up one-thousand-fold if you work with them consciously and closely.

Merger with Your Spiritual Teacher

If you have just one spiritual teacher or guru, such as His Holiness, the Lord Sai Baba, then call during meditation for complete merger with and overlighting by that teacher. However, be sure that teacher is worthy of such an invocation.

Secondary Overlighting Mergers

There are usually groups of teachers you will work with alternatively, both consciously and unconsciously. I, personally, work very closely with Djwhal Khul, Lord Maitreya, and Melchizedek. However, I have what I call secondary overshadowing mergers with His Holiness, the Lord Sai Baba, the Lord of Sirius, the Lord of Arcturus and the Arcturians, Metatron, and Sanat Kumara. Request in meditation, if you like, a secondary overshadowing by these masters or by angels or others you feel an affinity for and an attunement with.

Anchoring the Ascension Seats

As you move through your initiations, call forth first at the planetary level and then after ascension at the solar, galactic, and universal levels for the permanent anchoring of the various ascension seats into your own consciousness and many-body system. After ascension, call in the solar ascension seat of Helios. After the completion of your ascension, call in the galactic ascension seat. After the completion of your seventh initiation, call in the anchoring of your universal or Melchizedek ascension seat on a permanent basis. This universal seat can actually be anchored after you take the beginning of your seventh initiation. In a previous ascension technique, I recommended calling the ascension seats to anchor into your ascension column. This technique suggests anchoring and activating the seats permanently in your consciousness so you are living in one wherever you go.

Your Cosmic Bodies

It is possible to begin to anchor and activate on an extremely subtle level your bodies that exist beyond the twelve I have mentioned. The twelfth body is, of course, the universal body, which connects you with the twelfth dimension. There are four other bodies that can be called forth. The highest body, which connects you directly with the Godhead, is the Lord's Mystical body. It cannot be permanently anchored or activated, but a feeling of it can definitely come in. Below it are the three overself bodies that lie far beyond the twelve dimensions that form a type of ring-pass-not for realization in this planetary mystery school called Earth. The three cosmic bodies beyond the twelve bodies are the Elohistic Lord's body, the Paradise Son's body, and the Order of the Sonship body. Call these in when you are doing your cosmic meditation work.

Melchizedek's Light Grid of Protection

I asked Melchizedek how to prevent alien implants from being reinstituted once they have been cleared. He told me it isn't so much a shield that protects you at the higher initiation levels but rather a Light grid that becomes permanently anchored. Call to Melchizedek, Melchior, Helios, and Sanat Kumara to place a permanent Light grid of protection around you.

The Overself and the Seven Cosmic Bodies

Another model for understanding cosmic ascension other than the Keys of Enoch terminology (the Lords Mystical Body, the Elohistic Lords Body, the Pradise Sons Body and the Order of the Sonship Bodies) is to realize that there are seven cosmic bodies that correlate with the seven cosmic planes. In other words, there is a cosmic physical body, cosmic astral body, comic mental body, cosmic buddhic body, cosmic atmic body, cosmic monadic body, and cosmic logoic body. Previously I had refered to the cosmic monad. This can also be referred to as the "overself." The overself is different than the oversoul. The oversoul is like the higher self. It is a higher counterpart to the monad. The overself is the cosmic monad. When one merges with the monad, they achieve planetary ascension. When one merges with the overself, they achieve "cosmic ascension." To merge with ones overself one must merge with the seven overself bodies I have listed above. It is potentially possible in this earthly school to anchor as much as five to ten percent of this cosmic level on Earth. This does not really begin until you complete your seven levels of initiation first, then the twelve bodies.

Removal of Etheric Weapons and Auric Tears

Call forth to your own migthty I Am Presence and the ascended masters of your choice and request the removal of all etheric weapons and the healing of all auric tears.

The Twelve Cosmic Rays

Call forth to the Cosmic Council of Twelve at the 352nd level of the Mahatma to send forth the twelve cosmic rays. It must be understood that the twelve rays that we utilise are really subrays that have been toned down a million fold. As one moves beyond ascension it is possible to begin going beyond our twelve planetary rays and accessing a small portion of these cosmic rays. Request to go to the golden chamber of Melchizedek and sit in the ascension seat there and request Melchizedek's help in receiving this prayer request. It is more appropriate to do this after you take your ascension, however, it can be experimented with a little before this. See the Cosmic Map which shows these cosmic rays emanating from the Cosmic Council of Twelve. Each council memeber is in charge of one of these cosmic rays.

A Special Divine Dispensation

Upon attaining the stabilized 98% Light quotient level and the seventh sublevel of the seventh initiation, I asked Melchizedek if it would be possible to request a special divine dispensation to begin anchoring the cosmic Light quotient level. He had already told us that it would take two years to fully anchor and fully activate all fifty chakras and all twelve bodies. At the completion of the seven levels of initiation and the 99% Light quotient, the process of anchoring and fully activating chakras thirty-seven through fifty begins. The process of anchoring and fully integrating and activating bodies eight through twelve also begins. Melchizedek originally said it would take two to four years; however, we were invoking the super-crash course so we could be of greater service. After we made this special request, Melchizedek took out a scroll while we sat in his Golden Chamber, and he told us that we were being given permission now to anchor 1% of the cosmic Light quotient. Remember, the 99% planetary Light quotient is only 7% to 9% of the cosmic Light quotient. We were being allowed to anchor 1% of the cosmic Light quotient, the cosmic chakras, and the cosmic bodies.

My sense was that this is not normally done, but that since we had come up with the question, and since we had already begun the process of anchoring the eighth- and ninth-dimensional chakra grids and the twelve bodies and were manifesting self-discipline and commitment to service, we were granted our prayerful request. To handle such an increase in Light, the above-mentioned levels must have been achieved and the purpose for requesting them must be to be of greater service.

Mahatma Cosmic Walk-in Request

If you have not done this, then you absolutely must do it right now: call to the Mahatma and request to be his cosmic walk-in on Earth and beyond until you reach your planetary and cosmic ascensions. If you have already done this, then request, right now, a deeper penetration and overlighting by his energy on an ongoing and permanent basis.

The Galactic, Universal, and Cosmic Christ

Call in meditation for an anchoring of and merger with those cosmic beings in God's infinite universe who embody the Planetary Christ, the Solar Christ, the Galactic Christ, the Universal Christ, the multi-universal Christ, and the cosmic Christ at the three hundred fifty-second level of the Godhead. Go through each from bottom to top and take a minute or two to assimilate and absorb each cosmic master's energy. Request that this be done on a permanent basis.

The Holy Grail Benediction and Blessing

The Holy Grail is the chalice Jesus used during the Last Supper. Many authors throughout the past two thousand years have written about its glorious spiritual significance. In a conversation I had with Jesus and Sanat

Kumara, they suggested that I end this book with a Holy Grail blessing and benediction to you, my reader. They now offer you on the inner plane, in your right hand, the Holy Grail with holy water contained therein. If you like, you can even get a glass of "real" physical water and they will bless it for you.

Their instructions to me were to have you, inwardly or outwardly or both, hold your Holy Grail chalice in the air and receive the toast and blessing they are now giving you. Sanat Kumara, as the spokesperson for the Spiritual Hierarchy, says, "We thank you and bless you for your devotion, commitment, and service to the Divine Plan. We congratulate you in your process as you walk down the path of Light. We now lift our glass in a toast to you. We honor you in this moment and wish you the greatest success on your path of ascension and the highest success on your personal service mission in the Light."

Blessings to all!

Conclusion

On December 12, 1994 (the 12:12), as Djwhal Khul had prophesied, I began the first stage of the seventh sublevel of my seventh initiation. (In the Brian Grattan system it would be called the first stage of my twelfth initiation.) From that point on, service has been my only reason for being here. It is my single, all-consuming desire to give back to humanity and all other kingdoms the love, the grace, and the freedom I now humbly receive.

As Djwhal Khul has said, "Much has been given and much is now expected." I gladly take on this mantle which, in truth, I have been wearing all along. My vow to you, brothers and sisters, is that I will not rest until every being on Planet Earth and throughout God's infinite universe shares this mantle with me!

Be diligent, disciplined, and eternally focused in your quest. Help your brothers and sisters in God's infinite family at every opportunity. Spread the teachings of the Spiritual Hierarchy by sharing these books. Let go of all negative ego, separation, selfishness, fear, and competition. Djwhal Khul has said that it is now possible to move from the third initiation to the sixth initiation in only six years. Take advantage of this exciting moment. There has never been a better time in the history of the Earth to be incarnated if you are interested in achieving ascension. In the past, masters took whole lifetimes to pass just one initiation. Now you can move through all seven initiations in ten or fifteen years if you focus your energies on that goal.

The material in this book is on the cutting edge; it is part of the universal dispensation for the future. However, if you do not apply yourself and practice the exercises, the book will not take you to your ultimate goal. You must now have the eyes to see and the ears to hear: acknowledge that you have tapped into a gold mine of spiritual information and go forward with it. As Jesus said, "Be ye faithful unto death and I will give thee a crown of life!"

Afterword: What's Next?

I am one self, united with my Creator.

A Course in Miracles

One of the interesting questions I have begun to ask myself now is, what goes on after you complete the seven levels of initiation? Certainly the first and most important answer is complete and total absorption in service. Any focus on achieving more initiations is meaningless because there are no more that can be taken on Planet Earth. Any focus on building your Light quotient is meaningless because you cannot go beyond 98% or 99% so, as Melchizedek said, you move from a vertical focus to a more horizontal focus and attend to serving humanity.

I have come to realize that there is personal growth that can and does take place even though there are no further initiations. First of all, I am currently working on fully anchoring, activating, and actualizing the eighth- and ninth-dimensional chakra grids. At the completion of the seventh initiation, the thirty-sixth chakra is in the crown. It is possible to anchor chakras thirty-six through forty-nine (and up to 99.99% of the fiftieth chakra) into the crown while still maintaining a physical body. That last .01% means losing the physical body. So in a sense, you can move up the dimensional attunement scale even though you are not taking new initiations or building Light quotient.

I asked Melchizedek if, once my forty-ninth (or fiftieth) chakra was in my crown (which he said would occur during the Wesak Festival of May 1995), that meant I would be operating out of the ninth dimension of reality. Melchizedek said that the merger with the forty-ninth chakra (and up to 99.99% of the fiftieth chakra) did not mean that I would be in the ninth dimension, but rather more attuned to it.

Djwhal Khul told Marcia and me that we could, however, move into and up through the eighth dimension in this physical vehicle. He said we could not move into the ninth because we would lose the physical vehicle if we did.

So there is still dimensional movement that can take place, even though the initiation level and Light quotient remain the same. You can still, obviously, continue to refine your physical, emotional, and mental vehicles. You can gain knowledge and wisdom. You can learn to release more and more negative ego, fear, and separation consciousness. You can begin doing work to prepare for future initiations that you will be taking after this incarnation. You can lay the groundwork. The main point is that there is always spiritual growing to be done, although it should come about mainly through immersion in world service.

In our meditation this week, Lord Melchizedek clarified this final step. He told us that just as our initiation process would stop at the completion of the seventh sublevel of the seventh initiation (or the twelfth initiation, in Brian Grattan's system), the same was true of the Light quotient and the anchoring of the fifty chakras. In other words, the Light quotient can be built to 99.99%. If you go to the 100% Light quotient level you lose the body. This is the same in terms of the eighth initiation. If you take the eighth initiation in the Alice Bailey system you lose the body; if you take the thirteenth initiation in the Brian Grattan system you lose the body. (Again, the twelfth initiation in the Brian Grattan system is the same as the completion of the seventh in the Alice Bailey system.)

As of this writing, we have just about built our Light quotient to the 97% level and have anchored the thirty-sixth chakra in the crown. We were told that in six months we could build our Light quotient to the 99.99% level which, interestingly enough, falls on the Wesak Festival of 1995, which is the beginning of mass ascension on Planet Earth. We were told that it would take approximately another full year, until the Wesak of 1996, to anchor the eighth- and ninth-dimensional chakra grids and 99.99% of our fiftieth chakras into our crowns.

I share this with you to give you a sense of the speed and timing at which this can potentially be done and to suggest that in your prayers and invocations you time your goals according to the Wesak festivals which occur at the full moon of May. It is at Wesak that Sanat Kumara and Melchizedek conduct all the major initiations.

Another area that can be continually worked on after the completion of the seven levels of initiations is the anchoring of the twelve strands of DNA from the etheric body into the physical body. The first step is to build them into the etheric body; the second step is to build them into the physical vehicle.

Yet another other area of growth you can concentrate on after you complete your seven levels of initiation is the developing and refining of advanced ascension skills such as telepathic abilities, teleporting, bilocating, transfiguration, shapeshifting, multidimensional consciousness, dematerialization, and the ability to materialize objects, to name a few. Many of these abilities are not required development, so they remain an area for potential growth.

The final goal is to help humanity achieve all seven levels of initiation instead of focusing on your own. In truth, you live as much in your brother and sister as you live in yourself. To help your brother and sister is to help yourself, for your brother and sister are you, since God has only one child. Any time you hold back on giving to your brother and sister due to competition, ego factors, or separation, you are, in truth, just shorting yourself. Your brother and sister are mirrors, and what you receive in this incarnation is exactly what you give — no more and no less. Make the choice never to compete or compare and, for the most part, to keep the statistical aspects of your spiritual growth to yourself, for in truth, all are God, whether they have taken any initiations or not. As Sai Baba has said, the true definition of God is man minus ego.

The statistical references can be extremely helpful in charting your progression, but it is essential that you use them only in the service of your soul and that you not allow the negative ego to use them for self-aggrandizement. Comparing and competing are traps that even sixth- and seventh-degree initiates can still fall prey to. It is something to watch out for.

Always remember, you do not have to be a famous channel, teacher, writer, or psychic to pass your initiations. God couldn't care less about fame. All God cares about is that you fulfill your part of the Divine Plan perfectly. That could mean being a parent, schoolteacher, secretary, computer worker, friend, networker, artist, musician, comedian, policeman . . . it means following the path that is right for you, not following someone else's path. The initiations are given from the perspective of a team rather than that of an individual. Play the role that best helps the group consciousness; that is the key to the initiation process. Everyone on the team will take an initiation at the same time, regardless of who has more worldly fame. Indeed, it often happens that people in leadership positions have a harder time because of ego factors and power issues that come up and slow down their progress.

Lastly, I just want to say you do not have to be perfect to pass your initiations. I know this for a fact! I know a great many sixth- and seventh-degree initiates who still have emotional lessons to learn and battles to fight with their negative egos as well as physical health problems.

This might surprise you, but it is true. Be glad that God has not made the requirements so stringent that no one can pass them.

Completing the seven levels of initiation in this lifetime is within reach of every single person who is reading this book. Just study the materials and practice the meditations, and demonstrate your divinity at every opportunity. Most importantly, be loving, joyful, and happy at all times. Don't take things too seriously!

Namasté.

A Special Thank You

This book would not be complete if I did not say a very special thank you to Raney Alexandre for the incredible assistance she has given me in putting this material into book form. The spiritual path is much like a puzzle and each person on Earth has a very special part to play. Without Raney's help in editing, packaging, putting it on computer, graphics, and design, this book would never have been ready for my publisher. Raney has literally been a godsend to me in my work and has allowed me to avoid getting burdened by the more mundane aspects of writing these books. Her selfless and devoted help has allowed my energies to be freed up for other creative projects and service missions.

I am eternally grateful and appreciative. I am proud to be able to call her my friend and compatriot in Djwhal Khul's ashram!

Namasté.

Bibliography

A Course in Miracles. Tiburon, CA: Foundation for Inner Peace, 1975.

Bailey, Alice A. *Initiation, Human and Solar*. New York: Lucis Publishing Co., 1922.

——. *The Rays and the Initiations*. New York: Lucis Publishing, 1993.

——. *I AM Discourses*, Vol. 12. Schaumburg, IL: St. Germain Press, 1987.

Hurtak, J. J. *The Book of Knowledge: The Keys of Enoch*. Los Gatos, CA: Academy of Future Science, 1987.

McClure, Janet. Scopes of Dimensions. Sedona, AZ: Light Technology Publishing, 1989.

Milanovich, Norma. *We, the Arcturians*. Albuquerque, NM: Athena, NM, 1990.

Redfield, James. *The Celestine Prophecy*. New York: Warner Books, 1994.

Stone, Joshua David. *The Complete Ascension Manual: How to Achieve Ascension in This Lifetime*. Sedona, AZ: Light Technology Publishing, 1994.

Stone, Joshua David. *Soul Psychology: Keys to Ascension*. Sedona, AZ: Light Technology Publishing, 1994.

Subject Guide

For further information,
Dr. Joshua David Stone
can be contacted
through the publisher
or at
5252 Coldwater Canyon, #112
Van Nuys, CA 91410
(818) 769-1181

BOOK MARKET

A reader's guide to the extraordinary books we publish, print and market for your enLightenment.

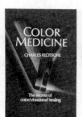

COLOR MEDICINE
The Secrets of Color Vibrational Healing
by **Charles Klotsche**

A practitioners' manual for restoring blocked energy to the body systems and organs with specific color wavelengths by the founder of "The 49th Vibrational Technique."

$11.95 Softcover 114 pp. ISBN 0-929385-27-6

THE STORY OF THE PEOPLE
by **Eileen Rota**

An exciting history of our coming to Earth, our traditions, our choices and the coming changes, it can be viewed as a metaphysical adventure, science fiction or the epic of all of us brave enough to know the truth. Beautifully written and illustrated.

$11.95 Softcover 209 pp. ISBN 0-929385-51-9

THE NEW AGE PRIMER
Spiritual Tools for Awakening

A guidebook to the changing reality, it is an overview of the concepts and techniques of mastery by authorities in their fields. Explores reincarnation, belief systems and transformative tools from astrology to crystals and healing.

$11.95 Softcover 206 pp. ISBN 0-929385-48-9

THE SEDONA VORTEX GUIDEBOOK
by **12 various channels**

200-plus pages of channeled, never-before published information on the vortex energies of Sedona and the techniques to enable you to use the vortexes as multidimensional portals to time, space and other realities.

$14.95 Softcover 236 pp. ISBN 0-929385-25-X

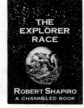

COMING SOON!
THE EXPLORER RACE
A channeled book
by **Robert Shapiro**

In this expansive overview, Zoosh explains, "You are the Explorer Race. Learn about your journey before coming to this Earth, your evolution here and what lies ahead." Topics range from ETs and UFOs to relationships.

$24.95 Softcover 650 pp. ISBN 0-929385-38-1

BEHOLD A PALE HORSE
by **Bill Cooper**

Former U.S. Naval Intelligence Briefing Team Member reveals information kept secret by our government since the 1940s. UFOs, the J.F.K. assassination, the Secret Government, the war on drugs and more by the world's leading expert on UFOs.

$25.00 Softcover 500 pp. ISBN 0-929385-22-5

SHINING THE LIGHT
by **Light Technology Research**

Revelations about the Secret Government and their connections with ETs. Information about renegade ETs mining the Moon, ancient Pleiadian warships, underground alien bases and many more startling facts.

$12.95 Softcover ISBN 0-929385-66-7

SHINING THE LIGHT BOOK II
by **Light Technology Research**

Continuing the story of the Secret Government and alien involvement. Also information about the Photon Belt, cosmic holograms photographed in the sky, a new vortex forming near Sedona, and nefarious mining on sacred Hopi land.

$14.95 Softcover ISBN 0-929385-70-5

LIVING RAINBOWS
by **Gabriel H. Bain**

A fascinating "how-to" manual to make experiencing human, astral, animal and plant auras an everyday event. Series of techniques, exercises and illustrations guide the simply curious to see and hear aural energy. Spiral-bound workbook format.

$14.95 Softcover ISBN 0-929385-42-X

BOOK MARKET

EXPLORING LIFE'S LAST FRONTIER

by **Dr. Heather Anne Harder**

By becoming familiar with death, the amount of fear and grief will be reduced, making the transition and transformation of Earth more joyful. A manual for learning acceptance and letting go.

$15.95 Softcover 315 pp. ISBN 1-881343-03-0

COMING SOON!

THE ALIEN PRESENCE
Evidence of secret government contact with alien life forms.

by **Ananda**

Documented testimony of the cover-up from a U.S. president's meeting to the tactics of suppression. The most significant information yet available.

$19.95 Softcover ISBN 0-929385-64-0

LIFE ON THE CUTTING EDGE

by **Sal Rachelle**

To explore some of the most significant questions of our time requires a cosmic view of reality. From the evolution of consciousness, dimensions and ETs to the New World Order, this is a no-nonsense book from behind, about and beyond the scenes. A must-read!

$14.95 Softcover 336 pp. ISBN 0-9640535-0-0

BOOKS BY VYWAMUS / JANET MCCLURE

FOREVER YOUNG

by **Gladys Iris Clark**

You can create a longer younger life! Viewing a lifetime of nearly a century, a remarkable woman shares her secrets for longevity and rejuvenation. A manual for all ages. She explores the tools for optimizing vitality, nutrition, skin care, Tibetan exercises, crystals, sex and earth changes. A fascinating guide to transforming.

$9.95 Softcover 109 pp. ISBN 0-929385-53-5

The Story of **SANAT KUMARA**
Training a Planetary Logos

Vywamus
Channeled and Edited by Janet McClure

SANAT KUMARA
Training a Planetary Logos

Vywamus through **Janet McClure**

How was the beauty of this world created? The answer is in the story of the evolution of Earth's Logos, the great being whose name is Sanat Kumara. A journey through his eyes as he learns the real-life lessons of training along the path of mastery.

$11.95 Softcover 179 pp. ISBN 0-929385-17-9

THE SOURCE ADVENTURE

VYWAMUS
Channeled by Janet McClure
Edited by Lillian Harben

THE SOURCE ADVENTURE

Vywamus through **Janet McClure**

Life is discovery, and this book is a journey of discovery "...to learn, to grow, to recognize the opportunities—to be aware." It asks the big question, "Why are you here?" and leads the reader to examine the most significant questions of a lifetime.

$11.95 Softcover 157 pp. ISBN 0-929385-06-3

AHA! THE REALIZATION BOOK

Vywamus through **Janet McClure** with **Lillian Harben**

If you are mirroring your life in a way that is not desirable, this book can help you locate murky areas and make them "suddenly...crystal clear." Readers will find it an exciting step-by-step path to changing and evolving lives.

$11.95 Softcover 120pp. ISBN 0-929385-14-4

Light Techniques

VYWAMUS
Channeled by Janet McClure
Edited by Lillian Harben

LIGHT TECHNIQUES THAT TRIGGER TRANSFORMATION

Vywamus through **Janet McClure**

Expanding the Heart Center... Launching Your Light... Releasing the destructive focus... Weaving the Garment of Light...Light Alignment and more. A wonderfully effective tool for using Light to transcend and create life as a Light being. Beautiful guidance!

$11.95 Softcover 145 pp. ISBN 0-929385-00-4

SCOPES OF DIMENSIONS

How To Experience Multi-Dimensional Reality

VYWAMUS
Channeled by Janet McClure
Edited by Lillian Harben

SCOPES OF DIMENSIONS

Vywamus through **Janet McClure**

Vywamus explains the process of exploring and experiencing the dimensions. He teaches an integrated way to utilize the combined strengths of each dimension. It is a how-to guidebook for living in the multidimensional reality that is our true evolutionary path.

$11.95 Softcover 176 pp. ISBN 0-929385-09-8

BOOK MARKET

BOOKS BY TOM DONGO

NEW! UNSEEN BEINGS UNSEEN WORLDS
by **Tom Dongo**
Venture into unknown realms with a leading researcher. Discover new information on how to communicate with nonphysical beings, aliens, ghosts, wee people and the Gray zone. Many photos to depict ET activity and inter-action with humans.
$9.95 Softcover 122 pp.   ISBN 0-9622748-3-6

THE QUEST The Mysteries of Sedona III
by **Tom Dongo**
Fascinating in-depth interviews with 26 who have answered the call to Sedona and speak of their spiritual experiences. Explores the mystique of the area and effect the quests have had on individual lives. Photos/illustrations.
$8.95 Softcover 144 pp.   ISBN 0-9622748-2-8

OUT-OF-BODY EXPLORATION A Guide to New Dimensions of Self-realization
by **Jerry Mulvin**
Techniques for traveling in the Soul Body to achieve absolute freedom and experience truth for oneself,. Discover reincarnation, karma and your personal spiritual path.
$8.95 Softcover   ISBN 0-941464-01-6

THE ALIEN TIDE The Mysteries of Sedona II
by **Tom Dongo**
The UFO and ET events and para-normal activity in the Sedona area and nationwide are investigated and detailed by a leading researcher who cautions against fear of the alien presence. Intriguing information for all who seek new insights. Photos/illustrations.
$7.95 Softcover 128 pp.   ISBN 0-9622748-1-X

THE MYSTERIES OF SEDONA
by **Tom Dongo**
An overview of the New Age Mecca that is Sedona, Arizona. Topics are the famous energy vortexes, UFOs, channeling, Lemuria, metaphysical and mystical experiences and area para-normal activity. Photos/illustrations.
$6.95 Softcover 84 pp.   ISBN 0-9622748-0-1

BOOKS BY RUTH RYDEN

THE GOLDEN PATH
Channeled by **Ruth Ryden**
"Book of Lessons" by the master teachers explaining the process of channeling. Akashic Records, karma, opening the third eye, the ego and the meaning of Bible stories. It is a master class for opening your personal pathway.
$11.95 Softcover 200 pp.   ISBN 0-929385-43-8

BOOKS BY WES BATEMAN

KNOWLEDGE FROM THE STARS
by **Wes Bateman**
A telepath with contact to ETs, Bateman has provided a wide spectrum of scientific information. A fascinating compilation of articles surveying the Federation, ETs, evolution and the trading houses, all part of the true history of the galaxy.
$11.95 Softcover 171 pp.   ISBN 0-929385-39-X

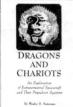

DRAGONS AND CHARIOTS
by **Wes Bateman**
An explanation of spacecraft, propulsion systems, gravity, the Dragon, manipulated Light and inter-stellar and intergalactic motherships by a renowned telepath who details specific technological information he has been given through contact with ETs.
$9.95 Softcover 65 pp.   ISBN 0-929385-45-4

LIVING THE GOLDEN PATH Practical Soul-utions to Today's Problems
Channeled by Ruth Ryden
Guidance that can be used in the real world to solve dilemmas – to strengthen inner resolves and see the Light at the end of the road. Covers the difficult issues of failure, addictions, drugs, personal tragedies, rape, abortion, and suicide.
$11.95 Softcover 186 pp.   ISBN 0-929385-65-9

BOOK MARKET

BOOKS BY PRESTON B. NICHOLS/PETER MOON

THE MONTAUK PROJECT
Experiments in Time
by Preston B. Nichols with Peter Moon

The truth about time that reads like science fiction! Secret research with invisibility experiments that culminated at Montauk, tapping the powers of creation and manipulating time itself. Exposé by the technical director.

$15.95 Softcover 160 pp. ISBN 0-9631889-0-9

MONTAUK REVISITED
Adventures in Synchronicity
by Preston B. Nichols with Peter Moon

The sequel unmasks the occult forces that were behind the technology of Montauk and the incredible characters associated with it.

$19.95 Softcover 249 pp. ISBN 0-9631889-1-7

PYRAMIDS OF MONTAUK
Explorations in Consciousness
by Preston B. Nichols with Peter Moon

A journey through the mystery schools of Earth unlocking the secret of the Sphinx, thus awakening the consciousness of humanity to its ancient history and origins.

$19.95 Softcover 249 pp. ISBN 0-9631889-1-7

ACUPRESSURE FOR THE SOUL
by Nancy Fallon, Ph.D.

A revolutionary vision of emotions as sources of power, rocket fuel for fulfilling our purpose. A formula for awakening transformation with 12 beautiful illustrations.

$11.95 Softcover 150 pp. ISBN 0-929385-49-7

SOUL RECOVERY & EXTRACTION
by Ai Gvhdi Waya

Soul recovery is about regaining the pieces of one's spirit that have been trapped, lost or stolen either by another person or through a traumatic incident that has occurred in one's life.

$9.95 Softcover 74 pp. ISBN 0-9634662-3-2

I'M O.K.
I'm Just Mutating!
by the Golden Star Alliance

Major shifts are now taking place upon this planet. It is mutating into a Body of Light, as are all the beings who have chosen to be here at this time. A view of what is happening and the mutational symptoms you may be experiencing.

$6.00 Softcover 32 pp.

AN ASCENSION HANDBOOK
by Serapis through Tony Stubbs

A practical "how-to" guide for Lightworkers for increasing the frequency of energy bodies to emerge as self-realized Masters. Ascend with grace, ease and fun.

$11.95 Softcover 140 pp. ISBN 0-880666-08-1

E.T. 101:
COSMIC INSTRUCTION MANUAL
Emergency Remedial Edition,
Co-created by Mission Control and Diana Luppi

A witty guide for evolving beyond the programming and manipulation.

$12.95 Softcover 86 pp. ISBN 0-9626958-0-7

OUR COSMIC ANCESTORS
by Maurice Chatelain

A former NASA expert documents evidence left in codes inscribed on ancient monuments pointing to the existence of an advanced prehistoric civilization regularly visited (and technologically assisted) by ETs.

$9.95 Softcover 213 pp. ISBN 0-929686-00-4

BOOKS BY LYNN BUESS

CHILDREN OF LIGHT: CHILDREN OF DENIAL
by Lynn Buess M.A., Ed.S.

In his fourth book Lynn calls upon his decades of practice as counselor and psychotherapist to explore the relationship between karma and the new insights from ACOA/ Co-dependency writings.

$8.95 Softcover 150 pp. ISBN 0-929385-15-2

NUMEROLOGY: NUANCES IN RELATIONSHIPS
by Lynn Buess M.A., Ed.S.

Provides valuable assistance in the quest to better understand compatibilities and conflicts with a significant other. A handy guide for calculating your/his/her personality numbers.

$12.65 Softcover 239 pp. ISBN 0-929385-23-3

NUMEROLOGY FOR THE NEW AGE
by Lynn Buess M.A., Ed.S.

An established standard, explicating for contemporary readers the ancient art and science of symbol, cycle, and vibration. Provides insights into the patterns of our personal lives. Includes life and Personality Numbers.

$9.85 Softcover 262 pp. ISBN 0-929385-31-4

BOOK MARKET

BOOKS BY HALLIE DEERING

LIGHT FROM THE ANGELS

Channeled through Hallie Deering for the Angel Academy

Now those who cannot attend the Angel Academy in person can meet the Rose Angels who share their metaphysical wisdom and technology in this fascinating book.

$15.00 Softcover   ISBN 0-929385-72-1

Do-It-Yourself POWER TOOLS

Channeled through Hallie Deering for the Angel Academy

Assemble your own Power Tools using the patterns in this book and a few inexpensive supplies. You will build ten angelic instruments worth $700.

$25.00 Softcover   ISBN 0-929385-63-2

PRISONERS OF EARTH Psychic Possession and Its Release

by **Aloa Starr**

The symptoms, causes and release techniques in a documented exploration by a practitioner. A fascinating study that de-mystifies possession.

$11.95 Softcover 179 pp.   ISBN 0-929385-37-3

SEDONA POWER SPOT, Vortex and Medicine Wheel Guide

by **Richard Dannelley**

An exploration of the vortex legends and their effects on the mind and spirit. Meditations, maps and photographs to guide the reader to profound transformation.

$9.95 Softcover   ISBN 0-962945-2-3

THE LEGEND OF THE EAGLE CLAN

by **Cathleen M. Cramer** with **Darren A. Robb**

The emotionally charged story of Morning Glory, a remembrance of her life 144 years ago as part of the Anasazi, the ancient ones. This book is for the ones who need to remember who they are.

$12.95 Softcover   ISBN 0-929385-68-3

THIS WORLD AND THE NEXT ONE

(AND THERE IS A NEXT ONE)

BY AIELLO

(This Is About Your Life Before Birth and Your Life After Death)

A Handbook of How and Why

THIS WORLD & THE NEXT ONE

by **Aiello**

A handbook about your life before birth and your life after death, it explains the "how" and "why" of experiences with space people and dimensions. Man in his many forms is a "puppet on the stage of creation."

$9.95 Softcover 213 pp.   ISBN 0-929385-44-6

BOOKS BY ROYAL/PRIEST

PRISM OF LYRA

by **Lyssa Royal & Keith Priest**

Traces the inception of the human race back to Lyra, where the original expansion of the duality was begun, to be finally integrated on earth. Fascinating channeled information.

$11.95 Softcover 112 pp.   ISBN 0-9631320-0-8

VISITORS FROM WITHIN

by **Lyssa Royal & Keith Priest**

Explores the extraterrestrial contact and abduction phenomenon in a unique and intriguing way. Narrative, precisely focussed channeling & firsthand accounts.

$12.95 Softcover 171 pp.   ISBN 0-9631320-1-6

PREPARING FOR CONTACT

by **Lyssa Royal & Keith Priest**

Contact requires a metamorphosis of consciousness since it involves two species who meet on the next step of evolution. A channeled guidebook to ready us for that transformation., it is engrossing.

$12.95 Softcover 188 pp.   ISBN 0-9631320-2-4

BOOKS BY DOROTHY ROEDER

THE NEXT DIMENSION IS LOVE

Ranoash through **Dorothy Roeder**

As speaker for a civilization whose species is more advanced, the entity describes the help they offer humanity by clearing the DNA. An exciting vision of our possibilities and future.

$11.95 Softcover 148 pp.   ISBN 0-929385-50-0

REACH FOR US Your Cosmic Teachers and Friends

Channeled by **Dorothy Roeder**

Messages from Teachers, Ascended Masters and the Space Command explain the role they play in bringing the Divine Plan to the earth now!

$13.00 Softcover 168 pp.   ISBN 0-929385-69-1

CRYSTAL CO-CREATORS

Channeled by **Dorothy Roeder**

A fascinating exploration of 100 forms of crystals, describing specific uses and their purpose, from the spiritual to the cellular, as agents of change. It clarifies the role of crystals in our awakening.

$14.95 Softcover   ISBN 0-929385-40-3

BOOK&TAPE MARKET

HOT OFF THE PRESSES AT . . .

LIGHT TECHNOLOGY PUBLISHING

THE ASCENSION BOOK SERIES by Joshua David Stone

THE COMPLETE ASCENSION MANUAL: How to Achieve Ascension in This Lifetime

BOOK I A synthesis of the past and guidance for ascension. This book is an extraordinary compendium of practical techniques and spiritual history. Compiled from research and channeled information, it offers specific steps to accelerate our process of ascension — here and now!
ISBN 0-929385-55-1   **$14.95**

SOUL PSYCHOLOGY: Keys To Ascension

BOOK II Modern psychology deals exclusively with personality, ignoring the dimensions of spirit and soul. This book provides ground-breaking theories and techniques for healing and self-realization.
ISBN 0-929385-56-X   **$14.95**

BEYOND ASCENSION: How to Complete the Seven Levels of Initiation

BOOK III This book brings forth incredible new channeled material that completely demystifies the seven levels of initiation and how to attain them. It contains revolutionary new information on how to anchor and open our 36 chakras and how to build our light quotient at a rate of speed never dreamed possible.
ISBN 0-929385-73-X   **$14.95**

ASCENSION ACTIVATION MEDITATION TAPE

How to anchor and open your 36 chakras and build your light quotient at a speed never dreamed possible. Hundreds of new ascension techniques and meditations directly from the galactic and universal core.
S101   **$10.00**

TREE OF LIFE ASCENSION MEDITATION TAPE

S102   **$10.00**

THE ANGEL ACADEMY SERIES by Hallie Deering
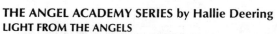
LIGHT FROM THE ANGELS

CHANNELED THROUGH HALLIE DEERING FOR THE ANGEL ACADEMY
Angelic Technology manifesting on Earth!

Meet the Rose Angels, who share their metaphysical wisdom and technology in this fascinating book. Now those who cannot attend the Angel Academy in person have a unique opportunity to learn about major metaphysical topics from the angels themselves. Here is a treasure chest waiting to be opened, with healing and meditation tools that can change your life dramatically. Topics include making and using Power Tools, angelic medicine, healing with dolphins, understanding the subtle bodies and the chakras, finding your twin soul, and much more.
ISBN 0-929385-72-1   **$15.00**

DO-IT-YOURSELF POWER TOOLS

CHANNELED THROUGH HALLIE DEERING FOR THE ANGEL ACADEMY

Angelic Power Tools are interdimensional windows that flood your psychic centers with angelic energy. Treasured by lightworkers around the world.
HOT DEAL! The Power Tools you can make with this book are worth $700! You get ten superb Power Tools channeled from the Rose Angels.
Assemble your own amazing glass disks that holographically amplify energy to heal trauma, purify auras, open the heart and mind, destroy negative thought forms, tune the base chakra and other powerful work with the subtle energies of the body. Using only the patterns in this book and a few inexpensive supplies found in any stained glass shop you will build ten authentic, versatile angelic instruments for healing, channeling and self-transformation.
ISBN 0-929385-63-2   **$25.00**

B O O K M A R K E T O R D E R F O R M

BOOKS PUBLISHED BY LIGHT TECHNOLOGY PUBLISHING

		NO. COPIES	TOTAL
ACUPRESSURE FOR THE SOUL *Fallon*	$11.95	___	$ _____
ALIEN PRESENCE *Ananda*	$19.95	___	$ _____
BEHOLD A PALE HORSE *Cooper*	$25.00	___	$ _____
CHANNELLING *Vywamus/Burns*	$9.95	___	$ _____
COLOR MEDICINE *Klotsche*	$11.95	___	$ _____
EXPLORER RACE *Shapiro*	$24.95	___	$ _____
FOREVER YOUNG *Clark*	$9.95	___	$ _____
LEGEND OF THE EAGLE CLAN *Cramer*	$12.95	___	$ _____
LIVING RAINBOWS *Bain*	$14.95	___	$ _____
MAHATMA I & II *Grattan*	$19.95	___	$ _____
NEW AGE PRIMER	$11.95	___	$ _____
PRISONERS OF EARTH *Starr*	$11.95	___	$ _____
SHINING THE LIGHT	$12.95	___	$ _____
SHINING THE LIGHT — BOOK II	$14.95	___	$ _____
SEDONA VORTEX GUIDE BOOK	$14.95	___	$ _____
SHADOW OF S.F. PEAKS *Bader*	$9.95	___	$ _____
STORY OF THE PEOPLE *Rota*	$11.95	___	$ _____
THIS WORLD AND NEXT ONE "*Aiello*"	$9.95	___	$ _____

Arthur Fanning

SOULS, EVOLUTION & the FATHER	$12.95	___	$ _____
SIMON	$9.95	___	$ _____

Wesley H. Bateman

DRAGONS AND CHARIOTS	$9.95	___	$ _____
KNOWLEDGE from the STARS	$11.95	___	$ _____

		NO. COPIES	TOTAL
Lynn Buess			
CHILDREN OF LIGHT ...	$8.95	___	$ _____
NUMEROLOGY: Nuances	$12.65	___	$ _____
NUMEROLOGY for the NEW AGE	$9.85	___	$ _____
Hallie Deering			
LIGHT FROM THE ANGELS	$15.00	___	$ _____
DO-IT-YOURSELF POWER TOOLS	$25.00	___	$ _____
Dorothy Roeder			
CRYSTAL CO-CREATORS	$14.95	___	$ _____
NEXT DIMENSION IS LOVE	$11.95	___	$ _____
REACH FOR US	$13.00	___	$ _____
Ruth Ryden			
THE GOLDEN PATH	$11.95	___	$ _____
LIVING THE GOLDEN PATH	$11.95	___	$ _____
Joshua David Stone, Ph.D.			
COMPLETE ASCENSION MANUAL	$14.95	___	$ _____
SOUL PSYCHOLOGY	$14.95	___	$ _____
Vywamus/Janet McClure			
AHA! THE REALIZATION BOOK	$11.95	___	$ _____
LIGHT TECHNIQUES	$11.95	___	$ _____
SANAT KUMARA	$11.95	___	$ _____
SCOPES OF DIMENSIONS	$11.95	___	$ _____
THE SOURCE ADVENTURE	$11.95	___	$ _____
EVOLUTION: LOOP OF EXPERIENCING	$14.95	___	$ _____

BOOKS PRINTED OR MARKETED BY LIGHT TECHNOLOGY PUBLISHING

ASCENSION HANDBOOK *Stubbs*	$11.95	___	$ _____
DEDICATED TO THE SOUL ... *Vosacek*	$9.95	___	$ _____
E.T. 101 INSTRUCTION MANUAL *Mission Control/Luppi*	$12.00	___	$ _____
EXPLORING LIFE'S ... *Harder*	$15.95	___	$ _____
"I'M OK ..." *Golden Star Alliance*	$6.00	___	$ _____
I WANT TO KNOW *Starr*	$7.00	___	$ _____
GREAT KACHINA *Bader*	$9.95	___	_____
LIFE ON THE CUTTING EDGE *Rachelle*	$14.95	___	$ _____
OUR COSMIC ANCESTORS *Chatelain*	$9.95	___	$ _____
OUT OF BODY EXPLORATION *Mulvin*	$8.95	___	$ _____
PRINCIPLES TO REMEMBER *Maile*	$11.95	___	$ _____
SEDONA POWER SPOT/GUIDE *Dannelley*	$9.95	___	$ _____
SONG OF SIRIUS *McManus*	$8.00	___	$ _____
SOUL RECOVERY/EXTRACTION *Waya*	$9.95	___	$ _____

SPIRIT OF THE NINJA *Siege*	$7.95	___	$ _____
TALKS WITH JONATHON *Miller*	$14.95	___	$ _____
Tom Dongo: Mysteries of Sedona			
MYSTERIES OF SEDONA—Book I	$6.95	___	$ _____
ALIEN TIDE—Book II	$7.95	___	$ _____
QUEST—Book III	$8.95	___	$ _____
UNSEEN BEINGS ...	$9.95	___	$ _____
Preston B. Nichols with Peter Moon			
MONTAUK PROJECT	$15.95	___	$ _____
MONTAUK REVISITED	$19.95	___	$ _____
PYRAMIDS OF MONTAUK	$19.95	___	$ _____
Lyssa Royal and Keith Priest			
PREPARING FOR CONTACT	$12.95	___	$ _____
PRISM OF LYRA	$11.95	___	$ _____
VISITORS FROM WITHIN	$12.95	___	$ _____

ASCENSION MEDITATION TAPES

Joshua David Stone, Ph.D.

Ascension Activation Meditation	$10.00	___	$ _____
Tree of Life Ascension Meditation	$10.00	___	$ _____

Vywamus/Barbara Burns

The Quantum Mechanical You (6 tapes)	$40.00	___	$ _____

Brian Grattan

Seattle Seminar Resurrection 1994 (12 tapes)	$79.95	___	$ _____

YHWH/Arthur Fanning

On Becoming	$10.00	___	$ _____
Healing Meditations/Knowing Self	$10.00	___	$ _____
Manifestation & Alignment w/ Poles	$10.00	___	$ _____
The Art of Shutting Up	$10.00	___	$ _____
Continuity of Consciousness	$25.00	___	$ _____
Black Hole Meditation	$10.00	___	$ _____
Merging the Golden Light Replicas of You	$10.00	___	$ _____

BOOKSTORE DISCOUNTS HONORED

SEND ☐ CHECK OR ☐ MONEY ORDER
(U.S. FUNDS ONLY) PAYABLE TO:

LIGHT TECHNOLOGY PUBLISHING
P.O. BOX 1526 • SEDONA • AZ 86339
(520) 282-6523 Fax: (520) 282-4130
1-800-450-0985

NAME/COMPANY _____

ADDRESS _____

CITY/STATE/ZIP _____

PHONE _____ CONTACT _____

All prices in US$. Higher in Canada and Europe.

SUBTOTAL: $ _____

SALES TAX: $ _____
(7.5% – AZ residents only)

SHIPPING/HANDLING: $ _____
($3 Min.; 10% of orders over $30)

CANADA S/H: $ _____
(20% of order)

TOTAL AMOUNT ENCLOSED: $ _____

CANADA: Cherev Canada, Inc. 1(800) 263-2408 Fax (519) 986-3103 • ENGLAND/EUROPE: Windrush Press Ltd. 0608 652012/652025 Fax 0608 652125